Pre-Industrial Canada 1760-1849

Readings in
Canadian Social History
Volume 2

Edited by
Michael S. Cross
and Gregory S. Kealey

McClelland and Stewart

McClelland and Stewart Limited
The Canadian Publishers
25 Hollinger Road
Toronto, Ontario
M4B 3G2

Canadian Cataloguing in Publication Data
Main entry under title:
    Pre-industrial Canada, 1760-1849

(Readings in Canadian social history; v. 2)
Includes bibliographies.
ISBN 0-7710-2461-4

1. Canada – Social conditions – To 1867 – Addresses,
essays, lectures.* 2. Canada – Economic conditions –
To 1867 – Addresses, essays, lectures.* I. Cross,
Michael S., 1938-   II. Kealey, Gregory S., 1948-
III. Series.

FC400.P73   971.03   C82-094041-0
F1032.P73

Printed and bound in Canada by Webcom Ltd.

Contents

Abbreviations

APQ   Archives de la Province de Québec
CHAR Canadian Historical Association *Report*
CHR   *Canadian Historical Review*
OH   *Ontario History*
PAC   Public Archives of Canada
TPL   Toronto Public Library

General Introduction
– The Series

The emergence of social history has been perhaps the most significant development of the last fifteen years in Canadian historical writing. Historians young and old have brought new approaches and new perspectives to Canada's past, revealing areas previously overlooked and offering new interpretations of old areas. The result has been what historian Ramsay Cook has called the discipline's "golden age." This five-volume series of readers in social history is intended to make the fruits of that "golden age" readily available to teachers, students, and general readers.

Modern social history is an approach rather than a specific subject matter. Where once social history was seen as what was left over after political and economic history was written, social history now is a "global" discipline, which can embrace politics and economics as well as the history of social groups or charitable institutions. The ideal of social history is to write the history of society, to study all of the ways in which people, groups of people, and classes of people interact to produce a society and to create social change. Such a global picture may never be drawn but its goal of an integrated history underlies recent study in Canada. The social historian, then, may write about a small subject over a limited period of time. However, that historian must be conscious of the links to the larger reality; of how local politics, say, indicate the relations of social classes, how they react with ideological assumptions of provincial politicians, how they affect local social customs.

It is a new field and that means its effort has been scattered. Canadian social history has embraced everything from the study of women's groups to computer analysis of population changes to the history of disease. It also has been marked by some sharp differences of opinion. The editors of this series, as practitioners and partisans, make no claim to objectivity in assessing these differences. Broadly, some historians treat social history as an extension of previous historical writing and share its assumptions about the general sweep of Canadian development: its liberal-democratic character; its fluid class structure; its peaceful and orderly growth. Others, however, break from that interpretation and argue for a different picture: a more rigid and influential class structure; a greater degree of conflict and violence; an emphasis on the working class. Which interpretation will prevail remains to be seen. The essays chosen for the series attempt to present as many viewpoints as possible, but the overall structure clearly reflects the judgment of the editors, which favours the second approach, the "working class" approach.

Rather than being structured along the traditional political divisions, the volumes in the series have been organized around dates which seemed most appropriate to social history.

I   New France to the Conquest, 1760

II Pre-Industrial Canada, from the Conquest to the end of the imperial economic system, 1760 to 1849

III The Age of Industry, from the coming of the railway to the full flowering of industrialism, 1849 to 1896

IV The Consolidation of Capitalism, from the beginnings of economic monopoly to the Great Crash, 1896 to 1929

V   The Emergence of the Welfare State, from the origins of large-scale state intervention to the present, 1930 to 1981.

Again, the internal divisions of the volumes have been chosen to illustrate basic themes that represent building blocks in social history. Not all themes could be included and some historians might argue with the particular choices made here. We would suggest several rationales for the selection: these themes seem important to us; the volume of writing and research on them, completed and underway, suggests that many others find them important; and they have proven useful in teaching social history.

Different periods and the availability of good literature require some variance from volume to volume. The general structure, however, is consistent. Each volume begins with an essay on the major economic developments of the period, for we work from the assumption that changing economic forms underlie most social changes. The second theme is that of social structure and social institutions, of the classes and groups of Canadian society and the way in which they interact. This theme will embrace subject matter as diverse as politics, religion, and landholding patterns.

Certain groups have emerged to centre stage historically in recent years. One is workers, the third theme in each volume. Workers and their work have been perhaps the area of richest development in historical writing in the last decade; social history has made its most profound impact in reshaping historical knowledge in this area. The fourth theme is one in which social history has had a similarly important influence, if only because interest in it is so recent. That is violence and protest, now receiving close attention from historians, sociologists, and criminologists. Violence and protest involved many Canadians and touched the lives of many more, and therefore are significant in their own right. However, they also provide a sharply defined picture of the structures and values of the society in which they occurred. The things people consider important enough to fight and protest about give us some indication of the values of particular groups. The attitudes of the leadership of society emerge in the fifth theme, social control. This theme studies the checks placed on violence and protest and inappropriate behaviour, as well as the institutions created to mould appropriate behaviour.

Along with workers, the other group to receive due attention from social history is women. No area, perhaps, was so neglected for so long as the study of women, outside of occasional writing on the suffrage movement. Recently, however, there has been a flood of literature, not just on feminism and women's organizations, but on women's productive and reproductive work. In a field devoted to creation of an integrated picture of society, this is a welcome and exciting development. Some of the trends in women's history, and some of the major achievements, are illustrated in these volumes.

The structure adopted here is offered as a useful one which will open to teachers and to students an exciting area of Canadian studies. It makes no claim to comprehensiveness; it is very much a starting point for that study. The additional readings suggested will help to move beyond that starting point and to introduce the controversies which cannot be reflected adequately in the small number of essays reprinted here. These volumes, however, do serve as a report on some approaches we have found helpful to students of social history and on some of the best literature available in this new field. More, they are collected on the premise that the investigation of social change in Canadian history, the ideas exposed and the questions raised, may allow students to understand more fully the nature of the Canadian society in which they live.

M. S. Cross
G. S. Kealey
Halifax and
St. John's,
July, 1981

Introduction
to Volume 2

It began and ended with British troops in the streets of Montreal. The colonial period, the pre-industrial period, can be dated from September, 1760, when British forces entered Montreal after its capitulation and ended 150 years of the French regime. The pre-industrial period came to a symbolic conclusion in April, 1849, when the 71st Highlanders struggled to suppress a rioting mob led by the commercial interests of Montreal. Taken together, the two events suggest many of the broad outlines of Canadian society in the colonial era.

The imperial presence, and its military support, was a central fact of life in these clustered colonies known as British North America. From the time imperial soldiers entered Montreal in 1760, British North America was subject to pervasive influence from the home country. The British Empire dominated life in many ways. The colonies received versions of the British constitution. This elaborate and complicated form of government – with its governor, executive council, legislative council, popular assembly, and civil service – was often unsuited to new, sparsely settled colonies. They were encumbered by an expensive administration with a multitude of offices. This, in turn, meant that the rise of governing elites was almost inevitable. The British form of government demanded educated administrators, sufficiently cultured to associate with aristocratic governors. There were few such men, and the result was the concentration of office among the handful who were qualified. Dubbed the Family Compact in Upper Canada (Ontario), the Chateau Clique in Lower

Canada (Quebec), the Council of Twelve in Nova Scotia, these powerful office-holders held sway until the mid-1830's.

Colonial conservatives were fond of claiming that the provinces enjoyed the image and transcript of the British constitution. While the governor was not the king and the legislative council fell short of the dignity of the House of Lords, a distinctively British style of government was established in British North America, for better and all too often for worse. A sophisticated administration added a tone of stability to struggling colonies in their early years; its conservatism, its inability to adjust to colonial growth, helped make the governmental structure one of the causes of rebellion in 1837.

The British connection also established the Church of England as the state religion, with the Church of Scotland holding only a slightly less exalted position. In an age when religious disputes could trigger riots and topple governments, the privileges of the Anglicans became a very sore point. Although it enjoyed huge land endowments totalling one-seventh of Upper Canada and the newly opened parts of Lower Canada, education privileges, and political appointments for its leaders, the Anglican Church was a minority institution in the colonies. Catholics always had predominated in Lower Canada, Baptists and Presbyterians in Nova Scotia, Methodists and then Catholics in Upper Canada. The Church of England played a significant role in establishing grammar schools and colleges, serving the native peoples, and adding a tone of sophistication to colonial society. However, its privileged position was a source of controversy and anger throughout the colonial period. The goals and ideology of the established church are probed in this volume in S. F. Wise's article on sermon literature. Among other things, it demonstrates that Anglicanism supplied a respectable intellectual tradition to the rude colonies.

Canada was part of an economic empire as well as a political one. British merchants dominated the trade of the colonies, their commercial efforts supported by imperial law. Under the Navigation Acts, trade to and from the colonies could be carried only in British ships. The Navigation Acts persisted until 1849. Imperial trade was shielded also by an elaborate series of protective tariffs. These acts placed duties on goods entering Britain from outside the empire, thus giving a financial advantage to products of Britain and the colonies. This protection was most important to the timber trade. Canada produced relatively small amounts of ship masts and other timber in the first years after the Conquest. However, Britain's struggle with Napoleon became an economic war and European supplies of timber to England were endangered by the French emperor. The British answer was to develop domestic supplies by "differential duties." After 1808, tariffs were raised against foreign wood, providing a large advantage to timber from the colonies. The result was a frantic development of timbering in Canada and a booming colonial prosperity.

What the colonial system gave it could take away. In 1842, preferences were slashed on timber. The reduction of timber duties in the 1840's was part of a general British retreat from empire. When the troops entered Montreal in 1760 they were closely followed by fur traders from other parts of the empire – ambitious Scots, experienced merchants from Albany in the colony of New York – who knew that trade followed the flag, that Britain would support their commercial enterprises. For eighty years Britain did foster the prosperity of her merchants. In the 1840's, however, England embraced free trade, the removal of barriers to commerce, the philosophy of free enterprise. Now the predominant industrial power in the world, able to compete successfully in markets everywhere, Britain no longer needed artificial protection. Nor, incidentally, did she need either the markets or the produce of the colonies. So the mainstays of Canadian development, the timber duties and the Corn Laws – which had provided a protected market for colonial wheat – disappeared between 1842 and 1846.

These British actions produced a panic in Canada. The situation was worsened by a general depression in the western world and by the Irish famine migration. The failure of the potato crop in Ireland caused widespread starvation and disease. Tens of thousands fled the disaster; in 1847 alone, some 100,000 set out for the North American colonies. Many died along the way, but the survivors arrived in the colonies bringing with them their diseases and their poverty. An economy already disrupted by depression and free trade reeled under the impact of the Irish hordes. The colonial mind, conditioned by the experience of the imperial system of the past, could conceive of few solutions to the compound crisis of the 1840's.

The events of April, 1849, in Montreal demonstrated this failure of imagination. The flashpoint was the Rebellion Losses Bill, a piece of legislation passed by the legislature of the Province of Canada that compensated Lower Canadians who had suffered property losses during the Rebellion of 1837. Tories charged that rebels would be paid for their treason. Behind their anger, however, lay other factors: anti-French prejudice; opposition to the political innovation of responsible government, implemented in 1848; and frustration over losing the election of 1847-48. The commercial problems of the 1840's, however, were the background noise for the crisis. The riots that began in Montreal on 25 April 1849 were led by Tory merchants, men whose livelihood had been threatened by free trade, depression, and famine Irish. Bred within the imperial system they could not imagine functioning without it. Their future seemed hopeless; they were alone in a highly competitive world. Their frustration boiled over in the Rebellion Losses riots, when they burned the parliament buildings, attacked the governor general, Lord Elgin, and threw Montreal into chaos. That autumn they took the next logical step and circulated the Annexation Manifesto, calling for Canada to join the United States. With one empire gone, the merchant reaction was to find another.

The Manifesto failed to gain support beyond the mercantile community and prosperity soon began to return. Canada could survive outside of the imperial womb. In part that survival rested on the beginning of capitalism, especially the construction of railways that fuelled the economy in the 1850's. The crucial year of 1849 saw the symbolic end of the old order with the repeal of the ancient source of the imperial system, the Navigation Acts. It also saw the beginning of the new order in the passage of the Guarantee Act by the Canadian parliament. Providing government guarantees for railway loans, it heralded not only the railway boom to come, but the intimate relationship of government and industry that would mark Canadian development.

This imperial structure underlay the staple economy described by Harold Innis in the present volume. Staple products, along with military concerns, were what made colonies attractive to the mother country; masts for men-of-war and square timber for construction were as much the raison d'être of colonial British America as beaver hats had been for New France. For most people in the colonies, however, the domestic economy was more important – the family farm and the village market. That is the focus of the selection from Fernand Ouellet in what is, admittedly, a controversial interpretation of the French-Canadian economy.

Within this grand context of empire and commerce, increasing numbers of people lived out their lives. As Judith Fingard describes in her essay in this volume, "The Poor in Winter," many were more affected by the climate than by imperial policy. Nevertheless, English needs had much to do with the structure of society that did emerge. The mother country's reluctance to lose manpower while fighting in Europe meant few migrated from Britain before 1815. Instead, the colonies – especially Nova Scotia and Upper Canada – had received much of their immigration from the United States. A Yankee cast of manners, of assumptions about social mobility and forms of agriculture and domestic architecture were stamped indelibly on the colonies. They would never be fully British.

England turned on the taps after the Napoleonic Wars and poured her surplus population on British North America. Her requirements shaped the character of the migration and ultimately of Canadian society. British North America received large numbers of the poor and unskilled and an undue proportion of gentle folk – retired military officers on half-pay, younger sons of the upper middle class, and the like. Compared to the United States, Canada received relatively few of the most productive workers, artisans, and capitalists. After the early 1830's, the immigration was dominated by Irish, fleeing their dying country and encouraged to leave by landlords and the British government. The contours of Canadian society were shaped by this selective immigration.

It was in many ways an unstable society, as the article by Ruth Bleasdale suggests. The rapidity of the peopling of Canada almost guaranteed that instability as disparate elements, different nationalities, different religions, and different classes were thrown together in a new environment. Friction and disorder were inevitable, especially when one of the elements, the Irish, had long traditions of disrespect for authority and of violence. To these factors were added ethnic and religious discrimination, as well as the economic oppression that tormented groups such as the canal workers.

The state played an increasing role in mediating between groups and in controlling their behaviour. This was especially true in the 1840's. The Rebellions had shown the danger in unrest and the necessity to control it before it grew into insurrection. The friction in a mixed society suggested the need to establish common patterns of behaviour and common economic, social, and political goals. Institutions of social control emerged to meet this need. Some were frankly coercive, such as police forces and prisons, mechanisms to frighten people into appropriate behaviour. Others were more subtle. The school became the most important institution of social control, a place where good citizenship, personal hygiene, the idea of progress, and respect for authority all would be inculcated in the young. Many in 1849 believed that if the schools were successful the disorder of a pioneer society would be a thing of the past.

Not all areas suffered the pressures of immigration and economic development. Sylvia Van Kirk discusses the special problems of women on the fur trade frontier. That frontier was a disorderly and often bloody place as two great fur companies, the North West Company of Montreal and the English Hudson's Bay Company, struggled for supremacy on the Prairies and across the Rockies. The chief victims of this war were the native peoples, debauched by traders' whiskey, their societies disrupted by white interference. The West quieted after the two companies merged in 1821 as the enlarged Hudson's Bay Company. Permanent settlements developed, the most important that at Red River, site of present-day Winnipeg. Indian society, however, would not recover from the ravages of the fur war and the tragic future of the native peoples already was written.

Women, east or west, always lived on a kind of frontier. They were isolated by custom from much of the mainstream of society, from politics and commerce and high decision-making. They nevertheless played an essential role, especially in the farm economy. They organized the household, managed the garden that produced most of the family's food, preserved food for the winter, and carried out a thousand and one necessary tasks. More, they produced the children who were the hope of the future; children were a vital labour force and they were old-age pensions for their parents, the only hope that mother and father would have at least subsistence when they were unable to work the farm. This importance gave rural women some measure of status, which was lacking for town women who had less significant roles.

Children were the hope of the future. But this did not mean they were pampered or coddled. They lived under a stern morality, which demanded that, in many essentials, they behave like small adults. They even looked like small adults, for clothing was basically the same for all ages. And they were expected to work.

When young, they worked with mother in the garden and at domestic tasks. When older, the boys went to the fields with father. It was a harsh regime, but the realities of life in a new world demanded that it be so.

It was a society with its diversions, however. Religion was perhaps the most important – services brought people together, people who might be isolated the rest of the week. The camp meetings held by the Methodists especially were emotional, evangelical gatherings that provided psychological release for many. And there were other diversions. Market days were chances to get together, drink, and, often, fight. Drink itself was important as a release and consumption was enormous, either at the numerous taverns or at home. Politics, too, provided an emotional outlet. In Canada, as everywhere, people found ways to temper the grimness of everyday life.

The essays in this volume will help to flesh out the picture of Canadian society in the pre-industrial period. They will help us understand how something distinctly British North American was emerging, as the echoes of the boots of British soldiers died away.

I
Economic Overview

Discussion of the pre-industrial economy has produced sharp controversy. The traditional view has been dominated by economist Harold Innis, one of the great original thinkers Canada has produced. His staples theory of economic growth stressed the dominating influence of natural products for export–furs, timber, wheat, minerals. No theory of similar general application has challenged the staples thesis, which even found new life in the 1960's and 1970's through Innis's disciple Marshall McLuhan and through a group of young nationalists who fastened on it as a distinctively Canadian explanation of development.

Other areas of interest have gripped economists and historians, such as landholding, agriculture, and immigration. The integration of economic and political history is well-advanced, especially in the work of Fernand Ouellet. While he is very much a historian, he works within a French tradition unfamiliar to English Canadians. He uses detail and statistics to build a broad interpretation. It is a controversial interpretation, for some other Quebec historians reject not only his negative conclusions about French-Canadian nationalism but even his picture of the physical reality. In particular, Jean-Pierre Wallot and Gilles Paquet have argued that there was no agricultural crisis at the beginning of the nineteenth century and advance their own set of statistics to support their view. They contend that both peasants and nationalists acted more rationally than Ouellet has suggested. This war of ideologies and statistics is likely to go on for some time to come.

FURTHER READING:
Some of Ouellet's articles, as well as an important piece by W. H. Parker, "A New Look at Unrest in Lower Canada," are collected in Ramsay Cook, ed., *Constitutionalism and Nationalism in Lower Canada* (Toronto, 1969). The major elements in the Lower-Canadian controversy can be sampled in two articles in the *Canadian Historical Review*: T. J. A. LeGoff, "The Agricultural Crisis in Lower Canada, 1802-12: A Review of a Controversy," LV, 1 (1974), 1-31; and G. Paquet and J. P. Wallot, "The Agricultural Crisis in Lower Canada, 1802-12: mise au point. A Response to T. J. A. LeGoff," LVI, 2 (1975), 133-68. On the merchant community, see Gerald J. J. Tulchinsky, *The River Barons* (Toronto, 1977). There is an extensive literature on timbering; the most comprehensive study is Arthur R. M. Lower, *Great Britain's Woodyard* (Montreal, 1973). A controversial discussion of land is Paul Phillips, "Land Tenure and Development in Upper and Lower Canada," *Journal of Canadian Studies*, IX, 2 (1974), 35-45. A radical view is that of Leo Johnson in "Land Policy, Population Growth and Social Structure in the Home District, 1793-1851," *Ontario History*, LXIII, 1 (1971), 41-60. The strongest defence of the classic staples theory is M. H. Watkins "A Staple Theory of Economic Growth," in W. T. Easterbrook and M. H. Watkins, eds., *Approaches to Canadian Economic History* (Toronto, 1967), 49-73.

Harold Adams Innis was head of the Department of Political Economy and Dean of Graduate Studies at University of Toronto. He was the author of such economic studies as *The Cod-Fisheries* (1940) and works in communications theory, including *The Bias of Communication* (1951). He died in 1952. **Fernand Ouellet**, author of *Histoire économique et sociale du Québec, 1760-1850* (1968), is Professor of History at Université d'Ottawa.

The Importance of Staple Products

by Harold Adams Innis

Fundamentally the civilization of North America is the civilization of Europe and the interest of this volume is primarily in the effects of a vast new land area on European civilization. The opening of a new continent distant from Europe has been responsible for the stress placed by modern students on the dissimilar features of what has been regarded as two separate civilizations. On the other hand communication and transportation facilities have always persisted between the two continents since the settlement of North America by Europeans, and have been subject to constant improvement.

Peoples who have become accustomed to the cultural traits of their civilization – what Mr. Graham Wallas calls the social heritage – on which they subsist, find it difficult to work out new cultural traits suitable to a new environment. The high death rate of the population of the earliest European settlements is evidence to that effect. The survivors live through borrowing cultural traits of peoples who have already worked out a civilization suitable to the new environment as in the case of the Indians of North America, through adapting their own cultural traits to the new environment, and through heavy material borrowing from the peoples of the old land. The process of adaptation is extremely painful in any case but the maintenance of cultural traits to which they have been accustomed is of primary importance. A

Reprinted from Harold A. Innis *The Fur Trade in Canada: An Introduction to Canadian Economic History* by permission of University of Toronto Press. © University of Toronto Press 1970.

sudden change of cultural traits can be made only with great difficulty and with the disappearance of many of the peoples concerned. Depreciation of the social heritage is serious.

The methods by which the cultural traits of a civilization may persist with the least possible depreciation involve an appreciable dependence on the peoples of the homeland. The migrant is not in a position immediately to supply all his needs and to maintain the same standard of living as that to which he has been accustomed, even with the assistance of Indians, an extremely fertile imagination, and a benevolent Providence such as would serve Robinson Crusoe or the Swiss Family Robinson on a tropical island. If those needs are to be supplied he will be forced to rely on goods which are obtainable from the mother country.

These goods were obtained from the homeland by direct transportation as in the movement of settlers' effects and household goods, involving no direct transfer of ownership, or through gifts and missionary supplies, but the most important device was trade. Goods were produced as rapidly as possible to be sold at the most advantageous price in the home market in order to purchase other goods essential to the maintenance and improvement of the current standard of living. In other words these goods supplied by the home country enabled the migrant to maintain his standard of living and to make his adjustments to the new environment without serious loss.

The migrant was consequently in search of goods which could be carried over long distances by small and expensive sailboats and which were in such demand in the home country as to yield the largest profit. These goods were essentially those in demand for the manufacture of luxuries, or goods which were not produced, or produced to a slight extent, in the home country as in the case of gold and of furs and fish. The latter was in some sense a luxury under the primitive conditions of agriculture in Europe and the demands of Catholic peoples. The importance of metropolitan centres in which luxury goods were in most demand was crucial to the development of colonial North America. In these centres goods were manufactured for the consumption of colonials and in those centres goods produced in the colonies were sold at the highest price. The number of goods produced in a north temperate climate in an area dominated by Pre-Cambrian formations, to be obtained with little difficulty in sufficient quantity and disposed of satisfactorily in the home market under prevailing transport conditions, was limited.

The most promising source of early trade was found in the

abundance of fish, especially cod, to be caught off the Grand Banks of Newfoundland and in the territory adjacent to the Gulf of St. Lawrence. The abundance of cod led the peoples concerned to direct all their available energy to the prosecution of the fishing industry which developed extensively. In the interior, trade with the Indians offered the largest returns in the commodity which was available on a large scale and which yielded substantial profits, namely furs and especially beaver. With the disappearance of beaver in more accessible territory, lumber became the product which brought the largest returns. In British Columbia gold became the product following the fur trade but eventually lumber and fish came into prominence. The lumber industry has been supplemented by the development of the pulp and paper industry with its chief reliance on spruce. Agricultural products – as in the case of wheat – and later minerals – gold, nickel, and other metals – have followed the inroads of machine industry.

The economic history of Canada has been dominated by the discrepancy between the centre and the margin of western civilization. Energy has been directed toward the exploitation of staple products and the tendency has been cumulative. The raw material supplied to the mother country stimulated manufactures of the finished product and also of the products which were in demand in the colony. Large-scale production of raw materials was encouraged by improvement of technique of production, of marketing, and of transport as well as by improvement in the manufacture of the finished product. As a consequence, energy in the colony was drawn into the production of the staple commodity both directly and indirectly. Population was involved directly in the production of the staple and indirectly in the production of facilities promoting production. Agriculture, industry, transportation, trade, finance, and governmental activities tend to become subordinate to the production of the staple for a more highly specialized manufacturing community. These general tendencies may be strengthened by governmental policy as in the mercantile system but the importance of these policies varies in particular industries. Canada remained British in spite of free trade and chiefly because she continued as an exporter of staples to a progressively industrialized mother country.

The general tendencies in the industrial areas of western civilization, especially in the United States and Great Britain, have had a pronounced effect on Canada's export of staples. In these areas machine industry spread with rapidity through the accessibility of the all-year-round ocean ports and the existence of ample supplies of coal and iron. In Great Britain the nineteenth century was characterized by increasing industrialization[1] with greater dependence on the staple products of new countries for raw material and on the population of these countries for a market. Lumber, wheat, cotton, wool, and meat may be cited as examples of staple imports. In the United States[2] the Civil War and railroad construction gave a direct stimulus to the iron and steel industry and hastened industrial and capitalistic growth. These two areas began to draw increasingly on outside areas for staples and even continental United States has found it necessary with the disappearance of free land, the decline of natural resources, and the demand for new industrial materials, notably rubber, to rely on outside areas as shown in her imperialistic policy of the twentieth century. Canada has participated in the industrial growth of the United States, becoming the gateway of that country to the markets of the British Empire. She has continued, however, chiefly as a producer of staples for the industrial centres of the United States even more than of Great Britain, making her own contribution to the Industrial Revolution of North America and Europe and being in turn tremendously influenced thereby.

I THE FUR TRADE

The history of the fur trade in North America has been shown as a retreat in the face of settlement. The strategic campaigns in that retreat include the Conquest of New France, the Quebec Act of 1774, the American Revolution, the Jay Treaty of 1794, the amalgamation of 1821, the Oregon Treaty of 1846, and the Rupert's Land Act of 1869. The struggle continues in the newly settled areas of the Dominion. The trade has been conducted by large organizations from the artificial and natural monopolies of New France to the Northwest Company and the Hudson's Bay Company which still occupies an important position. It has depended on the manufactures of Europe and the more efficient manufactures and cheaper transportation of England. Control of the fur trade was an index of world importance from the standpoint of efficient manufactures, control of markets, and consumption of luxuries. The shift from Paris to London of the fur trade was significant of the industrial growth of France and England – just as possession of Canada after the American Revolution was significant of the industrial limitations of the United States. The demands of the Indians for cheaper and greater quantities of goods were determining factors in the destiny of the northern half of North America.

The crises which disturbed the history of the fur trade were determined finally by various important factors including the geographic background and the industrial efficiency of England. These long-run factors were obscured by a complexity of causes which centred about each crisis. In the first half of the seventeenth century the Indian trading organization was essential to the trade. In the latter part of the century the French trading organization to the interior became more effective and the market became flooded with furs. Finally the geographic limits of the trade with the canoe were reached with the extension of the trade to the Saskatchewan in the first half of the eighteenth century. In the second half of the century transport became more efficient with the development of lake transport supplementary to the canoe and the trade was extended with increased capital resources and efficient business organization to the Pacific. With continued decline in the supply of beaver, the development of a more efficient transport and of a more elastic business organization from Hudson Bay, amalgamation became inevitable and the canoe disappeared as the dominant form of transport in the fur trade. Dependence on the York boat rather than the canoe was symbolic of the increasing importance of capitalism. After the amalgamation, improved transport facilities from the south led to the disappearance of monopoly control in 1869 and to the reign of competition which has become increasingly severe since that date. The beaver became less important after the amalgamation and the trade more dependent on other varieties of furs. Supply decreased less rapidly and in spite of competition the trade continued on a more permanent basis. Severe fluctuations were the result, throughout the period, of the discoveries of new territory and new Indians but especially of wars. These fluctuations were more serious in the earlier period of the French *régime* and occasioned serious results for the colony and the mother country. They became less serious after the Conquest and were less disastrous to the mother country. With the disappearance of these fluctuations, business organization became more efficient. But in the long run improved transport combined with geographic advantages reigned supreme. It was significant, however, that business organization was of vital importance to the trade and, combined with geographic advantages, maintained a strong position. This combination favoured the growth of capitalism which became conspicuous in the later days of the Northwest Company and in the succeeding Hudson's Bay Company especially after 1869.

The early history of the fur trade is essentially a history of the trade in beaver fur. The beaver was found in large numbers throughout the northern half of North America. The better grades of fur came from the more northerly forested regions of North America and were obtained during the winter season when the fur was prime. A vast north temperate land area with a pronounced seasonal climate was a prerequisite to an extensive development of the trade. The animal was not highly reproductive and it was not a migrant. Its destruction in any locality necessitated the movement of hunters to new areas.

The existence of the animal in large numbers assumed a relatively scant population. It assumed an area in which population could not be increased by resort to agriculture. Limitations of geological formation, and climate and a cultural background dependent on these limitations precluded a dense population with consequent destruction of animal life. The culture was dependent on indigenous flora and fauna and the latter was of prime importance. Moose, caribou, beaver, rabbit or hare, and fish furnished the chief supplies of food and clothing. This culture assumed a thorough knowledge of animal habits and the ability of the peoples concerned to move over wide areas in pursuit of a supply of food. The devices which had been elaborated included the snowshoe and the toboggan for the winter and the birch-bark canoe for the summer. This wide area contained numerous lakes and difficult connecting waterways, to which the canoe was adapted for extensive travel. Movement over this area occasioned an extended knowledge of geography and a widespread similarity of cultural traits such as language.

The area which was crucial to the development of the fur trade was the Pre-Cambrian shield of the northern half of the North American continent. It extended northwesterly across the continent to the mouth of the Mackenzie River and was bounded on the north by the northwesterly isothermal lines which determined the limits of the northern forests and especially of the canoe birch (*B. papyrifera*). The fur trade followed the waterways along the southern edge of this formation from the St. Lawrence to the Mackenzie River. In its full bloom it spread beyond this area to the Pacific drainage basin.

The history of the fur trade is the history of contact between two civilizations, the European and the North American, with especial reference to the northern portion of the continent. The limited cultural background of the North American hunting peoples provided an insatiable demand for the products of the more elaborate cultural development of Europeans. The supply of European goods, the product of a more advanced and specialized technology, enabled the Indians to gain a livelihood more easily – to obtain their supply of food, as in the case of moose, more quickly, and to hunt the beaver more effectively. Unfortunately the rapid destruction of the food supply and the revolution in the methods of living accompanied by the increasing attention to the fur trade by which these products were secured, disturbed the balance which had grown up previous to the coming of the European. The new technology with its radical innovations brought about such a rapid shift in the prevailing Indian culture as to lead to wholesale destruction of the peoples concerned by warfare and disease. The disappearance of the beaver and of the Indians necessitated the extension of European organization to the interior. New tribes demanded European goods in increasingly large amounts. The fur trade was the means by which this demand of the peoples of a more limited cultural development was met. Furs were the chief product suitable to European demands by which the North American peoples could secure European goods.

A rapid and extensive development of the trade followed accessibility to the vast areas of the Canadian Shield by the St. Lawrence and its numerous tributaries and by the rivers of the Hudson Bay drainage basin. Following a rapid decline in the supply of beaver in more accessible territory and the necessity of going to more remote areas, the trade began in the Maritime Provinces, extended rapidly by the Saguenay and later by the St. Lawrence and the Ottawa to the Great Lakes, and northwesterly across the headwaters of the rivers of Hudson Bay drainage basin from Lake Superior to Lake Winnipeg, the Saskatchewan, the Churchill, across the headwaters of the Mackenzie River drainage basin to Mackenzie and Peace rivers, and finally to the headwaters of rivers of the Pacific coast to New Caledonia and the Columbia. The waterways along the edge of the Canadian Shield tapped the rich fur lands of that area and in the smaller rivers of the headwaters of four drainage basins provided an environment to which the canoe could be adapted.

The extension of the trade across the northern half of the continent and the transportation of furs and goods over great distances involved the elaboration of an extensive organization of transport, of personnel, and of food supply. The development of transportation was based primarily on Indian cultural growth. The birch-bark canoe was borrowed and modified to suit the demands of the trade. Again, without Indian agriculture, Indian corn, and dependence on Indian methods of capturing buffalo and making pemmican, no extended organization of transport to the interior would have been possible in the early period. The organization of food supplies depended on agricultural development in the more favourable areas to the south and on the abundant fauna of the plains area. Limited transportation facilities, such as the canoe afforded, accentuated the organization and production of food supply in these areas. The extension of the fur trade was supported at convenient intervals by agricultural development as in the lower St. Lawrence basin, in southeastern Ontario, and areas centring about Detroit, and in Michilimackinac and Lake Michigan territory, in the west at Red River, though the buffalo were more important in the plains area in the beginning, and eventually in Peace River. On the Pacific coast an agricultural base was established on the Columbia.

The increasing distances over which the trade was carried on and the increasing capital investment and expense incidental to the elaborate organization of transport had a direct influence on its financial organization. Immediate trade with Europe from the St. Lawrence involved the export of large quantities of fur to meet the overhead costs of long ocean voyages and the imports of large quantities of heavy merchandise. Monopoly inevitably followed, and it was supported by the European institutional arrangements which involved the organization of monopolies for the conduct of foreign trade. On the other hand, internal trade, following its extension in the interior and the demand for larger numbers of *voyageurs* and canoes to undertake the difficult task of transportation and the increasing dependence on the initiative of the trader in carrying on trade with remote tribes, was, within certain limits, competitive. Trade from Quebec and Montreal with canoes up the Ottawa to Michilimackinac, La Baye, and Lake Superior could be financed with relatively small quantities of capital and was consequently competitive. Further extension of trade through Lake Superior by Grand Portage (later Kaministiquia) to Lake Winnipeg, the Saskatchewan, Athabasca, the Mackenzie River, and New Caledonia and the Pacific coast involved heavy overhead costs and an extensive organization of transportation. But the organization was of a type peculiar to the demands of the fur trade. Individual initiative was stressed in the partnership agreements which characterized the Northwest Company. The trade carried on over extended areas under conditions of limited transportation made close control of individual partners by a central organization impossible. The Northwest Company which extended its organization from the Atlantic to the Pacific developed along lines which were fundamentally linked to the technique of the fur trade. This organization was strengthened in the amalgamation of 1821 by control of a charter guaranteeing monopoly and by the advantages incidental to lower costs of transportation by Hudson Bay.

The effects of these large centralized organizations characteristic of the fur trade as shown in the monopolies of New France, in the Hudson's Bay Company, and in the Northwest Company were shown in the institutional development of Canada. In New France constant expansion of the trade to the interior had increased costs of transportation and extended the possibilites of competition from New England. The population of New France during the open season of navigation was increasingly engaged in carrying on the trade over longer distances to the neglect of agriculture and other phases of economic development. To offset the effects of competition from the English colonies in the south and the Hudson's Bay Company in the north, a military policy, involving Indian alliances, expenditure on strategic posts, expensive campaigns, and constant direct and indirect drains on the economic life of New France and old France, was essential. As a result of these developments control of political activities in New France was centralized and the paternalism of old France was strengthened by the fur trade. Centralized control as shown in the activities of the government, the church, the seigniorial system, and other institutions was in part a result of the overwhelming importance of the fur trade.

The institutional development of New France was an indication of the relation between the fur trade and the mercantile policy. The fur trade provided an ample supply of raw material for the manufacture of highly profitable luxury goods. A colony engaged in the fur trade was not in a position to develop industries to compete with manufactures of the mother country. Its weakness necessitated reliance upon the military support of the mother country. Finally the insatiable demands of the Indians for goods stimulated European manufactures.

The importance of manufactures in the fur trade gave England, with her more efficient industrial development, a decided advantage. The competition of cheaper goods contributed in a definite fashion to the downfall of New France and enabled Great Britain to prevail in the face of its pronounced militaristic development. Moreover, the importance of manufactured goods to the fur trade made inevitable the continuation of control by Great Britain in the northern half of North America. The participation of American and English merchants in the fur trade immediately following the Conquest led to the rapid growth of a new organization[3] which was instrumental in securing the Quebec Act and which contributed to the failure of the American Revolution so far as it affected Quebec and the St. Lawrence. These merchants were active in the negotiations prior to the Constitutional Act of 1791 and the Jay Treaty of 1794.[4] As prominent members of the government formed under the Quebec Act and the Constitutional Act, they did much to direct the general trend of legislation. The later growth of the Northwest Company assured a permanent attachment to Great Britain because of its dependence on English manufactures.

The northern half of North America remained British because of the importance of fur as a staple product. The continent of North America became divided into three areas: (1) to the north in what is now the Dominion of Canada, producing furs, (2) to the south in what were during the Civil War the secession states, producing cotton, and (3) in the centre the widely diversified economic territory including the New England states and the coal and iron areas of the middle west demanding raw materials and a market. The staple-producing areas were closely dependent on industrial Europe, especially Great Britain. The fur-producing area was destined to remain British. The cotton-producing area was forced after the Civil War to become subordinate to the central territory just as the northern fur-producing area, at present producing the staples, wheat, pulp and paper, minerals, and lumber, tends to be brought under its influence.

The Northwest Company and its successor the Hudson's Bay Company established a centralized organization which covered the northern half of North America from the Atlantic to the Pacific. The importance of this organization was recognized in boundary disputes, and it played a large role[5] in the numerous negotiations responsible for the location of the present boundaries. It is no mere accident that the present Dominion coincides roughly with the fur-trading areas of northern North America. The bases of supplies for the trade in Quebec, in western Ontario, and in British Columbia represent the agricultural areas of the present Dominion. The Northwest Company was the forerunner of the present confederation.

There are other interesting by-products of the study which may be indicated briefly. Canada has had no serious problems with her native peoples since the fur trade depended primarily on these races. In the United States no point of contact of such magnitude was at hand and troubles with the Indians were a result. The existence of small and isolated sections of French half-breeds throughout Canada is another interesting survival of this contact.[6] The half-breed has never assumed such importance in the United States.

"The lords of the lakes and forest have passed away" but their work will endure in the boundaries of the Dominion of Canada and in Canadian institutional life. The place of the beaver in Canadian life has been fittingly noted in the coat of arms. We have given to the maple a prominence which was due to the birch. We have not yet realized that the Indian and his culture were fundamental to the growth of Canadian institutions. We are only beginning to realize the central position of the Canadian Shield.

II THE FOREST INDUSTRIES

Canada emerged as a political entity with boundaries largely determined by the fur trade. These boundaries included a vast north temperate land area extending from the Atlantic to the Pacific and dominated by the Canadian Shield. The present Dominion emerged not in spite of geography but because of it. The significance of the fur trade consisted in its determination of the geographic framework. Later economic developments in Canada were profoundly influenced by this background.

The decline of the fur trade in eastern Canada which followed the export of furs from the Northwest through Hudson Bay after 1821 necessitated increased dependence on other staple exports.

Wheat and potash had become increasingly important but they were overshadowed by the rise of the lumber trade. The transport organization and personnel of the fur trade and its capitalistic beginnings were shifted to the development of new lines of trade.[7] An extended financial organization under the fur trade was attested by the plans for the first establishment of a bank in Canada with the strong support of Phyn and Ellice[8] and the establishment of the Bank of Montreal in 1817[9] with John Gray, an old fur trader, as president and John Richardson of Forsyth, Richardson & Company, as a strong supporter. McGill University persisted as a memorial to the wealth acquired by James McGill. Edward Ellice became an important figure in London with strong colonial interests and Simon McGillivray retained an interest in colonial activities. On this basis, with the advantages of preference in England and abundant and cheap shipping after the war, the lumber exports to Great Britain increased rapidly in the face of Baltic competition.

As with the fur trade the development of the lumber trade depended on water transportation. A bulky commodity, it was restricted in the early period to the large rivers. The buoyant softwoods could be floated in rafts down the St. Lawrence and the Ottawa to Quebec for shipment to England. The largest and best trees were in demand for the square-timber trade. Square timber was in demand in England for the wooden shipbuilding industry, exports of which reached a peak in 1845.[10] As the largest trees were cleared out it became necessary to go farther from the large rivers for timber and with smaller streams the long, square timber was more difficult to handle. Moreover, the cutting off of the forests and destruction by fires caused a decline in the flow of water in the streams and enhanced the difficulties and cost of transport. Decline in the use of wooden sailing vessels and increase in the use of iron steamships had an important effect on the square-timber trade. The saw-log trade developed with the improvement of sawmills which sprang into existence at an early date in response to the local demands of settlements. With decline in the size of logs, improvement of sawmill technique, and the hastening of transport in steamships, deals became of greater importance and, in the period prior to 1867, reached a peak in 1862.

The lumber industry created an important problem of overhead costs. Ships sailing from Quebec with lumber were in search of a return cargo which emigration provided.[11] "Coffin ships" suitable for the lumber trade were employed to take out emigrants. Immigration and settlement brought an increase in imports of manufactured products and in exports of potash, wheat, lumber, and other products. With agricultural development, labour and supplies were available for the seasonal prosecution of the lumber industry. With the westward movement settlement increased in Upper Canada and the middle west, the forests were cleared, and the St. Lawrence and the Great Lakes became more important as a transport route. The export of commodities[12] from the territory above Niagara Falls and in Upper Canada and the western states was shown in an increase from 54,219 tons of traffic in 1836 to 1,045,821 tons in 1851 passing through the Erie Canal. Wheat exported through the Welland Canal increased from 210,105 bu. in 1831 to 1,579,966 bu. in 1841, and merchandise increased from 736 tons in 1831 to 4,051 tons in 1841. The completion of the Welland Canal made possible the export of timber from the territory above Niagara Falls. Exports of staves increased from 137,718 in 1831 to 2,776,161 in 1841, square timber (cu. ft.) from 75,992 in 1832 to 1,155,086 in 1841, lumber (ft.) 986,888 in 1831 to 3,580,911 in 1841, saw logs, 4,187 in 1831 to 11,300 in 1841.

With increase in exports and imports to Upper Canada the demand for improved communication on the upper St. Lawrence became more insistent. Rafts of timber could be floated down the rapids but loads of grain and merchandise both up- and downstream became more difficult to handle. The demand of settlers for cheaper transport was an important factor in the struggle over the control of revenue to finance the construction of canals. The Act of Union of 1840 offered a solution and was followed by rapid construction of canals in the decade to 1850. Improvements of waterways were rendered obsolete through the disadvantage of water transportation, especially on the St. Lawrence with its northerly direction and its long closed season, and the construction of railroads to the seaboard in the United States. Railway lines were built after 1850 to shorten the water routes as in the road from Toronto to Collingwood. The Grand Trunk was extended from Sarnia to Montreal and Portland on the open seaboard. These railways not only joined the important settlements along the waterways but provided for the settlement of territory distant from the lakes and rivers. They provided an all-year-round outlet for lumber and agricultural produce from

Canada and the United States, and for the import of merchandise.

The improvement of transportation in canals and railways had important effects on the lumber trade in providing for an extension of the supply of raw material and of the market for the finished product. The increasing demand for lumber in the United States following the rapid development of settlement in the Middle West and the growth of towns, as Chicago, stimulated the production of planks and boards. Decline in the size of trees and an increase in the number of saw logs and of smaller logs facilitated the introduction of modern sawmill technique with gang saws and band saws adapted to mass production. More recently the decline in supplies of American lumber and the rise in price of lumber hastened production on a large scale. Machine industry became increasingly important to the lumber industry. Dependence on water transportation for the raw material and the finished product, and on water power for sawing (latterly on steam power), was responsible for concentration of the industry at the mouths of large rivers as in New Brunswick. Mills were located at points accessible to large vessels along the coast and the Great Lakes as on Georgian Bay and at important waterfalls on the large rivers of the interior – the Saguenay, the St. Maurice, and the Ottawa. With the concentration, railways increased the supply of raw material as in the construction of the Canada and Atlantic Railway from Ottawa to Parry Sound by J. R. Booth.

The increasing demand for paper in the United States and the exhaustion of more available supplies of pulpwood were factors responsible for the development of the pulp and paper industry especially after 1900. Machine industry in lumber production provided a basis for the pulp and paper industry with its demands for large quantities of capital. Lumber interests were in control of substantial timber limits, of large sources of power, of skilled labour especially in the woods sections, and of capital. The decline of white pine and the existence of large quantities of spruce on the limits facilitated the shift to pulp and paper production. The migration of capital, skill, and technique from the United States hastened the movement. The forest industries concentrated about the mouths of the large rivers of the Atlantic and later the Pacific coast, the pulp and paper industry being dependent on those tributaries of the Atlantic and the Pacific which furnished abundant supplies of power.

III CAPITALISM AND THE STAPLES

The lumber industry of eastern Canada was largely responsible directly and indirectly for the improvement of waterways and for the construction of railways prior to Confederation. Canal and railway construction was synonymous with heavy capital investment. Capital was obtained through private enterprise and substantial guarantees and aid from the imperial and colonial governments. Heavy expenditures involved the development of a strong centralized government in Canada. Canada's financial organization had been greatly strengthened through the strains incidental to the lumber industry. The crises in Great Britain and the United States in 1825-26, 1837, 1847, and 1857 had serious effects on construction industries and on the trade of a country interested in the export of lumber. The collapse of weaker banks in these periods contributed to the centralization of banking structure which became conspicuous in the period after Confederation. The fur trade and the lumber industry contributed the basic features essential to expansion after Confederation.

Capital investment in the transport improvement of eastern Canada brought serious problems. Immigration, settlement, and agriculture were hastened by the railroads but these were not adequate to support the overhead costs incidental to the heavy initial outlay in railroad construction and early railroad finance. Railway materials had been supplied by the rapidly expanding industry of Great Britain, and English financiers, as well as the Canadian government, were anxious to promote measures increasing traffic and reducing overhead. Sir Edward Watkin with the concurrence of the Duke of Newcastle proposed to extend the Grand Trunk to the west as a means of guaranteeing the successful operation of the road and as an escape from bankruptcy. Capital expenditures on canals had been largely responsible for the Act of Union and the additional expenditures on railways were largely responsible for Confederation and its provisions for the inclusion of the area westward to the Pacific.

Grand Trunk interests[13] in 1863 acquired control of the Hudson's Bay Company in London. This step was followed by Confederation in 1867, the sale of Rupert's Land to Canada in 1869, and finally the construction of the Canadian Pacific Railway. At one stroke Imperial interests and Grand Trunk interests favourable to the new technique replaced Hudson's Bay Company interests favourable to the fur trade. The large central organization in the fur trade facilitated the transfer and the organization of the new technique over a wide area. The fur trade and its personnel[14] continued to be fundamentally important. The fur trade had not only produced a centralized organization but it had produced a succession of fur traders who were typically self-reliant, energetic, and possessed of keen bargaining ability and high organizing capacity. D.A. Smith, later Lord Strathcona,[15] was not only an important official in the Hudson's Bay Company, trained in the school of the fur trade, but he was an influential force in the construction and management of the Canadian Pacific Railway which heralded the new industry. The relationship which existed with the opening of western Canada, in which important officials of the Hudson's Bay Company were prominent in the activities of the Bank of Montreal, of the Canadian Pacific Railway Company, and of the Dominion government, was not accidental.

The superposition of machine industry on an institutional background characteristic of the fur trade was effected with remarkably little disturbance. The rapidity with which the Industrial Revolution has swept across the North American continent was a result of the centralized organization which had paved the way for immediate growth. The economic organization of the fur trade was dependent on the Canadian Shield for a supply of furs and on the development of agriculture at convenient intervals to support the heavy cost of transportation. The economic organization of modern industrial Canada has depended on these agriculturally developed areas and more recently on the Canadian Shield. Agriculture and other lines of economic activity were started in suitable territory south of the Canadian Shield under the direction of the fur trade. The organization of the fur trade occasioned the organization of other lines of trade. The forwarding of supplies to the interior and the heavy one-way, in most cases upstream, traffic of the trade stimulated the development of trade in exports other than furs. The Hudson's Bay Company shifted from the fur trade to the retail and wholesale trade as the large number of their department stores in western Canada attests. The development of transportation organization in the recent gold rush from Hudson to Red Lake along lines already opened by the Hudson's Bay Company is evidence to the same effect. Early agriculture in Red River paved the way for the extensive production of wheat on the plains following the construction of the railroads. The parallel between wheat and furs is significant. Both involve a trunk line of transportation from Montreal to Winnipeg and feeders, in the case of the fur trade, to the north, and, in the case of wheat, to the south. Both were staples dependent on industrialized Europe for a market.

The construction of the Canadian Pacific Railway to the Pacific implied a marked advance in technology such as characterized the construction of transcontinental roads in the United States, notably cheap production of iron and steel and high explosives and standardized methods of railroad construction. The westward movement in the United States which had been speeded up with the steamboat and the railroad, eventually reached the northern part of the plains area. The stretch of level and agricultural territory in western Canada was settled during the period at which industrialism had gained momentum on the North American continent. The construction of a railway across the Canadian Shield added to the overhead costs incidental to earlier construction in eastern Canada. Rapid settlement of the prairies, rapid increase in the export of wheat and in imports of manufactured products, were encouraged as a means of increasing traffic. Wheat became a new staple export demanded to an increasing extent by the industrially deficient countries and produced, transported, and manufactured on a large scale only through the efficiency of modern industrialism.[16] With the addition of other transcontinental lines the main framework of the railway system was completed and Canada came under the full swing of modern capitalism with its primary problems of reducing overhead costs.

The problems of wheat incidental to overhead costs are of primary importance. Wheat is a plant grown in a north temperate land area. Its production has increased at a rapid rate over a long period; it affords a pronounced seasonal traffic especially as it is largely dependent on seasonal navigation; it has decided variations in yield and it occasions a pronounced one-way traffic. Wheat is shipped to the elevators on Lake Superior, to Georgian Bay ports, to Port Colborne and down the St. Lawrence to Montreal, and to Buffalo and New York. Shipping in the Great Lakes is suspended during the closed season and overhead costs on grain boats and elevators contribute to the general problem of the railroads.[17] Numerous devices have been followed in solution of the problem. The tariff has been invoked for the encouragement of a return traffic from the industrial east. The rapid industrial growth of eastern Canada and the growth of its metropolitan centres hastened the development of mixed farming. Heavy one-way traffic of vessels calling for wheat at Montreal provides for cheap freight on imports of raw material. The production of power on the proposed St. Lawrence waterway will hasten the tendency toward increased manufactures. The wheat flow has been reduced by increasing shipments through the all-year-open port of Vancouver and the Panama Canal. Industries of the Canadian Shield including lumbering, pulp and paper, mining, power development, and agriculture have been stimulated. The tourist traffic has been fostered. At the western extremity of the railroads in British Columbia overhead costs have been reduced through the rapid increase in the production of lumber, pulp and paper, minerals, agricultural products, canned salmon and halibut, and the export of wheat. The early rapid progress of the colony resulting from gold discoveries, and its feverish later development, were stabilized through railway construction, steamship connections with the Orient, and machine industry.

In the fundamental problem of reduction of overhead costs, mining has occupied an important position necessitating the importation of large quantities of mining supplies to the Canadian Shield and providing for constant operation without appreciable seasonal fluctuations. The location of the mines within relatively short distances from the railroads has been a factor minimizing the problem of overhead charges. The pulp and paper industry has also contributed in its constant export of the finished product and its constant demands for labour and supplies. The development of surplus power, chiefly a result of the pulp and paper industry, has stimulated manufactures as in the conspicuous example of Arvida on the Saguenay. The problems consequent to a decline in the mining towns and to the exhaustion of resources will in part be solved by a shift in the use of power in these industries to manufactures. The industries of the Canadian Shield represent a direct contribution to the reduction of overhead costs–a contribution which promises to become even more important with the opening of the Hudson Bay region. The Maritime Provinces have unfortunately been outside the main continental developments although they have contributed to the main task through exports of coal, iron and steel, brains, and brawn. It is quite probable that they will become more closely linked with the movements following the opening of the Hudson Bay route.

The relation of the government of Canada to general economic growth has been unique. The heavy expenditures on transport improvements, including railways and canals, have involved government grants, subsidies, and guarantees to an exceptional degree. The budget debates on the heavy debt of the Canadian National Railways are an annual reminder of the relation between transport and government. The Canadian government has been an important contributor to the prosperity of the Canadian Pacific Railway and to the maintenance of the Canadian National Railways. The unique character of this development has been largely a result of the sudden transfer of large areas tributary to the fur trade to the new industrialism. The British North America Act, like the Act of Union, has provided for a strong central government. The prairie provinces as producers of wheat were controlled from Montreal and Ottawa as they were controlled in the earlier period as producers of fur under the Northwest Company. With the United States, residuary powers[18] were left with the states whereas in Canada they remain with the federal government or rather with eastern Canada. Canada came under the sweep of the Industrial Revolution at one stroke whereas the westward movement of the United States was a gradual development. There are no transcontinental railroads controlled by one organization in the United States. In Canada transcontinental roads are distinct entities controlled in eastern Canada. Similarly in financial institutions the branch bank system with headquarters in the east has been typical of Canada but not of the United States. No such tendency toward unity of structure in institutions and toward centralized control as found in Canada can be observed in the United States. The Canadian government has a closer relation to economic activities than most governments. The trade in staples, which characterizes an economically weak country, to the highly industrialized areas of Europe and latterly the United States, and especially the fur trade, has been responsible for various peculiar tendencies in Canadian development. The maintenance of connections with Europe, at first with France and later with Great Britain, has been a result. The diversity of institutions which has attended this relationship has made for greater elasticity in organization and for greater tolerance among her peoples. This elasticity of institutions facilitated the development of the compromise which evolved in responsible government[19] and the British Empire. Having failed in her own colonial policy England was able to build up an empire in Canada on the remarkable success of French colonial policy. The fur trade permitted the extension of the combination of authority and independence across the northern half of the continent. Moreover, the business structure shifted from the elastic organization characteristic of the Northwest Company along the St. Lawrence from the Atlantic to the Pacific, to the more permanent organization from Hudson Bay. The diversity of institutions has made possible the combination of government ownership and private enterprise which has been a further characteristic of Canadian development. Canada has remained fundamentally a product of Europe.

The importance of staple exports to Canadian economic development began with the fishing industry but more conspicuously on the continent with the fur trade. The present boundaries[20] were a result of the dominance of furs. The exploitation of lumber in the more accessible areas followed the decline of furs. The geographic unity of Canada which resulted from the fur trade became less noticeable with the introduction of capitalism and the railroads. Her economic development has been one of gradual adjustment of machine industry to the framework incidental to the fur trade. The sudden growth occasioned by the production of wheat and the development of subsequent staples in the Canadian Shield have been the result of machine industry. It is probable that these sudden changes will become less conspicuous as a result of a more closely knit unity and of the constant pressure of heavy overhead costs, and that Canadian growth will proceed on a more even keel. Revolutions in transport, which have such devastating effects on new countries producing raw materials, will become less disturbing even though full allowance is made for the effects of the Hudson Bay railway.

NOTES

1. C. R. Fay, *Great Britain: An Economic and Social Survey from Adam Smith to the Present Day* (London, 1928).
2. Charles A. and Mary R. Beard, *The Rise of American Civilization* (New York, 1927-1942), 4 vols.
3. M. G. Reid, "The Quebec Fur-Traders and Western Policy, 1763-1774," *CHR*, VI (1925), 15-32.
4. Wayne E. Stevens, *The Northwest Fur Trade, 1763-1800* (Urbana, Ill. 1928).
5. *Ibid*.
6. Marcel Giraud, *Le métis canadien: son rôle dans l'histoire des provinces de l'Ouest* (Paris, 1945).
7. F. W. Howay, "The Fur Trade in Northwestern Development," in *The Pacific Ocean in History: Papers and Addresses Presented at the Panama-Pacific Historical Congress* (New York, 1917).

8. For an advertisement of the Canadian Banking Company, see: R. M. Breckenridge, *The Canadian Banking System, 1817-1890* (Toronto, 1894), 18.

9. Bank of Montreal, *The Centenary of the Bank of Montreal, 1817-1917* (Montreal, 1917).

10. A. R. M. Lower, "A History of the Canadian Timber and Lumber Trade prior to Confederation" (M.A. thesis, University of Toronto, 1923).

11. Helen I. Cowan, *British Emigration to British North America: The First Hundred Years* (Toronto, 1928; reprint, 1961).

12. J. L. McDougall, "The Welland Canal to 1841" (M.A. thesis, University of Toronto, 1923).

13. Sir E. W. Watkin, *Canada and the States: Recollections, 1851 to 1886* (London, 1887). On the problems of the period, see: R. G. Trotter, *Canadian Federation, Its Origins and Achievements: A Study in Nation-building* (Toronto, 1924); Trotter, "British Finance and Confederation," *CHAR* (1927), 89-96.

14. Professor O. D. Skelton, in a review of H. A. Innis, *History of the Canadian Pacific Railway* (London, 1923; reprint, Toronto, 1971), in *CHR*, IV, 2 (1923), has pointed out the neglect of personality in the development of the railway. The importance of the fur trade would appear to strengthen his contention.

15. It is an interesting conjecture that the dramatic episode in the House of Commons in which Mr. D. A. Smith was in a position to oust the Macdonald administration from the government in 1873 was in part related to his connections to the fur trade. Rumours were current that Sir Hugh Allan was engaged in promoting a rival fur company to operate in the Northwest and his position as president of the Canadian Pacific Company to whom the charter for the construction of the transcontinental road had been given made this possibility unusually alarming. Mr. D. A. Smith as fur trade commissioner of the Hudson's Bay Company may have found his task in deciding the fate of the project during the debate on the Pacific scandal somewhat easier than is ordinarily supposed. See Beckles Willson, *The Life of Lord Strathcona and Mount Royal (1820-1914)* (Toronto, 1915), 337. For a most suggestive biography of Lord Strathcona, see John Macnaughton, *Lord Strathcona* (Toronto, 1926).

16. For an interesting description of the importance of machine industry in the United States, see: Thorstein B. Veblen, "The Price of Wheat Since 1867," *Journal of Political Economy*, I (1892), 69-103.

17. The importance of wheat to the overhead problems of the Canadian Pacific Railway has been described in Innis, *History of the Canadian Pacific Railway*.

18. O. D. Skelton, *The Life and Times of Sir Alexander Tilloch Galt* (Toronto, 1920), especially on Galt's place in the Confederation movement; also, W. B. Munro, *American Influences on Canadian Government* (Toronto, 1929), ch. I, and W. P. Kennedy, "Canada: Law and the Customs in the Canadian Constitution," *Round Table* (December, 1929), 143-60.

19. Georges Vattier, *Essai sur la mentalité canadienne-française* (Paris, 1928).

20. David Thompson was probably recommended by Ogilvie to help in the boundary commission: J. J. Bigsby, *The Shoe and the Canoe* (London, 1850), chs. II, V. J. B. Tyrrell became interested in Thompson through his work on the Dominion survey. Tyrrell bridges the gap between the fur trade, settlement (survey), and mining, the most recent development. See the biography of Tyrrell by W. J. Loudon, *A Canadian Geologist* (Toronto, 1930).

The Rural Economic Crisis in Lower Canada

by Fernand Ouellet

The golden age of the fur trade – merchant adventurers, *coureurs des bois*, and close economic ties between Indians and whites and between the east and the far west – was virtually a thing of the past by the beginning of the nineteenth century. With the Napoleonic wars as a stimulus, lumber emerged as a new staple trade. Without it the collapse of the fur economy would have been disastrous.

In the early years of the new century, wheat production tended increasingly to fall behind a burgeoning population growth, to a point where, by 1830, Lower Canada had become a major importer of wheat. The decline, of course, progressed more rapidly in some regions than others, and some producers were slower than others to read the writing on the wall and abandon the old, wasteful agricultural methods. But not a single rural parish was spared, and by 1840 the entire farming population was more or less seriously affected.

A major shift in production structures occurred as wheat production failed even to fulfil subsistence requirements and farmers turned to other crops, notably oats and potatoes, and discovered a new interest in livestock. But the basic problem remained,

From Fernand Ouellet, *Lower Canada, 1791-1840: Social Change and Nationalism,* translated and adapted by Patricia Claxton (Toronto, 1980), 117-8, 119-29, 131-4, 137-8, 140-2. Reprinted by permission of The Canadian Publishers, McClelland and Stewart Limited.

namely the inadequacy of farming methods resulting in disappointing yields and quality. A proportion of farmers found outlets locally for their produce, but it became increasingly difficult to be competitive in the urban marketplace. With growing rural dependence on imported wheat, self-sufficiency became impossible. The agricultural crisis became a social one, whose effects spilled from the rural districts into the cities.

Despite the convergent ill winds of falling agricultural production and a general decline in prices, certain sectors of the economy were making progress. Trade in Upper-Canadian and American produce to fill the vacuum in both the Lower-Canadian and imperial markets stimulated growth for the transportation sector and for the city of Montreal. The new trade patterns and the lumber economy necessitated the appearance of banks. With the end of the continental blockade Great Britain continued to protect her colonies with preferential tariffs, and the lumber trade, far from returning to its previous marginal state as feared by Quebec City merchants, continued to flourish.

Forestry became the dominant economic activity in the Ottawa Valley and many townships, and while local contractors and the middle classes of Quebec profited most from it, it also provided a supplementary source of income for much of the population in the rural parishes, especially in the Quebec district.

Thus the economy of Lower Canada changed, but remained profoundly affected by the crisis in agriculture, the sector whose fortunes weighed most heavily on the lives of the greatest number of individuals and especially on the future of the French-speaking population. . . .

I THE AGRICULTURAL CRISIS

The picture of changing agricultural structures obtainable from the various indicators shows the decline in wheat production beginning around 1802 overall, and earlier in certain regions.[1] The principal variables at work were three, soil fertility, stability of landholdings, and population growth. Providing the soil was fertile and landholdings stable, in all cases peak yields were attained toward the end of the first major phase of settlement in a given region, with stagnation or decline thereafter. In the oldest parishes where, even in the eighteenth century, settlement was rapid, cultivation intense, and subdivision under way, the decline in production began between 1790 and 1802. In certain parishes the progress of urbanization was an important factor in patterns of change. Such was the case with the parish of Montreal, where the English-speaking led the way in commercializing agriculture; there the wheat decline was reflected in a shift toward oats and particularly potatoes.

Thus a transformation occurred between 1800 and 1840 which saw wheat fall from between 60 and 70 per cent of all agricultural production (the level which had prevailed since the seventeenth century) to 21 per cent in 1831 (a good crop year) and to 4.4 per cent in 1844. Production per farm family in good crop years from 1760 to 1802 had averaged between 100 and 200 *minots*, but was only 56.5 *minots* in 1831 and 12 *minots* in 1844. In 1831 the average per family was less than 50 *minots* in 37.9 per cent of the parishes and less than 100 *minots* in 76 per cent; in 1844 the average was less than 50 *minots* in 98 per cent of the parishes. Attempts were made to increase the production of other grains such as barley, rye, and buckwheat from which flour might be made, either alone or with some wheat content. They succeeded only marginally, the reason of course being the same as for the decline in wheat production.

By 1833, though he was consuming less bread, the *habitant* was dependent for his very subsistence on grain produced by his competitors in Upper Canada, and he was to remain so. The roles were now reversed. Over the long term the wheat crisis, along with the lumber trade, was to strengthen the economic ties between the Canadas. Isolation in self-sufficiency was now impossible in any event. Wheat was no longer the mainstay of the *habitant's* diet and his source of supplementary income but a commodity to be bought if he could afford it.

A change in production structures was inevitable, but the *habitant*, alas, was slow to change his habits until forced to do so. W. H. Parker's conclusion that the decline of wheat began after 1830 with a blight of wheat flies and that oats became a major replacement crop[2] does not appear to be borne out by the records. Tithe reports between 1805 and 1831 and parish inventories of 1827 and 1831 show that in most seigneuries the proportion of oats to total harvest remained about the same as during the French Régime. It is true, however, that the proportion of oats rose to 33 per cent by 1844, but there is no indication that oatmeal acquired importance in the French-Canadian diet. Most of the oat mills were probably built to serve the English population.

The principal replacement crop was in fact potatoes, a rich source of nourishment. Modest quantities had earlier been grown for feeding pigs, but during the difficult years from 1813 to 1816 the *habitant*, having insufficient bread, discovered a liking for this food and it soon came to have a place of honour on his table. In 1819 a contemporary observed, "Potatoes were introduced in Canada only after the Conquest of 1760; and all now grow them in abundance. The quantity sown every year has increased four-fold since 1816, because they were almost the only recourse in that year of shortage."[3] Parish inventories of 1827 and 1831 show potatoes accounting for 47 and 46 per cent of total harvests. It seems, however, that the French Canadians did not grow them for sale. In the cities, lumber camps, and even rural areas there was a fairly strong local market, but the biggest producers were English-speaking, and it was they who supplied that market. For the French Canadians potatoes were a subsistence crop, but, grown by traditional methods, they proved after 1830 to be sub-ject to adverse conditions and also costly in soil fertility.

With the dwindling supply of wheat and less money in rural hands, the rural diet contained not only less bread but less im-ported sugar, about the same amount of peas, more maple sugar and above all, along with potatoes, more pork. In 1784, a hog count of over four per household was registered in 41 per cent of seigneurial parishes; in 1831 the proportion was 75 per cent, but fell to 11 per cent during the following decade. Demand was strong and prices on the whole fairly good; some of the rural folk were undoubtedly raising hogs to increase or maintain their in-comes, but the majority were more concerned with subsistence than sales. The hog-raiser with pork surpluses, moreover, had difficulty competing with foreign producers in the urban market and by and large was obliged to sell his product in the rural districts. With the new emphasis on hog-raising, the *habitant* once again paid the price of poor farming methods and found himself in most difficult straits in the post-1830 depression. Be-tween 1831 and 1842, the average number of hogs per farm in the Montreal district dropped from 4.7 to 3.3.

The decline in rural incomes after 1815 also forced the *habitant* to turn to his own devices to clothe himself. In 1819 it was ob-served, "Flax is grown in great quantity at present in this district [Quebec] and a rough linen is made from it for domestic use. The farmer now finds himself more obliged to pay attention to this ar-ticle and [also] to increase the number of his sheep in order to have enough to clothe himself while the products of the land are at such low price on the markets of Great Britain."[4] And in 1821, in the midst of a market crisis, "Unless the habitants of the district of Montreal begin more generally to make their own cloth with which to dress, they will soon be unable to protect themselves from the rigours of the seasons."[5] Sheep-raising in this period increased considerably in comparison with that of the eighteenth century. Parish inventories show an average of more than four sheep per farm in 87 per cent of the parishes in 1831 and the same in 1844 (68 per cent in 1784). In regions of sheep-raising on a larger scale, however, the size of flocks diminished after 1832, the proportion of parishes with an average of over 16 sheep per farm falling from 10 per cent to 2 per cent by 1844. Here again, the produce of the seigneuries was uncompetitive in the marketplace. Only the English-speaking attempted textile manufacturing on a commercial scale.

Similar observations can be made regarding cattle-raising for milk, butter, cheese, leather, and meat. Deficiencies in local production kept prices from following the general decline after 1815, and after 1820 there was an increase in the size of cattle herds; in 1831, 16 per cent of the parishes registered average herds of more than 10 "*bêtes á cornes*" per farm, but the proportion was only 8 per cent in 1844 (3 per cent in 1784). Since English-speaking farmers were the most active in this domain, they were the most severely affected by the post-1830 depression.

As the scarcity of new, fertile land became acute, the inadequacy of farming methods began to have disastrous consequences. European practice forbade the sowing of wheat two years in a row in the same field because it would impoverish the soil and produce poor-quality grain, but the *habitant* ignored the rule, often in contravention of the terms of his concession. When the soil began to show unmistakable signs of exhaustion, or when the needs of a growing family required, or when export market demand encouraged it, he would turn to newly cleared land. When subdivided, the land would lose its fertility all the more quickly. During the second half of the eighteenth century, the average wheat yield per *arpent* had been between six and twelve *minots*, but by 1831 it was only about three *minots* and even less in the following decade. Agricultural societies, noting the effectiveness of experiments in the British Isles, campaigned with little success for crop rotation and for fertilization with manure, which was ordinarily thrown into rivers or dumped in some far corner of the farm. They also tried to stop the *habitant* from denuding his land of trees, which not only destroyed his reserves of wood but contributed to the impoverishment of the soil. Even before 1820, the agent for the seigneury of Laprairie was writing that "none of the concessions of the seigneury of Laprairie has any wood left either for firewood or fences."[6]

Resistance to change pervaded all aspects of farmwork. Ploughing and harrowing were shallow, as they had always been, for farm implements were essentially the same as had always been used; there were often more thistles in a field than wheat. The agricultural societies organized exhibitions of the latest equipment used in Great Britain; some progress was noted but more often the lack of it, for while some farmers did begin to modernize their equipment, most clung to their old implements and customs. A change to horses as draft animals in place of oxen was progressing, but slowly. The proportion of parishes with an average of less than two horses per farm in 1831 and 1844 was 46 per cent and 53 per cent respectively (76 per cent in 1784). . . .

The *habitant* was no more inclined to give up growing wheat than to improve his farming methods. A contemporary observed in 1821, "The price of wheat naturally affects the price of labour and of all agricultural production; perhaps in this country more than any other, for here wheat forms by far the greatest part of the habitant's food."[7] Declining production, vanishing surpluses, and the reluctance or refusal of the *habitant* to change his ways brought progressive constriction to what was already a chronically poverty-stricken rural existence. Most of the scant surpluses a farmer might possess passed into the hands of seigneurs, merchants, and clergy. . . .

In the eighteenth century, as estimated by several contemporaries, the *habitant* had consumed 3 pounds of bread a day, representing an annual per capita consumption of 13 *minots* of wheat. Gauldrée-Boileau, French consul in Quebec from 1858 to 1863, estimated the Gauthier family's wheat harvest of 165 *minots* to be divided as follows: food for the family of nine, 118 *minots*; seed, 25 *minots*; tithes, 6 *minots*; surplus, 16 *minots*.[8] Another observer estimated 40 *minots* to be the minimum necessary for a colonist, his wife, and three children,[9] the equivalent of 72 *minots* for a family of nine. In poor crop years a family either ate poorly in order to keep enough for seeding or ate reasonably well and had nothing left, and then would have to buy seed. On a farm in the seigneury of Murray Bay over the period 1838 to

1849, the wheat yield varied between 8.4 and 2.2 *minots* per *minot* sown; the amount sown, 8 to 40 *minots*, was thus 11 to 45 per cent of the amount harvested.[10] Surveys made in the poor crop years of 1813, 1816, 1826, and 1833 show a high rate of indebtedness; in 1833 most of the debts contracted in 1826 had yet to be repaid.

Besides food and seed, there were fixed obligations in bad years as in good, such as the *cens et rentes* paid to the seigneurs. The fee at seigneurial mills was about 1/13 of the wheat brought for milling. In the seigneury of Laprairie in 1806, the *rente* brought a total of 646 *minots*, and milling fees 2,400 *minots*. Revenue for 1815 from *lods et ventes*, payable by sellers of land at the rate of 1/12 of the price of sale, amounted to 9,171 French *livres*.[11] There is no doubt that the small producer's obligations to the seigneur weighed more and more heavily as production declined and prices eroded. The church also extracted its share. The tithe, the basis of the curés' personal incomes, took 1/26 of all grain harvested; reports of 46 parishes in the Montreal region for the years 1834, 1835, and 1836 show that 16 curés collected between 1,000 and 3,000 *minots* and 18 others between 500 and 1,000 *minots*.[12] Parishioners also made personal gifts to their curés. Then there were pew rentals, Sunday and holy-day collections and the Quête de l'Enfant-Jésus (a subscription to which each gave according to his means), masses to be paid for, fees for baptisms, marriages, and burials, and special contributions for church construction and repair. Like the seigneurs, the curés, both personally and as administrators of the *Fabriques*, had considerable quantities of agricultural produce for disposal in one way or another. The seigneurs and the curés in any event seem to have reaped considerably more than the farmers from the export and urban grain trade after the turn of the century.

The *habitant* had necessarily to sell some of his produce to meet his cash payments to the seigneur and the curé, and to obtain imported commodities he would need for his own consumption. The transactions were rarely to his advantage. Dealers, through agents known as *coureurs des côtes*, bought heavily in good crop years at low prices and sold dearly in bad years. Between the export market and the increasingly important domestic market such speculation became very complex, the new local merchants acting as middlemen. The average *habitant* was invariably vulnerable. In the eighteenth century his lot had been bearable since he often had surpluses to sell and he and his sons could earn extra money in the fur trade, but from 1800 on, with declining production, more frequent crop failures, and a waning fur trade, his condition worsened progressively, and after 1830 he was in sore straits indeed. A wheat harvest of 56 *minots* per family (an average of 6.4 persons) in the relatively good crop year of 1831 clearly reveals the depth of the crisis.

In the circumstances, the lumber trade began to play a major role in rural life, particularly in the townships, and in the district of Quebec where in 1831 nearly half the sawmills were located. Seigneurial land near Montreal, however, was already stripped of much of its timber and by this period it was here that the agricultural crisis was most cruelly felt.

II FOREST INDUSTRY DEVELOPMENT

As overall prices tumbled in Europe and North America, the forest industries enjoyed unprecedented growth. An economic structure based on healthy agriculture and the fur trade yielded to one of ailing agriculture and the lumber trade. By reason of dependence on external factors, in particular protective tariffs, the growth in lumber was not seriously affected by agricultural deficiencies, though the two sectors were to some extent interdependent.

In response to demand from Great Britain and the West Indies and aided by dwindling resources in the United States, exports of Lower-Canadian forest products rose vigorously. Production for local use increased at the same time. With a few short-lived downturns, demand remained firm throughout this period, growing steadily for squared timber used in shipbuilding and railway development, for deals and for barrel staves, and more modestly and spasmodically for other categories such as squared oak, for which local supply was running low or becoming inaccessible. Exports of potash and pearl ash fluctuated with demand and particularly with local conditions; since there was little wood left on the farms in the seigneuries after the first decade of the century, exports of these products were dependent on availability of wood from new land-clearing and, increasingly, imports; after 1815 the Lower-Canadian share of export volume fell rapidly from 50 per cent to 30 per cent.

Without the mother country's protective tariffs, established in time of war to assure supplies and not to stimulate long-term development, there would have been no such growth in the industry, for Europe, the United States, and even New Brunswick had the advantage of more favourable location. Rising transportation costs rendered the early tariffs ineffectual and they were raised modestly a number of times and eventually more decisively in 1814 to 65 s. per load. Colonial suppliers were thus provided with an effective differential, and were further favoured by the beginning of a long-term price decline. While there was no guarantee that the tariffs would remain after the return of peace, the post-war depression brought Great Britain to realize the importance of her colonies as outlets for her products and surplus population, and she found it expedient to maintain the system as a matter of policy. Besides, it became apparent that without the lumber industry the Lower-Canadian economy would become more and more anaemic, which would jeopardize the upper colony's development and perhaps even cause the Canadas to look to the United States for salvation. Despite the post-war deflation, the 1814 tariff was maintained until 1821, when, in response to pressure from English merchants, the rate on Baltic timber was dropped from 65s. to 55s. per load and a duty of 10s. per load was imposed on wood from the colonies. This new tariff structure remained until after 1840. The colonial lumber industry was still protected well enough, for the Americans ceased to be a threat to it after 1830, and henceforth competition came only from northern Europe. Growing opposition to the mercantilist policy both in Britain and Canada, however, was a source of anxiety for Lower-Canadian businesssmen.

The boom in lumber brought a surge of activity to the ports of Lower Canada. In 1812, 362 ships were cleared through the port of Quebec; in 1823, 609 ships manned by 6,330 men; in 1825, 796 ships with 8,973 crewmen; in 1834, 1,213 ships with 13,341 crewmen. There were besides large numbers of schooners doing a coastal trade, steamships plying the St. Lawrence between Quebec and Montreal, and a miscellany of vessels moving between the same cities and ports in Upper Canada and the United States. After the lumber trade, the principal stimulus behind all this activity was agricultural produce from outside Lower Canada.

Since the Navigation Acts had created a kind of monopoly for British shipping in the transport of colonial produce and since, in any event, Quebec and Montreal businessmen had insufficient capital to finance the many ships needed for the trans-Atlantic trade, most of the ships built at Quebec were sold to British and

West Indies shipping interests; the local shipowners concentrated on tonnage for local traffic. The result was that profits from the lumber trade fell largely into the hands of British shipowners.

Since the transport of lumber meant far more export bulk than import, incoming ships arrived mostly in ballast, a situation which kept costs higher than on other routes and led ships' masters outbound from Britain to offer bargain rates to immigrants, who upon arrival would seek employment in lumbering, often in the hope of earning enough money to buy farms. In this sense the lumber trade stimulated immigration to Lower Canada. In 1832, though 50,000 immigrants disembarked at Quebec, 470 ships out of a total of 1,008 still arrived in ballast.[13]

The boom in lumber attracted considerable capital, some in investment by British interests and some brought by wealthy immigrants. Lumber profits aided the growth of the industry and also led to a certain diversification even in the country districts. With the new investment activity, banks soon became necessary. Imports, too, were stimulated, from the West Indies, Britain, and even China by way of Britain, but most markedly in agricultural produce from Upper Canada and the United States. For wool and other textiles statistics are unfortunately lacking.

Since import arrivals at Quebec and Montreal were destined for both Lower and Upper Canada, the influence of the lumber trade on consumption is difficult to evaluate. Upper Canada's rapid settlement alone could account for a large share of the sharp rise in purchases of foreign goods. Per capita consumption of wine and coffee, in demand by the upper classes, remained unchanged. Molasses, which was bought by all classes, remained stationary or perhaps declined. The use of imported sugar increased markedly despite a sharp rise in maple sugar production in Lower Canada. Imports of spirits dropped after 1818 but this was offset after 1825 by an increase in local distilling, an activity well-advanced even earlier in Upper Canada. The most spectacular rise was in the consumption of tea, to which the poor classes had taken great liking.

Despite criticism that the lumber trade left little profit in the colony and gave employment to few, the mass of the people, both urban and rural, unquestionably benefited from it. Shipbuilding employed many skilled and unskilled workmen in and around Quebec; the production of squared timber, though concentrated in the Ottawa Valley, employed a large number of loggers and raftsmen, and in time there appeared a class of dockers who took over the loading and unloading of ships which had previously been done by sailors. Subsidiary to the trade in squared timber, the mainstay of the industry, other activities developed: the production of deals for both the local and imperial markets progressed steadily throughout the period. There were 727 sawmills by 1831 and 911 by 1844; in 1831, 248 of them were in the district of Quebec and some of them were very large; elsewhere most were of modest size. Farmers produced staves, hoops, and barrel ends for the local and export market. Production of potash and pearl ash brought benefit to farmers who had woodlots or who were clearing land, as well as to contractors. In 1831 there were 489 potash installations, 462 of them in the district of Montreal.

Lumber was Lower Canada's salvation in the precarious context presented by the crisis in agriculture, for it became the mainstay of a large segment of the commercial class and a major prop to the standard of living of an appreciable proportion of the lower classes. In the colony's relationship to the mother country it assumed the place once held by the fur trade, but that relationship was now one of even greater dependence by virtue of the protection provided by the system of preferential tariffs. As long as the British Empire was virtually the sole market, Upper-Canadian lumber could not compete with Lower-Canadian; only around 1846 when the American market began to open did the industry begin to play a major role in Upper Canada's economy.

III WESTERN RESOURCES AND THE REVOLUTION IN TRANSPORT

As early as 1792 certain Montreal merchants connected with the fur trade had proposed a bank to resolve the problem of currency shortages and the diversity of coin in circulation, but nothing had materialized. After the beginning of the nineteenth century, new economic structures emerging made the need even more pressing. In 1808 John Richardson made a new proposal but encountered adamant opposition from the French-Canadian members of the assembly. The failure aroused bitter resentment in business circles, for at that time there were problems not only of currency but of financing new ventures. The success of the army bills during the War of 1812 did much to change the minds of many influential figures, for the war-time prosperity was widely attributed to the bills and the post-war depression to their disappearance. It was French-Canadian assembly members in fact who proposed that they be made permanent. Thereupon the English-speaking merchants made yet another proposal, and the following year, 1817, the Bank of Montreal was founded with a capital of £250,000; some years later a branch was opened in Quebec. The Quebec Bank and the Bank of Canada, in Quebec and Montreal respectively, were established in 1818, and then the City Bank of Montreal in 1833 and the Banque du Peuple in 1835, the latter founded by members of the French-Canadian élite with a capital of £80,000.[14] In 1831 the Bank of Canada was absorbed by the Bank of Montreal.[15] With the appearance of savings banks in the two cities the system was completed.

The pacesetter was the Bank of Montreal. Though its charter was modelled on that of the first American bank, it followed the traditionally cautious British banking practices and all the other banks followed suit, which accounts for their successful resistance to a series of financial crises. Lower Canadians did their business with a small number of strong banks rather than a large number of smaller and weaker ones.

Not surprisingly, there was much criticism of the banking system, particularly of the Bank of Montreal which was accused of trying to establish a monopoly for itself. Though a certain amount of the criticism came from the Bank of Montreal's competitors, some had obvious political undertones. After 1830 the *parti patriote*, seeing the system as a major source of power for the English-speaking, waged a bitter campaign against the banks, using arguments borrowed from the Jacksonian Democrats, but differently and in a different context. Anachronistically, the founders of the Banque du Peuple were not only rivals of the Bank of Montreal and certain of its directors but members of a political party whose leaders were opposed to banks. But criticism notwithstanding, the banks continued to gain strength, serving an economic territory which reached considerably beyond the borders of Lower Canada; though the financial crisis of 1837 forced them to suspend their operations for a time, the survival of the system was assured.

As the agricultural focus shifted westward, financed by the banks, major changes in transportation were in store. With the steady fall-off in wheat production in Lower Canada and declining prices and profits after 1815, the construction of the Erie Canal by the Americans and its completion in 1825 increased the threat of foreign competition, and the merchants' anxiety over the high cost of transport became acute; the need for a system of canals and deeper river channels along the St. Lawrence and its tributaries became imperative.[16]

John Molson's St. Lawrence steamboat service, begun in 1809, was the prelude to a transformation of great importance. Until 1840 the number of steamboats operating between Quebec and Montreal increased steadily.[17] In this period merchants were also attempting to establish a steamboat link with the Maritimes; in 1825 they declared, "these colonies are less acquainted with each other than with the most distant lands."[18]

Pressure for inland navigational improvements had been exerted since the middle of the first decade of the century. The problems were not really serious between Quebec and Montreal, but above Montreal, the port of trans-shipment on the St. Lawrence route, there were the redoubtable Lachine Rapids, and even if that obstacle were overcome the shallowness of Lac St-Pierre would still impose stringent limits on the size of vessels navigating that section of the river. With the Lachine Canal finally completed, in 1826 the Montreal merchants proposed that a channel be dredged through Lac St-Pierre,[19] but though the plan was described as "inexpensive" the Quebec merchants, fearing loss of business to Montreal, were unenthusiastic. Applicants for incorporation of a proposed St. Lawrence Company in 1835 cited in their preamble "difficulties in trade communication between the two Provinces and the resultant uncertainty, delays and loss of time and money . . . which greatly diminish trade and retard the progress of the Provinces and prevent them from deriving the full benefits of the preference accorded their products by the policies of the Mother Country and also prevent their products from competing with those of foreign countries."[20]

Controversy over canal construction inevitably became political. Once the problems had been espoused as articles of faith by opposing factions, solutions were bound to be no more than partial.

In 1815 the legislature of Lower Canada appointed three commissioners to study the Lachine Canal project and voted £25,000 for its realization, but the plan was set aside. In 1819 a private company was formed by a group of Montreal merchants to revive it, but two years later ran short of funds and ceased work. With even such a modest enterprise foundering for lack of funds, it was becoming apparent that there was insufficient private capital in the Canadas to finance a major canal system. In 1821 the government of Lower Canada took over the project itself, the assembly having revoked the company's charter and voted funds to reimburse the shareholders for their expenditures and for completion of the work, more than £100,000 all told. The canal, 8½ miles long, 20 feet wide and 5 feet deep, was opened for traffic in 1824; though only a small part of a larger system most urgently needed, it was a major stimulus to the development of Upper Canada and of Montreal.

A second government project, the Chambly Canal, was begun in 1830 but not completed until after the rebellions of 1837 and 1838. While a private company was building a railway between Laprairie and St-Jean,[21] the canal construction suffered one delay after another, due to cholera epidemics in 1832 and 1834, torrential rains in 1833 and 1835,[22] and spiralling prices in 1836. In view of the extraordinary predominance of imports over exports at the port of St-Jean, it is apparent that the assembly's preference for this project over further improvements to the St. Lawrence route was politically rather than economically motivated.

While the business community and the nationalists squabbled over St. Lawrence canals, the British government, with an eye more on military security than economic considerations, undertook to build a navigable waterway between Montreal and the Great Lakes by which Upper Canada might be supplied without risk in time of war, at a cost of over £1 million. The major phase of the project was the Rideau Canal linking Kingston and the present city of Ottawa through the Rideau Lakes, a distance of 133 miles. The work, supervised by Colonel By, a British military engineer, was begun in 1826 and finally completed in 1834. There remained a hazardous series of rapids on the Ottawa River; these were bypassed by small canals which only partly facilitated navigation.

With the completion of the Erie Canal in 1825 the Americans had a considerable margin of commercial advantage. The money spent on the Rideau-Ottawa route did nothing to help the Montreal and Upper-Canadian merchants regain the competitive ground they had lost, as they might have done had the British government spent it instead on the St. Lawrence route. The economic health of British North America was poorly served by such blind preoccupation with military security a decade and more after the end of the War of 1812.

A program of massive investment in canals along the St.

Lawrence route would inevitably weigh heavily on the public purse. Rationally, the two colonies needed to pool their resources in pursuit of a common goal. Money might then have been raised in the imperial market.[23] As it was, however, Upper Canada took that initiative by itself and thereby jeopardized its financial stability. Once again the rational course was defeated by political rivalry. In Lower Canada the necessary change of attitudes was not forthcoming, either toward redivision between the colonies of import duty revenues, the major source of public funds, or toward diversification of revenue sources and borrowing. The legislative assembly continued to oppose the principle of land taxes and the very idea of borrowing money. Only a small proportion of the colony's budget was voted for public works and canalling. Between 1823 and 1827 only 12 per cent of expenditures was allocated to canals, and between 1828 and 1832 only 10 per cent, whereas 15 per cent might have been adequate. The assembly of Lower Canada, notwithstanding its complaints of government disregard for its wishes, clearly had a predominating influence over the use of public funds. . . .[24]

IV THE POPULATION EXPLOSION

The demographic factor which was new was the nature and volume of immigration; between 1815 and 1840 nearly 400,000 immigrants arrived at the ports of Lower Canada. Most were bound for Upper Canada and the United States, but those who remained in Lower Canada to settle in the cities, seigneuries, and townships added to the already severe demographic pressures.

There was no significant change in the natural population growth rate. In the period 1800-1839 the birth rate dropped very slightly from that of 1790-1800, from 52.5 to 51 per 1,000, and the marriage rate from 8.7 to 8.5, revealing neither a change in attitude toward marriage nor a trend toward birth control[25] but perhaps reflecting emigration to the United States. The death rate, instead of increasing, declined slightly from 27 to 25.8 per 1,000, a consequence perhaps of the establishment of a medical profession or of the role of potatoes in the *habitant's* diet. Despite short-term fluctuations, influenced variously by good and bad harvests, epidemics, economic factors, the War of 1812, and the rebellions of 1837 and 1838, the long-term population growth in any event remained unchanged at 25.4 per 1,000. From

1815 to 1840 the French-Canadian population increase was almost 250,000, but from 1831 to 1844 the proportion of children under fourteen dropped from 49 to 45 per cent, a consequence perhaps of emigration to the United States.

Over the short term, the recorded death rates reflected the occurrence of epidemics more than economic conditions or military operations. Generally speaking, epidemics were less frequent and less severe in the nineteenth century than in the eighteenth. Between 1760 and 1800 the death rate exceeded 30 per 1,000 as many as nine times, but between 1800 and 1840 only five times, most strikingly in 1832 and 1834, years of crippling cholera epidemics; in 1832 the rate climbed to 45.7 per 1,000, and the statistics are incomplete at that. . . .

Immigration was massive after 1815, and the immigrants were wretchedly poor for the most part, fleeing economic depression and misery in the British Isles, and lured by visions of greener fields and by bargain fares offered by captains of lumber ships which, without them, would have to make the westward voyage in ballast. Most were English and Scottish until 1832, and then Irish, but the greater number of the latter enshipped for New York.

Most of them disembarked at Quebec. Between 1819 and 1825 roughly a third chose to remain in Lower Canada and the rest moved on to Upper Canada and the United States in more or less equal numbers. Thenceforth the proportion remaining in Lower Canada diminished: 23 per cent between 1825 and 1830, 14 per cent in 1831, 10 per cent in 1834, 8 per cent in 1835, and 4 per cent in 1836; half of those arriving in this period went to Upper Canada and the rest to the United States. Entrepreneurs did brisk business moving them out, but neither that nor the richer land available further west accounts for the immigrants' increasing disinclination to remain in Lower Canada. Nor should their distaste for seigneurial land-tenure be overestimated. Judging from the facts and from remarks by contemporaries, most were capable of overcoming that initial reaction. This was noted by the agent of the seigneur of Beauport: ". . . the emigrants no longer have any repugnance for seigneurial tenure, for they perceive that they can become possessors of farms without purchase."[26] The immigrants, with or without money for land purchase, appear indeed to have had a preference for land in the seigneuries, for it was more valuable and closer to the markets. As many as 225 obtained concessions from the seigneurs of Gaudarville and

Fossambault,[27] and an undetermined number from the seigneur of Portneuf. These and other examples belie the view that the seigneurial régime was the "shield of the French-Canadian nation." More important factors seem to have been the growing shortage of land in the seigneuries, the seigneurs' reluctance to concede land, the distance and poor communications involved in settling in the townships, and last but not least the political climate and nationalism.

According to the best-informed contemporary observers, an immigrant settling on a farm, in order to have something to live on while awaiting his first harvest, would need the equivalent of six months' to a year's subsistence for himself and his family; W. B. Felton, for example, estimated the minimum necessary for six months for a family of three at 18 *minots* of wheat, 270 pounds of pork, 100 *minots* of potatoes, and a cow, or else a sum of £21.[28] The merchant Isaac Man of Ristigouche observed that "a man setting himself up must have the means to provide himself and his family for at least a year after coming to his farm. . . . I have always considered twenty to twenty-five *louis* as the least sum a man must have when leaving Quebec to settle on a farm."[29] An immigrant might manage without some initial capital, according to Felton, only if the farm he acquired was close to market; "when he is favourably situated in the neighbourhood of an establishment and has a market for his work, the necessity of capital disappears; but his comfort will be greater and his progress hastened by possession of capital." Since, according to evaluations after 1830, the wealth of an immigrant averaged only £9 to £10, it is clear that a very large number were completely destitute. Before 1820 there appeared a sorely needed charitable organization, the Society for the Relief of Emigrants in Distress.

The immigrant without capital would have to find what employment he could in the city of Quebec, for even if he intended to move on to Upper Canada he would at least have to earn his steamboat fare. Lieutenant Skeene, who proposed the creation of an agency to advise immigrants on employment prospects and ways and means of acquiring farms, noted that "several of those who have had a few weeks of employment at the King's Shipyards have been able to go upriver."[30] From November, 1821, to November, 1822, 700 immigrants worked in the shipyards, where a system of monthly turnovers was established; their pay was 2s. 6d. per day. Immigrants would in fact accept whatever work and pay was offered. Many worked on farms or clearing land, often in the townships. Felton noted, "The usual wages given in the townships to good men experienced in country work or logging, are from twelve to fourteen *piastres* [dollars] per month, with food, washing and mending, during the six months of summer; these men rarely contract for a year, being principally young men looking to establish themselves. . . . Europeans who contract for a year are usually given seven to ten *piastres* per month, with food, and they are lodged and their clothes washed and mended; after the first year, many of these men earn as much as the labourers of the Country."[31]

The combined effect of massive immigration and the vigorous natural growth of the French-Canadian population caused a multiplicity of problems. These would no doubt have arisen in any event, but with lagging economic growth, a scarcity of easily available land, and widespread social discontent, excessive demographic pressure could only exacerbate existing tensions and conflicts. It certainly did much to stimulate French-Canadian nationalism – perhaps more than any other factor.

NOTES

1. Since parish tithes were set at one twenty-sixth of harvests, production volume of those crops subject to tithing (wheat, oats, barley, rye, buckwheat, and peas) can be estimated from the curés' tithe reports. With due allowance for the fact that these reports were made following pastoral visits, not annually, in the case of wheat the statistics obtainable show close correspondence between production and exports, as do those derived from the records of la Quête de l'Enfant-Jésus. Other useful sources are parish censuses, seigneurial dues and mill revenues paid in wheat, and the records of certain farms belonging to the Quebec Seminary. See Ouellet, "L'agriculture bas-canadienne vue à travers les dîmes et la rente en nature," in Ouellet, *Eléments d'histoire sociale du Bas-Canada* (Montréal, 1972), 37-88.
2. W. H. Parker, "A New Look at Unrest in Lower Canada in the 1830's," *CHR*, XL, 3 (1959), 209-18.
3. *Quebec Gazette*, 2 August 1819.
4. *Ibid*.
5. *Ibid*., 18 October 1821.
6. APQ, Jesuit Estates, correspondence of the seigneurial agent, Blondeau, to the commissioners.

7. *Quebec Gazette*, 3 September 1821.
8. P. Savard, ed., *Paysans et ouvriers canadiens d'autrefois* (Québec, 1968), 48-51.
9. Anonymous, *Canada: courte esquisse de sa position géographique, ses productions, son climat* (1860).
10. APQ, Fraser Papers, seigneurial agent's reports.
11. APQ, Jesuit Estates, seigneurial agent's quarterly reports.
12. *Rapport* de l'Archiviste de la province de Québec (1943-4), 243, 387.
13. *Journals* of the House of Assembly of Lower Canada (1832-3), Appendix PP.
14. R. C. McIvor, *Canadian Monetary, Banking and Fiscal Development* (Toronto, 1958).
15. *Journals* (1830), App. NN; (1831), App. M.
16. W. T. Easterbrook and H. G. J. Aitken, *Canadian Economic History* (Toronto, 1956), 254-67.
17. G. P. de T. Glazebrook, *A History of Transportation in Canada* (Toronto, 1964), I, 67-72.
18. *Journals* (1835).
19. *Ibid.* (1827).
20. *Ibid.* (1835), application for incorporation, St. Lawrence Co.
21. The Champlain and St. Lawrence Railway, completed by 1837.
22. In the summer of 1833 there were eighty-three days of rain; in 1835, ninety days: *Journals* (1835-6).
23. For figures on revenues, expenditures, borrowing, and investment in canals in Upper Canada, see: *Journals* (1847), App. KKK.
24. *Ibid.*
25. P. Goubert, *Beauvais et le Beauvaisis de 1600 à 1730* (Paris, 1960), 1-83.
26. *Journals* (1821), third report of the committee on settlement of Crown Lands, 133.
27. *Ibid.*, testimony of Hall and Duchesnay, 129, 137.
28. *Ibid.*, testimony of W. B. Felton, 131.
29. *Ibid.*, testimony of Isaac Man, 125.
30. *Ibid.*, testimony of Skeene, 140.
31. *Ibid.*, testimony of Felton, 132.

II
Social Structure

Some influences on Canadian life have been overlooked by historians, others have received attention but only recently have benefited from a social approach. Climate is a striking example of the ignored topic, religion of a subject given new focus by a social historian.

Climate is perhaps so pervasive and obvious that historians have not thought to explore its implications in colonial society. Judith Fingard's essay rectifies that oversight. In a unique picture of colonial social structure, she portrays the rhythm of life in the pre-industrial period, a rhythm powerfully affected by the climate. At the same time she reminds us of the significance of certain resources and how climate and resources acted on the relationship between classes. The paper stresses the importance in everyday life of such humble and usually forgotten resources as wood and dogs. It is a large part of the responsibility of social history to rediscover the ordinary–ordinary things and ordinary people–and restore them to their true significance in the making of society. Professor Fingard's success in doing so has made her work on climate among the most significant in Canadian social history. It also has made her one of the leading practitioners of the "new history" in Canada. Pioneered in Britain by E. P. Thompson and E. J. Hobsbawm, the new history is concerned with the rhythm of life that Fingard has found in British American port cities, a rhythm of season and work. Yet, these historians argue, that very rhythm allowed the lower orders to develop a coherence in their lives, a particular style that some historians have considered to be a "working-class culture."

Judith Fingard helps us to focus on the way in which the grand themes of Canadian history–economic development, immigration, the lives of the elite–interrelate with the humble. That effort, so successful here, is at the core of social history.

In studying Anglican divines, S. F. Wise moves us to the other end of the social spectrum from Fingard's poor. However, his is also an integrative study, bringing together religious thought, ideology, politics, and a powerful vision of Canada. Religion, obviously, can be studied purely on its own terms. Yet Wise demonstrates that, without doing violence to the integrity of religion, it can be employed as a signpost of social development.

Despite the fact that immigration diminished the Anglican proportion of the population, figures such as John Strachan, first Bishop of Toronto after 1839, continued to exert a powerful influence in Canadian society. Strachan did much to found the school system of Upper Canada, created a university–King's College–and, when it was secularized by the government in 1849, built another Anglican institution, Trinity College. When Strachan died in 1867, the funeral cortege was watched by what was said to be the largest crowd ever gathered in Toronto to that date.

FURTHER READING:
Among Fingard's many studies, especially important is "Attitudes Toward the Education of the Poor in Colonial Halifax," *Acadiensis*, 5, 1 (1975), 32-53. Another practitioner of the new history is Bryan Palmer: "Discordant Music: Charivaris and Whitecapping in Nineteenth-Century North America," *Labour/ Le Travailleur*, 3 (1978), 5-62. For the two ends of the social scale, see: Brereton Greenhous, "Paupers and Poorhouses: The Development of Poor Relief in Early New Brunswick," *Histoire Sociale*, 1 (1968), 103-26; M. S. Cross, "The Age of Gentility: The Creation of an Aristocracy in the Ottawa Valley," *Historical Papers* (1967), 105-17. A collection of readings on lower-class life is M. S. Cross, ed., *The Workingman in the Nineteenth Century* (Toronto, 1974).

Another good example of elite studies by Wise is "Tory Factionalism: Kingston Elections and Upper Canadian Politics, 1820-1836," *Ontario History*, LVII (1965), 205-25. J. L. H. Henderson has produced two useful studies on the Anglican leader: a biography, *John Strachan, 1778-1867* (Toronto, 1969);

and *John Strachan: Documents and Opinions* (Toronto, 1969). More general religious history is discussed in John S. Moir, *The Church in the British Era* (Toronto, 1972). A useful introduction to the major themes of religion in Canada is John S. Moir, ed., *Church and State in Canada, 1627-1827: Basic Documents* (Toronto, 1967).

Judith Fingard is chairperson of the History Department at Dalhousie University and author of a forthcoming book on the life of sailors in Canadian ports. **Sydney F. Wise** was head of the Armed Forces Historical Branch and is now Director of Canadian Studies at Carleton University. He is the author of the official history of the RCAF.

The Poor in Winter: Seasonality and Society in Pre-Industrial Canada

by Judith Fingard

No student of the history of society can afford to ignore the contribution of climate and the seasons to the moulding of human behaviour, social attitudes, and popular myths. Distinctive behavioural characteristics often derive their peculiarities from the climate. In northern climes, to cite one example, the transition from dreary, confining winter to the bright, warm days of spring was traditionally accompanied by a release of the human spirit – an explosion of energy after the long pent-up days of cold and isolation – a burst that alike affected the Russian peasant and the Canadian lumberjack and created springtime unruliness. Canadian notions of Caucasian superiority included a racial concept concerning the adaptation to winter. This was embodied in Canadian immigration policy, which until the mid-twentieth century subscribed to the view that blacks could not withstand the cold, that the climate was white. Canadian historians have not been particularly attracted to climatic explanations, which is strange in view of their partiality for environmentalism and geographic determinism. Despite the fact that scholars such as Margaret Atwood, Pierre Deffontaines, and Cole Harris recognize that our literature and our human and historical geography

This essay is an abridged and slightly revised version of "The Winter's Tale: The Seasonal Contours of Pre-industrial Poverty in British North America," Canadian Historical Association, *Historical Papers*, 1974, 65-94. Reprinted by permission of the author.

have been much influenced by the effect of winter on the style of life, the effect of winter on our history has been largely ignored. Historians have had something to say about myths associated with winter. Carl Berger's studies of late nineteenth-century Canadian nationalism emphasize the creation of the myth of the great northern race drawing its purity and superiority, its energy and strength from the invigorating, sparkling cold of the Canadian winter. But he left the glorification of the climate with the elite where he found it. The only climatic theme explicitly favoured by a historian has been W. L. Morton's wistful assertions that the need to combat the harsh winter climate, characteristic of most of Canada, acted as a unifying force, particularly between French and English, and materially contributed to the creation of that elusive commodity, the Canadian identity.[1] That kind of unity is an illusion.

Admittedly in nineteenth-century pre-industrial Canada, winter did indeed act as a unifying force. It united the well-to-do in a whole range of leisure activities designed to pass the commercially dormant days of winter, activities like sleighing, parties, legislative sessions, and such charitable pastimes as theatricals, bazaars, and balls. At the same time it united the poor in hardship: cold, hunger, and gloomy unemployment or underemployment were their lot until the welcome return of summer. Winter therefore was a great divide. The stark contrast between its effect on rich and poor constituted a persistent theme in the social commentary of the day. Newspaper editorials waxed Dickensian in their study of this contrast. The editor of a Quebec paper considered the Christmas season an appropriate time for calling to the attention of his readers:

the hordes who will be pining in wretchedness and hunger, while we are gathered in social festivity, and happiness, round a well furnished and luxurious board; blest with all that can render life an elysium. . . . How gloomy, how dark, how fraught with shuddering sympathy, the reverse of this joyous picture, when we turn to the dwellings of the poor of Quebec, on this anniversary, this day of common and universal jubilee? Round a cold, fireless hearth, the humble child of want sits in moody despair, watching the huddled groups of his famishing family, whose blue, pinched, features, painfully index the weakening inroads of long continued and gnawing hunger; a few worn rags covering their emaciated frames, shiveringly drawn yet closer and closer around them, being their only means of warmth.[2]

A poem called "Winter" printed in a Kingston newspaper in 1845 was equally instructive and drove home the moral implications:

"You're welcome Old Winter!" the rich man cries,
    With a bosom of proud content,
As round his carpeted halls his eyes
    With a meaning glance are sent:
For the fires burn bright, and the casements tall,
    Are curtained with drapery rare–
The winds may howl, and the snows may fall,
    But what doth the rich man care?

"You're welcome Old Winter!" the gay lad cries
    As he plunges into the snow
Or o'er the ice-bound streamlet flies,
    Like a shaft from the twanging bow;
For garments warm are about his form,
    And his sport is rich and rare!
Old Winter may bluster and rave and storm,
    But what doth the rich man care?

"Oh! Winter is dreary!" the poor man cries,
    As he wands along the street,
While the snow in his frost-nipp'd visage flies,
    And benumbs his unshod feet!
"Oh Winter is drear!" But there's none to hear
    The plea of the poor and old,
Straight on goes the crowd with unlistening ear–
    Who cares if the beggar is cold?

"Alas it is Winter! And wo is me!"
    The Widow exclaims and clasps
The shivering Orphans around her knee,
    In a wild and phrenzied grasp;
Through the frosted pane on the life-thronged way
    A laughing crowd she sees,
And merrily jingle the sleigh-bells gay,
    While the Widow and Orphans Freeze!

Ay! Winter is drear! O, ye rich ne'er smile
    At my simple and homely Muse,

Nor the tale of the poor man's woes revile,
  Nor a helping hand refuse;
For Heaven has blest you with stores of gold,
  And how should your thanks appear.
But by shielding the poor from hunger and cold,
  And making their lives less drear![3]

From this preoccupation couched in prose and verse, two questions emerge: what special contributions did the winter make to the problem of pre-industrial poverty, and how did the rich and poor respectively respond to the plight of the poor in winter? By far the greater number of the people who suffered in winter did so as a result of the paralysing interruption in their means of earning a living. The seasonal nature of economic activity based on North Atlantic shipping and on harvesting the soil and the sea entailed a total lack of job security for the lower classes. During the months of mercantile activity, April to November, labourers were normally much in demand in the towns and wages were relatively attractive. This meant that steerage immigrants (usually Irish) arriving in the busy ports of the east coast or the St. Lawrence in summertime were often tempted to take jobs as day labourers since they came badly prepared for "roughing it in the bush." In addition to private employment, major public works on roads, canals, and buildings were generally suited to summer employment and offered the immigrant no more than a few months of continuous employment. Unfortunately, employers failed to explain the seasonal nature of outdoor labour, and the new arrivals, often grossly misinformed about the colonial environment, learned too late that summer employment seldom compensated for winter distress. In November, dockwork in the ice-locked ports of Upper and Lower Canada ground to a complete halt. Even in the ice-free ports of the Atlantic coast the perils for North Atlantic shipping in the days of the sailing ship and the unsophisticated steamer severely reduced waterfront activity in winter. Urban workers, both immigrant and resident–day labourers, mill hands, truckmen, seamen, carpenters, and other building trades workers–who were thrown out of work in the autumn, thereafter competed with each other in their quest for the few remaining jobs and for regular or special relief. This competition was increased by the arrival in the towns of poor agricultural labourers discharged by the farmers at the end of the harvest and fishermen confined to shore by the weather, both looking for winter subsistence.

As the number of available jobs decreased during November and December and the labour market in each of the colonial towns became glutted, employed wage earners found themselves completely at the mercy of employers who took advantage of this surplus, as well as shorter winter hours, to reduce wages by 25 to 50 per cent for both skilled and unskilled workers. At the same time, the supply of imported and locally produced goods diminished and the needy had to pay the resulting inflated prices and seldom enjoyed credit facilities beyond those available in the pawn shop. Because of the inability of the poor to buy in quantity during seasons of moderate prices, their regular dependence on the winter markets invariably meant in effect they were paying more than the non-labouring classes. With what were at best subsistence and often starvation wages, the underemployed labourer was often forced in winter time to purchase bread, the favoured staple in his diet, at prices inflated by as much as 50 per cent, as well as firewood at exorbitant rates in the larger towns.

The poor man could seldom escape from this vicious situation. Even if he was able to save out of his summer earnings enough to provide for impending winter, he rarely had any place to store substantial quantities of potatoes or firewood or anywhere to bake bread if he managed to lay in a barrel of flour. Accordingly, he still had to purchase both "fuel and food from *hand* to *mouth* at a considerably advanced price."[4] The sufferings of the poor man's family were exceeded only by those of the widowed or helpless woman, frequently with a brood of dependent children and with even less chance of finding employment. In particularly severe years, the period of late winter-early spring was the time of greatest hardship, "the pinching season," according to one observer, "when every article of provision naturally advances in price and becomes by the poor almost unobtainable."[5] In Saint John, New Brunswick, the hardship was compounded for penniless poor tenants who customarily found themselves forced to move house on May day when their quarterly rents became due at the very moment when their means were completely exhausted. Indeed, the May day move became a Canadian urban tradition immortalized by Gabrielle Roy in her novel, *The Tin Flute*, set in 1930's Montreal.

A striking illustration of the predicament of the urban poor in winter is afforded by the difficulties they encountered in obtaining a major necessity of life – fuel. It is singularly ironic that during the decades when the British-American timber trade flourished, the poor suffered severely from a lack of cheap firewood. While insufficient attention to this prosaic matter might lead us to conclude that the poor man simply took his axe and felled a nearby tree, the degree of urbanization even by the 1820's precluded this obvious resource. For the poor of the island and near-island towns of Montreal and Halifax, marketable supplies of firewood were essential, because unfenced land had long been denuded of its wood and the standing timber on private property was carefully protected. In Nova Scotia, many outports along the south shore earned a living in winter by supplying the Halifax market with firewood carried to the city by boat, so that in those bitterly cold winters when the outport harbours froze solid the sufferings of the poor both in town and country greatly increased. Until the railway raised hopes of adequate supply in Montreal in the 1850's, the poor of that city looked for their wood to the small loads brought to town across the ice by the habitants' sleighs. At old Quebec, where the banks of the St. Lawrence were stripped of forests, firewood had to be brought down from the region of the St. Maurice and other tributaries to the north. Similarly in Saint John, at the mouth of the Saint John River, the markets relied on river traffic (before rail transportation). The difficulty was that all these water highways froze in winter.

The residents of towns surrounded by woods rather than by water could in theory supply their own needs, provided the households included healthy adults, storage space, and a sleigh. But even enterprise might be rewarded by practical obstacles. In Quebec and St. John's, Newfoundland, the local authorities, concerned for the safety of the inhabitants and their livestock, intermittently promoted measures which deprived the poor man of the dogs he needed for hauling wood. It was an age which saw both great fear of "hydrophobia" – that is, rabies – and experiments to protect the public health. The authorities insistently argued that overloading the dog as a beast of burden caused the thirst and fatigue which induced distemper. At the same time, fear of mad dogs and the prevalence of sheep and cattle killing in St. John's led to a regulation which sanctioned the shooting of stray dogs, a move which prompted one irate newspaper editor to point out that "The whole dependence of every poor family in the town for fuel is upon the Dog," and that an order to exterminate the dogs was tantamount to an instruction to exterminate the poor.[6]

On the other hand, many who were forced to rely on the town markets for fuel but had no storage space could not buy wood by the cord even if they had the money.

> Is it at all possible [asked one contemporary in Halifax] to crowd so much lumber [as a cord] into a moderate sized room, which is occupied by *five* families, the middle one of which '*takes in boarders*!' One half the houses that are occupied by the poor, have no yard room, and few have more than enough to 'swing a cat in'; besides if there were a yard to hold 6 cords of wood, owned by three persons, and the house is taken by half a dozen families, three of which are not prudent, is it not likely the latter would be now and then *borrowing* a stick of it while the former were asleep?[7]

Obliged to shop for two or three feet of wood at a time the poor were forced to pay more per cord than if they had been able to purchase it by the full cord from the local depot or direct from the supplier.

Contemporaries believed that the outlay for fuel represented a major, if not the greatest, expense borne by the poor city dweller in winter. In 1854 the editor of the *Montreal Gazette* estimated that factory labourers in that city were compelled to devote about 20 per cent of their wages to the purchase of wood, an expenditure he assumed rendered wages in this northern clime far less attractive than comparable wages in the United States. Indeed, one traveller in the Canadas at mid-century considered the high cost of fuel to be one of the great drawbacks to the progress of colonial settlement. When the supply of firewood eventually became exhausted as the woods rapidly receded and conservation was neglected, he reckoned that the cost of coal would bear so heavily on the poor that it would "prevent the peopling the country."[8] It was recognized that although fuel was costly, fire was indispensable in a cold climate in order to preserve life itself. William Kingston, a British observer who was intrigued by the logistics of fuel supply and the technology of domestic heating in Quebec during the 1850's, reported that the poor suffered "dreadfully in the winter from want of firing, especially the poor Irish, for the first two or three years after their arrival in the colony. . . . Many, after their day's work is over, go to bed directly they reach home, and remain there till it is again time to go off, as the only means they possess to escape being frozen."[9]

As if these obstacles were not enough, in their struggle to obtain the necessaries of life the poor were remorselessly haunted by the spectre of illness. Instances of malnutrition leading to starvation in winter were not uncommon, and even where relief in the shape of soup or cornmeal was available, it did not necessarily counteract illnesses caused by dietary deficiencies. Many immigrants among the poor were so unused to Indian meal–the staple relief provided by government–that the coarse food caused serious problems for weakened constitutions. Despite attention given by historians to summer epidemics of cholera and typhus, it was long winters that saw the height of regular illnesses such as smallpox, diphtheria, and measles and that considerably increased the rate of mortality among the very old and very young, the cumulative effect of dietary deficiencies and poor health being most noticeable in the early spring of especially hard seasons. And the cold itself was of course a killer. The deaths of helpless poor children from exposure in their ghastly dwellings were graphically described in contemporary accounts. In the severe winter of 1816-17 a jury in Quebec concluded that little Maria Louisa Beleau died of "a violent sore throat, and cold, produced by exposure to the inclemency of the weather." Like so many of the colonial poor, Maria Louisa belonged to a family without a male provider, the type of family most crippled by the lack of employment and regular poor relief. A witness at the inquest claimed that

The hovel in which the deceased had lived, with her mother, and two sisters, is not fit for a stable. It is open in many parts of the roof and on all sides. There is no other floor than the bare earth. It is a mere wooden stall; it has no window, nor any chimney. In the middle is a shallow hole made in the earth, in which there are marks of a fire having been made; and the smoke escaped through the open parts of the roof and sides. –When I was there on Tuesday last, there was no fire in the hole. . . .[10]

It was such heart-rending scenes as this that particularly caught the attention of the well-to-do who were concerned about the plight of the poor in winter for a variety of reasons. On the surface self-indulgence played an important part. Since winter was a time of leisure for the comfortably off, what better way had they to spend their time than in an enjoyable pastime–whether play, ball, concert, or tea and sale-that would also raise a little money for charity. Underneath, benevolence was undoubtedly stimulated by a blend of traditional religious duty and evangelical humanitarianism. The appeal, however, was to people's sentiments. As one newspaper editor remarked: "Is it not true, that our humane feelings are particularly excited by the approach of cold weather! There is not a human being, unless he has the stoney heart of a German fairy tale, but must at this season feel some pity for those who are destitute and comfortless."[11] Similarly, an editor in Saint John wrote:

> Winter is a terrible enemy to the destitute in this most rigorous climate. None but those who experience it, can tell the amount of suffering there is in this City, during five months in the year, among women and children. We see the pauper in the streets, in tattered garb and attenuated form, and he passes by and out of our mind in a moment. Could we follow him to his inhospitable abode, and see his little ones crouching around a single brand of fire, to keep themselves warm, and witness the scanty meal of which they are to partake, we should soon begin to learn something of the dark shades of human life, and incline towards charity.[12]

The charity might be the provision of a Christmas dinner for a poor family (how fortunate that Christmas occurred in winter), an extra offering in the plate during the annual winter sermon for the poor, a donation to a charitable society, or whatever it took to salve the seasonally activated conscience.

The funds collected by the innumerable winter associations which came and went during the period-societies with such evocative names as the Quebec Sick and Destitute Strangers Society, the Halifax Poor Man's Friend Society, The Kingston Female Benevolent Society, the Toronto Wesleyan Dorcas Society-were also used for peculiarly seasonal relief: soup kitchens were greatly favoured, as was warm clothing for pauper children, which might enable them to go to Sunday school for the good of their souls; and, in response to the insuperable difficulties which the poor encountered in obtaining firewood, many of the voluntary urban relief schemes concentrated on supplying the indigent with fuel. In the winter of 1828-9, the citizens of Saint John, aware of the distress suffered by a large number of newcomers and the high cost of firewood, organized a "Fuel

Day" to obtain wood to distribute to the poor. Owners of land in the outlying districts contributed stands of timber, volunteer axe-men offered their services, and the truckmen of the city donated a day of work to carting the wood to a fuel yard established for the purpose. In Quebec an association known as the Young Men's Charitable Firewood Society existed for several years. Founded in 1842, its object was to collect enough subscriptions to enable it to retail firewood to the poor at about half the regular market price. In the winter of 1843-4 the society delivered free of charge and distributed at half price or less 327¼ cords of wood to 314 families.

These small-scale benevolent enterprises were matched by small-scale assistance dispensed by provincial and municipal governments using funds raised by direct or indirect taxation. In the present age when the welfare state is taken for granted, it is in-structive to recall the early beginnings of government assistance: Elizabethan-style poor laws in the Maritime colonies, grants-in-aid of private enterprises in the Canadas. But every time the howling blast of winter winds and the anguished countenances of freezing, famished children focused local attention on the plight of the poor, the inadequacy of such public assistance brought the forces of voluntary charity into action. Voluntary relief, how-ever, involved considerable self-interest, particularly among the mercantile classes dealing in the staples and commerce which underpinned the colonial economy. As the major employers of seasonal labourers, merchants involved in the import-export trades wanted to maintain throughout the winter the level of labour in the peak summer season in order to facilitate the ready resumption of commercial activity in the spring. A correspon-dent in Halifax explained it this way: "In a climate like ours a very considerable number of labouring men in town, must be without employment, the greater part of the winter; otherwise the community must be very deficient of the quantity of labour re-quired in summer."[13] Vested interest in the maintenance of a surplus of labour meant that the names of prominent merchants were sure to head the subscription lists of charitable societies and to predominate in reports of public meetings. Michael Tobin, a merchant of Halifax, openly admitted that the merchants did not pay their labourers sufficient wages to see them through the winter and that the deficiency had therefore to be supplied by other means. "No man is better acquainted than I am with their actual condition," Tobin claimed at a relief meeting. "During summer the wages might support them well–but in the winter from December to March, such is the nature of our climate and commerce that employment is scarce, and remuneration so scanty as not to afford subsistence."[14] Other merchants worried less about their image in the community and placed additional obstacles in the way of their labourers' ability to get through the winter. The merchants of St. John's were notorious for cutting off the accustomed credit to the fishermen they had deliberately entrapped in debt as soon as the commercial season ended and for sending the unemployed, destitute fishermen in search of relief.

But some of the attitudes towards poor relief also reflected the concern of citizens for the progress of their society in an age noted for its emphasis on reform and improvement. It was not considered proper that a new country should be burdened with a disproportionate number of poor and helpless. If they could not be encouraged to take themselves off to the countryside or return from whence they came, they should be made to contribute towards the improvement of the community or, if completely unemployable, be shut away in a suitable institution out of sight and out of mind. Yet many of the institutions opened in the last decades of the pre-industrial cities–whether called hospitals or houses of industry–began as purely seasonal refuges against the cold and want of winter. As for the unemployed, though much of the rhetoric found in the discussion of their plight was derived from the international debate on the causes and effects of poverty, it too had peculiarly seasonal implications. For example, the concept of self-help, or helping the poor to help themselves, involved encouraging the seasonally employed to put away enough in the summer to see them through the winter. To this end savings banks were encouraged and spendthrift habits discouraged, such as the excessive consumption of alcohol which the temperance movement sought to control. Those who discerned winter unemployment as the crux of the problem of poverty were increasingly prone to argue that urban society would benefit from systematic employment relief. The work, of course, had to be sufficiently unattractive to discourage the regularly employed labourers in the towns and surrounding countryside from opting for subsidized winter employment. Employment was therefore always provided at a "less eligible" rate of wages than could be obtained in other jobs.

Not only were the wages "less eligible," but the jobs themselves were unattractively menial. Since most of the labourers in colonial towns were considered unskilled, hand labour with pick and shovel on roads, works, canals, railroads, and civic water works was promoted as the most suitable form of activity. Their promoters argued that such public works would provide a way "in which the necessities of the labouring poor could be made to dovetail with the general interest of the whole community, so that they might be benefited by receiving work, while those who pay for it might be equally benefited by having it done."[15] Outdoor winter works, however, did not readily lend themselves to an extensive system of relief. Large-scale operations such as road- and canal-building were normally halted by the onset of bad weather in the autumn. In Newfoundland, for example, road-building was finished by the end of October and therefore afforded only two months' relief after the fishery ended.

Nor could such schemes involving heavy labour benefit women, the group that comprised the greatest proportion of unemployed colonial poor. For, as one observer wrote, in comparison with men, "To find suitable employment for females, is more difficult, but not by any means less requisite, as they abound far more than the poor of the other sex."[16] On grounds both moral and humane, contemporaries thought that women as well as children had to be engaged indoors, and one of the earliest projects in the colonies was that organized in Halifax in the early 1820's whereby women and girls were employed in knitting and spinning in one of the town's free schools. The provision of indoor employment relief, however, had to await the factory of the industrial period, an institution with neither the welfare of the poor nor the interests of the community uppermost in the minds of its promoters.

Meanwhile the poor did not necessarily accept their winter destitution with resignation. The nearest they came to doing so in the popular mind was in the case of the French Canadians, the most traditionally acclimatized residents, who were said to "associate the idea of disgrace with the fact of destitution and with few exceptions proudly conceal any amount of privation with a sort of Indian stoicism."[17] Undeniably, this response demonstrates a full adaptation to the unrelenting realities of the climate and probably reflects the tendency of the poor to help one another, observers often noting that the poor comprised the most charitable segment of society and that it was the poor who supported the poor. But the mid-century marked also the period of substantial French-Canadian emigration to the United States. Certainly the most enterprising, effective response to the climate and its rigours, as well as to the lack of jobs in general, was to leave it and migrate either permanently or at least seasonally to more congenial climes. Indeed, as the editor of a Halifax paper observed, the climate contributed to the well-known transiency of the population of colonial towns:

> The exceedingly precarious nature of industrial pursuits with the hopelessness of looking elsewhere within a nearer distance than the American cities for employment, naturally creates a vast amount of poverty in our city. . . . So sensible are the poorer classes of this, that few who have undergone the privations incidental to a severe winter, ever risk the repetition, but with the close of the year pack up their few little traps and clear out for Boston.[18]

Because of the transiency caused partly by the climate and the seasonal limits it imposed on the pre-industrial economy, the poor were ineffective in organizing protests against the tendency of colonial employers to exploit the situation to their own narrow advantage. The composition of the lower class changed too rapidly in the first half of the nineteenth century and its members were too inured to the seasonality of employment for a vigorous campaign of protest to have been successfully launched against the inequities of winter. Admittedly, individuals and groups from time to time petitioned government for relief and jobs or demonstrated in favour of their right to employment at a living wage in winter. For example, labourers engaged on the roads in St. John's as part of a winter works program in the early spring of 1849 collectively petitioned against payments in sacks of meal. Similarly, Irish labourers on the first winter canal-building at Lachine in the outskirts of Montreal in 1842-3 withheld their labour as a protest against a seasonal cut in their truck wages instituted in the customary fashion by the contractors. Yet another illustration is presented by a mass meeting of two thousand to three thousand unemployed French-Canadian shipyard workers in Quebec in November of the severe depression year of 1857. Since building ships in winter had always been held out to French-Canadian farmers and labourers as a charitable favour by the shipbuilders, the formidable meeting of the destitute ship-wrights simply aimed at demanding an alternative form of winter relief. The aims of all these labourers were singularly short-term and show the kind of occasional collective outburst to be expected from men whose sole common denominator was hardship. They posed no threat to the seasonally adjusted *status quo*.

Nonetheless, the so-called benevolence of employers in winter had begun by mid-century to encourage the articulation of working-class resentment among outdoor workers. The remarks of a Halifax carpenter reported in 1852 were probably typical. "He asks if it be fair, that for five months in the year able and willing mechanics, are compelled to accept the alternative of walking the steets or working for wages which do not afford ample remuneration for the labour performed." Then, "after submitting to all this, with apparent resignation – after enriching their employers by the sweat of their brow, on terms which barely keep the thread of life from snapping – they are told with bare-faced effrontery that they were employed in charity."[19] The solution, according to this carpenter, lay in the organization of a trade union as a means of self-defence.

As for more primitive forms of protest, observers occasionally feared or at least noted with surprise the absence of mass demonstrations and violent crimes among the poor during the winters of greatest suffering, but such observers did not draw the probable conclusion that the poor had to preserve what little energy they possessed in order to sustain life itself. While the anticipation of winter hardship occasionally turned starving populations into lawless banditti who threatened or raided stores or perpetrated gang robberies, winter itself was a hopeless season for protest. Admittedly, poor individuals might commit misdemeanours in order to gain admission to the local jail for the coldest months. But the poor were far more likely to show their spirit during the season of employment after they had "thawed out" and as their expectation rose. When railway labourers in Saint John struck for higher wages and shorter hours in March, 1858, despite the employment provided for them during January and February by "benevolent" contractors, one unsympathetic observer complained: "Do as much as you may for them in their adversity, as soon as they get upon their feet and feel that they have strength and got you in their power, they will turn upon you and wring the last copper from your pockets."[20]

Workers were notorious for demanding high wages in season.

Who could blame them when summer employment might represent the sum total of their year's labour? To the immigrant–the uninitiated–the demand for high wages accorded with a high level of expectation produced by emigration propaganda, but to the experienced colonial labourer it reflected a primitive determination to enjoy to the full a season of plenty. This disposition among fishermen in Newfoundland caused one newspaper editor to draw a comparison with the habits of the British sailor who "will earn his money like a horse and spend it like an ass."[21] Enjoyment invariably led to excess, a tendency to feast and be merry for four or five months of the year rather than to live frugally for twelve. Critics also believed that a tradition of winter relief encouraged indolence and fretted that persons in Newfoundland "have been known to bask in the noon-day's sun during the very height of the fishery!"[22] Indeed, the rhythm of seasonal employment was complemented by the rhythm of seasonal relief. The seasonal labourer could not be abandoned to the savagery of winter. If no shipbuilding or stone-breaking for road works was available, the poor man, whether considered deserving or not, could usually obtain a donation of welfare provisions, a temporary refuge in an asylum, or a share of the alms doled out by private citizens and religious institutions. Such relief was never lavish or particularly attractive, but then neither were the rewards of providence and frugality.

The plight of the poor in winter left its legacy to modern Canadian society. Since neither the shift to an industrial economy nor modern technological change could resolve all the problems posed by winter, many pre-industrial features of seasonal poverty persisted. The marginal work force continued to confront winter hardship–firstly, because winter remained an ever-present reality reducing the opportunities for outdoor forms of labour year after year, decade after decade. Government statisticians in the 1920's, for example, found that one-tenth of workers in non-agricultural sectors, who were gainfully employed in late summer, were unemployed in winter "from seasonal causes alone."[23] Secondly, workers encountered hardship because most levels of government, faced with the inevitability of winter, accepted climatic determinism and readily translated it into a preference for an economy run on the principle of high unemployment.

Similarly, employers continued well into the industrial age regularly to exploit the winter surplus of labour by reducing wages at that time of year when the cost of living was the highest.

While employers of outdoor labour were able to argue with impunity in the absence of labour legislation that the shorter day demanded lower wages, this long-time rationale could not be used by factory owners who maintained the same hours in winter as in summer. But they were so accustomed to taking advantage of the surplus of labour created in winter that they continued to reduce wages. Employees of a tobacco factory in Montreal in the 1880's, for example, saw their wages cut 37½ per cent in winter for no other reason than capitalist adherence to established practice.[24]

In response, the poor continued to seek seasonal escapes from their predicament. Any ability to get through winter without relief owed more to increased credit facilities than to sufficient summer wages or to more extensive seasonal migration south to the United States for winter employment. In addition, the earlier spring protest of the able-bodied poor came increasingly to be exemplified by the timing of strikes. The common spring strike represented the worker's retrospective winter weakness as much as his prospective summer strength.

For these reasons, any historical study concerned with poverty or the related questions of unemployment-underemployment and social welfare has to recognize with Leonard Marsh, Canada's leading expert on these problems in the 1920's and 1930's, that Canada is an eight months' country.[25] For the old adage, "the poor are always with ye," Canadians must substitute the truism, winter is always with us. Poverty and winter were inseparable considerations in nineteenth-century Canada and the customs of that period contributed to the social problems and attitudes of modern Canada.

NOTES

1. Margaret Atwood, *Survival: A Thematic Guide to Canadian Literature* (Toronto, 1972); Pierre Deffontaines, *L'homme et l'hiver au Canada* (Paris, 1957); Cole Harris, "The Myth of the Land in Canadian Nationalism," in Peter Russell, ed., *Nationalism in Canada* (Toronto, 1966), 27-43; Carl Berger, "The True North Strong and Free," in *ibid.*, 3-26; Berger, *The Sense of Power: Studies in the Ideas of Canadian Imperialism, 1867-1914* (Toronto, 1970); W. L. Morton, "Victorian Canada," in Morton, ed., *The Shield of Achilles: Aspects of Canada in the Victorian Age* (Toronto, 1968), 313.

2. *Quebec Mercury*, 22 December 1842. For a full version of the documentation, readers should consult the original essay. Quotations only are footnoted here.

3. *Chronicle & Gazette*, Kingston, 18 January 1845.

4. *Acadian Recorder*, Halifax, 29 January 1825.

5. *Times*, St. John's, 18 October 1848.

6. *Patriot*, St. John's, 5 October 1850.

7. *Acadian Recorder*, 10 August 1833.

8. R. Everest, *A Journey through the United States and Part of Canada* (London, 1855), 46-7.

9. W. H. G. Kingston, *Western Wanderings or, a Pleasure Tour in the Canadas* (London, 1856), II, 167.

10. *Quebec Mercury*, 3 December 1816.

11. *Halifax Morning Post*, 13 December 1845.

12. *Morning News*, Saint John, 23 December 1850.

13. *Acadian Recorder*, 21 December 1816.

14. *Novascotian*, Halifax, 2 February 1825.

15. *New Brunswick Courier*, Saint John, 30 January 1858.

16. *Ibid.*, 14 January 1832.

17. *Quebec Mercury*, 1 February 1855.

18. *Times and Courier*, Halifax, 22 March 1849.

19. *Halifax Daily Sun*, 4 March 1852.

20. *Morning News*, 8 March 1858.

21. *Times*, St. John's, 21 October 1854.

22. *Ibid.*, 29 September 1847.

23. Leonard C. Marsh, *Employment Research* (Toronto, 1935), 182.

24. Royal Commission on the Relations of Labor and Capital, in 1889, *Evidence-Quebec*, part 1, 680.

25. Terry Copp, *The Anatomy of Poverty: The Condition of the Working Class in Montreal, 1897-1929* (Toronto, 1974), 141.

Sermon Literature and Canadian Intellectual History

by S. F. Wise

I

Canadian intellectual history must be concerned, almost of necessity, with the kinds of ideas that lie between the formal thought of the philosopher or the political theorist and the world of action, and probably closer to the latter. Since (to understate the matter) no connected history of formal thought in Canada is possible, the Canadian intellectual historian must be concerned primarily with the interrelationship between ideas and actions, and therefore the intellectual commonplaces of an age, its root notions, assumptions, and images, will be of more significance to him than the study of coherent bodies of abstract thought. This sort of interest, of course, applies not merely to Canada but to the history of ideas in other places at other times. The historian who wants to establish the connections between ideas and events during the Civil War period in England is much less interested in the political philosophy of Thomas Hobbes than in ideas, well-worn though they may be, to be found in the ephemeral writings of such politicians and pamphleteers as Hyde, Vane, Lilburne, Pyrnne, or Milton (the more so in this particular instance, since Hobbes' political behaviour was not even Hobbesian). But it seems necessary to state the nature of a Canadian intellectual history, because there has been so little of it written; perhaps

From Committee on Archives, United Church of Canada, *The Bulletin*, no. 18 (1965), 3-18.

through a conviction that nothing of the kind was possible in the absence of any vigorous tradition of original formal thought.

It is indeed true that the explicit structures of thought from which most Canadian ideas derive lie outside Canada. It can be shown, for example, that the commonplaces of political or social language by which British American Tories of the early nineteenth century justified their actions to themselves stem directly from such European thinkers, or their popularizers, as Burke, De Lolme, Montesquieu, and Blackstone. No doubt the stock of Canadian ideas is replenished every generation from European and American sources; and doubtless it should be an important function of the Canadian intellectual historian to perform the sort of operations that will trace Canadian ideas to their ultimate external source. But his major task, surely, is to analyse the manner in which externally derived ideas have been adapted to a variety of local and regional environments, in such a way that a body of assumptions uniquely Canadian has been built up; and to trace the changing content of such assumptions. What, for example, are the social assumptions implicit in the early nineteenth-century term "yeoman"? When is "yeoman" replaced by "farmer," and what is the significance of the change? What is the relationship between changing terminology, and hence changing social assumptions, and the actual social process? Do these changes, both intellectual and social, occur at the same time in different parts of Canada? Again, what is the content, at any given time, of such terms as "loyalty," "order," "liberty," "authority"; terms which are merely abbreviations for complex socio-political assumptions? The content of the words "respectability" and "interest" is radically different today from what it was a century and a half ago; the life history of either term would disclose a great deal about the intellectual history of Canada.

There are good grounds for saying that the content of social image terminology, or the constellation of notions inherent in a word like "orders," will vary from region to region in Canada, and not just between French- and English-speaking regions. This may be the result of varying rates of assimilation of externally derived ideas in different parts of the country, or perhaps because some are not received at all, being "filtered out" because of the nature of local institutions. Before anything convincing can be said about the possibility that life in different regions of Canada is organized around marginally different sets of assumptions, however, much work must be done in charting the history of ideological configurations. This is not to imply that an approach which employs "French and Catholic mind" and "English and Protestant mind" as its two categories is erroneous; but simply that it is inadequate, because it cannot explain Canadian variety and because it implies that the Canadian mind, of either category, is a constant. Useful statements about the Canadian mind, at least in its historical context, are likely only after a series of careful investigations of those source materials in which the dominant assumptions of any one age are chiefly to be found, used in a context which makes their current meaning plain.

In any period, political rhetoric is a good guide to the current scale of public values, and also can provide a measurement of the frequent lag between professed belief and actual behaviour through a comparison of what the politician says with what he does. Newspaper editorials, public and private correspondence, travel books by Canadians (especially about other countries), the literature of criticism in the arts: all these classes of material are of permanent value. Other kinds of material, however, are of more significance in a particular age than in any other. Institutional and corporate advertising, for example, embalms values important in the age of large-scale economic enterprise; and a study of the advertising of the Bank of Montreal, the Steel Company of Canada, or even O'Keefe Breweries, over a generation, would probably show some remarkable shifts and changes.

The main purpose of this essay is to show, through illustration, the peculiar value of sermon literature as a medium for the expression of conservative ideas in late eighteenth and early nineteenth-century British America. Sermon literature as a source for the history of ideas, though untapped in Canada, has been used extensively elsewhere. Christopher Morris's *Political Thought in England: Tyndale to Hooker* (London, 1953),[1] and William Haller's brilliant study, *The Rise of Puritanism* (New York, 1938), both rely upon the exploitation of a large body of sermons to reconstruct the intellectual movements of early modern England; R. B. Perry's studies of the New England mind draw partly upon sermons. The most casual check of standard bibliographies of Canadian imprints will disclose that large numbers of sermons were published in the eighteenth and early nineteenth centuries, while many more manuscript sermons of the time are preserved in libraries and archives. In the Ontario Archives, for example, are several substantial bundles of the sermons of John Strachan, covering approximately sixty years of our history. They have never been used by an historian. Yet his sermons, and those of his contemporaries, are indispensable to an understanding of the conservative mind of the age.

II

Most of the sermons printed in British North America between 1784 and 1820 were those of "churchmen," that is, clergy of the Church of England, the Church of Scotland, and the Congregational churches of Nova Scotia. Each of these churches, in the land of its origin, was an established church and a defender of the established order of things. It is hardly remarkable that the sermons of the colonial clergy of these churches were uniformly conservative in character. It might perhaps be argued that unpublished rather than published sermons are a more valid source for the dominant ideas of the time, since they were intended only for the minister's congregation. It is true that since printed sermons were frequently those given on such public religious occasions as the opening of the legislature, days of general fast and humiliation, or days of public thanksgiving, they tended to be concerned with such public matters as the relationship between the state and its enemies, the purposes of God in times of war and revolution, or the duties of the citizen; while unpublished sermons, on the whole, seem to be less taken up with such questions. Even so reputedly political a churchman as John Strachan rarely gave an overtly political sermon to his own congregation. Moreover, the language of manuscript sermons is less studied, less formal, and less concerned with creating an impression of classical erudition. Yet there seems to be no substantial difference in the social and political assumptions which can be found running through the two classes of sermons. Whether on public occasions, or in ordinary Sunday services, the churchman preached social and political conservatism as well as the gospel.

It is the strategic position of the churchmen of the revolutionary age that lends a special importance to the content of their sermons. Accepted as members of the small colonial upper class, and accorded special respect because of their superior education in a society in which the general level was low, the clergy of the Anglican, Presbyterian, and Congregational churches (and indeed those of the Catholic church as well) were well-placed to exert a considerable influence upon the political outlook and behaviour of a large part of the colonial population. It has been argued[2] that social rank and education cut the established clergy off from the "people," but this is so only in a restricted sense, because their influence reached well beyond their by no means negligible congregations. In defining the public philosophy and the public morality, the conservative clergy had little competition, and that chiefly from the judges of the high courts, whose jury charges invaded, periodically, the ideological monopoly of the ministers. Legislative debates were not reported at this time, and thus the politician was virtually stifled. The day of the journalist-politician had scarcely dawned. The popular press did not exist. Society was wholly Christian; freethinkers kept their thoughts to themselves. No challenge to the intellectual primacy of the clergy came from such dissenting denominations as the Baptists and the Methodists, who accepted the political and social, if not ecclesiastical and theological assumptions of the churchmen.

The position of the conservative clergy in the realm of ideas was reinforced by the outbreak of the French Revolution, and by the long wars which were its aftermath. Men knew that the Revolution had brought a new age, and whether they wished it well, or were horrified by it, they followed the shifts and changes of the huge drama with absorbed fascination. Even in the little societies of British North America, a weekly budget of despatches, letters, bulletins, treaties, atrocity stories, and propaganda borrowed by the infant colonial press from newspapers abroad or from the United States kept the reading public informed (a few months in arrears) of the enormous events that were shaking the old order to its foundations. The deadly antagonism between the Revolution and established ideas and institutions meant that everywhere conservatives rallied to attack it. The politician Edmund Burke, in his *Reflections on the Revolution in France*, provided both a defence of British institutions and an eloquent assault upon the Revolution and all its works, and of course his arguments made a deep impression upon British American conservatives as well as those of Great Britain. In the colonies, however, it was the clergy, not the politicians, who bore the chief responsibility for interpreting the meaning of Europe's convulsions to society at large, and because of this, they made a lasting contribution to the nature of Canadian conservatism. It can be seen in that combination of religious and secular elements which gave to colonial Toryism one of its most marked characteristics, and perhaps its only real claim to distinctiveness. This synthesis, worked out during the long crisis of the Revolution, the French wars, and the War of 1812, proved an extraordinarily durable one. Some illustrations of its beginnings follow.

III

That the French Revolution surpassed previous revolutions in scale and in the social depths to which it reached was not questioned, even by the Loyalist clergy of British North America. To Charles Inglis, the Loyalist Bishop of Nova Scotia, it was an event without precedent.

The state of France at the present day is an occurrence wholly new in the annals of the human race. The history of mankind . . . furnishes no instance . . . of so general a phrenzy seizing a populous and polished nation; a phrenzy that is not confined to any particular description, but diffused through all ranks and orders of people. The high and the low, the peer and peasant, the learned and the ignorant, are equally stimulated to the perpetration of the most atrocious crimes; delighting in slaughter and unbridled cruelty; sporting with the lives and property of mankind; destroying all religion and subordination; openly avowing atheism; and sinking into a total depravation of principles and manners![3]

That it might be possible to equate the revolutions in France and America does not seem to have occurred to Inglis;[4] it was not the degree of violence or the universality of upheaval that made the French Revolution so radical a break from previous experience, but the shock of such an explosion in a nation so "populous and polished." How could so ancient and civilized a people be "suddenly transformed into a race of sanguinary barbarians and ruffians"?[5] Had the French gone spontaneously mad? Or were there deeper causes for this apparent national insanity? Could an explanation be found in the instabilities of the volatile French character, or was the Revolution a product of causes which could operate anywhere, and not exclusively in France?

The sermons of the day were attempts to answer such questions. In them is to be found an anatomy of the Revolution, and of revolutions: the false ideas from which they spring, the nature and the motivation of the men who concoct and spread inflammatory ideas, the vast deception behind the protestations of reformers. It is not really important that these sermons were couched in the terms of traditional thought, despite some flashes of insight or felicities of phrase. What is important is their contribution to the formation of a conservative political ideology. The principles hammered home from the pulpits during the long crisis with France were those which were to condemn a Gourlay, a Mackenzie, or a Papineau in the years after the end of the wars, and were to endure, in modified form, long beyond the collapse of political Toryism.

According to the Reverend Andrew Brown, incumbent of the Protestant Dissenting Church in Halifax, the seeds of the French Revolution were planted by the free-thinking followers of Lord Herbert of Cherbury. Under the guise of defending the freedom of the press and the right of private judgment, they launched a subtle attack upon organized religion, and by degrees poisoned the arts, science, and philosophy with their sceptical doctrines. In this they had the assistance of the European aristocracy, who, out of a sense of guilt for their historic crimes, sought "a commodious apology for the disorders of their conduct."[6] Aristocratic complicity was crucial:

> Abandoned by the rich and fashionable, the church continued for a season to be a refuge to the poor and afflicted. But in time the lower orders learned to despise, in their hearts, those religious observances which they saw their more enlightened superiors treat with unreserved contempt. Copying their example with perverse ingenuity, they joined in the ridicule poured upon their clergy, and regarded every scandalous story which reflected on the church or the sacred office, as an invaluable piece of history which could not be too carefully recorded. . . . Amidst the indifference and depravity of a degenerate age, Christianity was publicly renounced by many in the upper ranks of life, and a speculative deism, in no respect distinguishable from actual atheism, was substituted in its room.[7]

It was a cardinal principle of Tory social psychology that the example set by the upper orders would always influence decisively the conduct of the mass of mankind. This is why a relatively few aristocratic followers of "Voltaire, Rousseau, Helvetius, D'Alembert, & c." could produce a "nation of Atheists."[8] Once "Reason" was enthroned, the way was clear for the perpetration of the shocking crimes of the Revolution. But this black page of history had a moral utility, could its lesson be understood:

> . . . from the general tenour of the affairs of France since its rulers abjured religion, the least instructed of mankind . . . may be enabled to institute a comparison between the effects of genuine Christianity, and of that sublime Philosophy which was to regenerate the human race. . . . no sooner had the sceptical philosophers usurped the powers of legislation than . . . strife and anarchy prevailed. The worst passions of the worst persons rioted without controul. . . . The prisons were crowded with victims; new modes of trial and execution were invented; and under the direful agency of a murderous tribunal blood flowed in a continual stream.[9]

The bloody events of the Revolution, then, were the natural and inevitable outcome of the abandonment of religion by the ruling classes of France. It was vain and self-deceiving to imagine that the enlightened principles of the philosophers had somehow been betrayed by weak men; the atrocities in France were, in fact, "inseparable from the nature of the new principles, and would mark their rule to the world's end."[10]

Here the conservative clergy were on familiar ground: the mutually supporting nature of religion and the state. While admitting that without government, man would long since have exterminated himself, Inglis argued, following Warburton,[11] that religion was necessary to rectify the imperfections of government. Secular laws, which rested upon force, could not reach "the source and spring of our actions," the conscience. Moreover, society cannot work without such "duties of imperfect obligation" as gratitude, hospitality, charity, and so on. Yet social duties, without which the state of society would be "miserable," cannot possibly be legislated. Indeed, society is incapable of sufficiently rewarding its members to ensure its own preservation. Aside from the very few persons who receive rank and emolument from serving the state, society provides for the general mass of citizens only the reward of mere protection, quite insufficient to stimulate preservative civic virtues. As man grows more numerous, new problems arise: the more populous the society, the larger the cities, the wealthier their citizens, then the greater the increase in crime as "the depraved appetites of mankind" are inflamed. A rise in material prosperity and urban population does not mean progress, but merely more inducements to greater crime. A government based upon secular philosophy, no matter how benign, is powerless against the forces of evil and destructiveness latent in society itself. There is only one principle that will bind up the warring elements within peoples, and that is the "superior principle" of religion. Only religion teaches that the government is ordained of God, a principle that gives the state an authority that no secular sanction can give it.[12] Only religion renders man conscious of the all-seeing eye of God and of his own ultimate accountability to God. Without instruction in his duty toward God, man inevitably falls victim to the ever-increasing temptations that surround him, and is drawn into enormous crimes. It is therefore "the avenging terrors of Almighty God" which are "the best support of Government."[13]

Brown's argument was similar, if a little less crudely put. Any system, he held, that considered this life as the whole of existence, and thought of death as an everlasting sleep, would hold out only "safety and self-aggrandisement" as the ends of life, and since man is not accountable for his behaviour, the pursuit of these ends "by all means, even the most atrocious," is justified. But when society is Christian, then "the gospel . . . moderates the passions of the rich, and supports the virtue of the poor."[14] These and other arguments concerned with the vital social and political utility of religion were to be vigorously employed by the next generation of clerical and lay conservatives in their defence of the principle of the connection between church and state, or at least the public recognition of the Christian nature of society through financial aid to churches other than the Church of England. To conservatives, the necessity of some connection between organized religion and the state had been triumphantly vindicated by the horrors which irreligion had caused in France, and by the final defeat of France herself. Andrew Brown, in the early years of the Revolution, had been confident that such would be the outcome of the great contest then beginning:

> To all arguments in (Christianity's) favour which past ages have furnished, will be added those alarming ones derived from the bloody history of the French revolution. . . . Chris-

tianity will thus be restored to new credit and influence. The vain babblings of philosophy will be consigned to everlasting perdition. Men will reject with detestation all the modifications of deism, and be solicitous to establish in their country, in their houses, and in their hearts, the genuine doctrines of the Cross of Christ.[15]

Although the first concern of the conservative clergy was to explain the French Revolution in terms of the abandonment of religion for the pernicious ideas of the free-thinkers, they also addressed themselves directly to radical French politics and the dangers French radicalism posed for British North America. Much is said, for example, of the character of the political innovator. Taken together, these remarks form a kind of compendium of the Tory rhetoric against reform, and are an illustration of a conventional pattern of thought that was to have a long life. To the churchmen, society was delicately and precariously balanced, an entity dependent upon the maintenance of an equilibrium between the desire of all its members for security in life and property, and the desire of each for self-aggrandisement. As we have seen, it was the function of religion to "subdue this restlessness and discontent," and to teach man to be "resigned to the will of God, and thankful for his allotment in the state of life where his providence has placed us."[16] The innovator, however, had more than the ordinary share of natural restlessness. He was a person in whom "ambition, self-interest, and humour" were in dangerous combination. "Not content with (his) proper rank in the scale of beings," he schemed to advance himself by stirring up others.[17] His tactics were ever the same: he called for redress of grievances in the name of patriotism, liberty, and the public welfare; he formed clubs, circulated inflammatory publications, got up petitions, spread rumours, worked up the multitude in the name of some great cause. He was a demagogue, who played upon the baser desires of the artless populace; he was a hypocrite, because "self-interest generally lies at the bottom" of the ringing ideals he professed. Such men rose on the hopes they created in the masses, and "secretly laugh at those who are the dupes of their artifices."[18] In this timeless game, the people were always deluded; indeed, doubly so: first by the deceitful demagogue who used them for his purposes, and second by their own illusion that programs of reform could have any beneficial effect upon their condition. Just as the state of France demonstrated the horrible consequences of irreligion, so also it showed the absurdity of impracticable schemes of political reformation, launched "under the specious names of *Fraternity, Equality,* and *Liberty.*"[19] Just as the deists had had the arrogant presumption to challenge eighteen centuries of Christianity, so the political philosophers had been dreaming dreams of perfection and calling them constitutions, when the teachings of both religion and history showed that the hard lot of man was to submit to his own imperfections and to put up with the institutions he had, which represented, after all, the wisdom of countless generations. How cruel to hoodwink the masses with glittering slogans!

> To meditate the establishment of equality . . . , that splendid delusion of the present age, the vision of the weak, and the pretext of the wicked, is in fact to meditate war against God, and the primary laws of creation. . . . In society inequality is just as natural as in the forest, but productive of much more salutary effects. Without inequality what would become of the necessary distinctions of parent and child, master and scholar, the employer and the employed![20]

Most clergymen were prepared to admit that there were times when political and social changes were necessary and even desirable, and that failure to change could bring upheavals like the French Revolution. But there were some, like Bishop Inglis, who saw no need at all for change in the present state of perfection. For him, religious history had come to a stop with the salutary changes of the Protestant Reformation, and political history with that culmination of the English genius, the Glorious Revolution of 1688:

> But, blessed be God, those times are now past. We enjoy the benefits resulting from those changes; we should be thankful to heaven for them; and look back with reverence to the fortitude and virtues of our ancestors who were instruments, in the hand of Providence, of conferring those signal blessings upon us. For we live in a period, when the Religion of Jesus Christ is professed and taught in its native purity, as contained in holy Scripture. We live under the best of Civil Constitutions; where we enjoy as much Liberty as is consistent with a state of Civil Society. . . . In these circumstances, to think the business of changing should still go on, and never stop, must surely pro-

ceed from [the] spirit of innovation, . . . or from something worse.[21]

Therefore, enjoined Inglis in the words of a text no longer in fashion, but then much used: "Fear thou the Lord and the King; and meddle not with them that are given to change."

Another important theme of the sermons of this period had to do with the meaning of the great struggle in which Britain and France were engaged. How could the larger purposes of God for man be reconciled with the necessity to justify a British victory? The interpretive framework upon which these sermons were preached was the providential theology, and, like other churchmen before and since, the clergy of the day were gradually drawn to identify the purposes of God with the policies of their own nation. Preaching in the first months of the war, Andrew Brown, "a short-sighted mortal," was wary of divining God's "precise purposes," but remained confident that He "never ordained impiety and anarchy to be perpetual among men."[22] Inglis was less cautious. He declared that "the judgments of God are actually abroad," and announced his conviction that the war against France was a sacred war. Surely it was "a contest in the cause of humanity against violence and blood, of order and government against anarchy and confusion, of right and justice against lawless rapacity, of real liberty against oppression and tyranny, of truth against falsehood, and of God against the most audacious Atheism."[23] Yet both Inglis and Brown asserted that the war was also a sore judgment of God against Britain and her allies for their transgressions, in which godless France was the divine instrument of punishment, just as God had used such pagan idolators as the Egyptians and Babylonians when Israel had strayed from the paths of righteousness. The war was monitory, therefore, and was to be seen as providing opportunity for a purifying repentance. Should the opportunity so presented be wasted, then Britain would be broken like a potter's vessel.[24]

But as the war went on, the emphasis upon British sinfulness became less strong, and more and more the clergy, especially the Anglicans, came to equate the aims of God and Great Britain. When Nelson won at Aboukir Bay, Mather Byles in Saint John adduced the victory as proof that the British people were "the favourites of God," and that France was Satan personified as a many-headed nation. Behind Great Britain was "the secret, irresistible scheme of Providence."[25] In a sermon celebrating the

same victory, Bishop Mountain at Quebec nodded to conve.
tional theology in acknowledging that God had used France to
chastise a sinful world, but professed to see that the British people, having passed through the refiner's fire of adversity, were
now "happily for ourselves, and for the world, made the instruments of chastising the arrogance, humbling the power of
France." Who could doubt that "we are engaged against an
enemy whom we may, without presumption, consider as much
more wicked than ourselves"?[26]

Mountain, and many another minister of the time, fell into the
classic error of accommodating Christianity to the current system
of values. They persuaded themselves, and many of their hearers,
that God was not merely using Britain to defeat atheistic France,
but that British victories meant also Divine approval of the
social, religious, and political institutions of the mother
country.[27] This delusion, always latent in British nationalism,
was given special strength by the zeal with which it was preached
during the many years' crisis, and was permitted to take firm
hold partly because there was nothing that could be called an "intellectual opposition" in colonial society. The notion that God
had staged the quarter-century of destruction as a kind of
massive lesson to benighted humanity of the superior virtues of
the British constitution in church and state (though never stated
quite so baldly) became an article of faith with British American
Tories. The special religious element in colonial Toryism owed
much to the inculcation, during the war years, of a crude providentialism, as did the fact that British American conservatives
had no provision in their scheme of things for orderly change, but
merely for the orderly acceptance of things as they were.

In the sermons of John Strachan, the "lessons" the conservative clergy thought the French wars had taught can be read
plainly. Unlike the other clergy mentioned to this point, Strachan
belonged essentially to the post-war period, but his ideas were
formed, once for all, before 1815. This fact, is of prime importance, because Strachan was teacher, mentor, and minister to a
whole generation of Tory politicians in Upper Canada, a central
figure in the politics of his province for at least twenty-five years
and a dominant influence in his church for many more years than
that. His impact upon the Ontario community in its formative
stage was very great, in one way or another, and yet it cannot be
said that his ideas have ever been adequately analysed. Plentiful
material for such an analysis is to be found in the large body of

sermons, printed and in manuscript, that he left behind him. These sermons establish clearly Strachan's intellectual debt to the clergy of the age of revolution, but also demonstrate that he was much more extreme in his conservatism than any of them.

Strachan's mind was rather like a megalithic monument: strong, crude, and simple. It moved in straight lines, was impatient of subtleties and qualifications (though often itself devious and self-deceiving), and was unleavened by what might be variously described as realism, a sense of proportion, or merely as a sense of the absurd. To such a mind, providentialism was heady wine, for Strachan pushed the conclusions to be drawn from it farther than did any of his contemporaries. Not for him the modest disclaimers of Brown, or even the more specious qualifications of Mountain. God's intentions could not be doubted; "never have so many unquestionable proofs of a superintending Providence appeared in so short a period."[28] The secular, egalitarian assumptions upon which the governments of the United States and France were, or had been based, had been judged and found wanting; "the two great experiments in America and France to constitute governments productive of virtues and happiness only . . . have completely failed." The lesson of the war was that "no great and decided amelioration of the lower classes of society can be reasonably expected: . . . that foolish perfectability with which they have been deluded can never be realized."[29] On the other hand, Strachan was not content to depict Britain as an instrument in the hands of God, used to accomplish His purposes, as had his clerical contemporaries. Just as God had revealed His truth to the Jews, thought Strachan, so had He in a later day to another nation. "Here, My Brethren," said Strachan, "I allude to the British nation, but not in the spirit of boasting or ostentation."[30] His victory sermon of 1814 and such other sermons as the Rebellion sermon of 1838[31] disclose that his deepest beliefs were that the British were God's peculiar people, and that their order in church, state, and society was providentially blessed. Among God's British, the Upper Canadians occupied a special position. This "remnant" of a once-great continental empire had been purified and united through struggle with the United States, the only country in the world to become the ally of France by free choice. The miraculous survival of tiny Upper Canada was a North American testimony to God's gracious dealings with those whom he designed specially to prosper. Strachan's sermon of 1814, preached in the first flush of victory over Napoleon and in the knowledge that Wellington's veterans were soon to be launched against the Americans, is an important document. It is a kind of manifesto for Upper-Canadian Toryism, but it contains not a program so much as an anti-program; that is, it lays down those things – the connection between church and state, the relative perfection of the British constitution, the delusiveness of projects of reform, and the suicidal dangers in listening to innovators – which the will of God as revealed in the verdict of the war had determined to be beyond challenge. Rid of her invaders, cleansed of her traitors and secure in her beliefs, Upper Canada would stand as a shining witness in North America. "Now," said Strachan, "the dawn of the happiest times is rising upon us."[32]

IV

One of the great difficulties in reconstructing the conservative mind (of any period) is the fact that the conservative is rarely explicit about his most cherished beliefs. He assumes certain things to be immutably true and established, and finds it unnecessary to explain them to his friends, and pointless to explain them to his enemies. When an Upper-Canadian Tory ran for election with a strong belief in the British constitution as his only declared platform, neither he nor his sympathetic constituents found such an appeal platitudinous or ludicrously inadequate. Such phrases stood for a whole set of conservative values.

At no time was the Tory less explicit than in explaining his social values. Quite possibly this was because the standard British arguments in justification of the principle of aristocracy seemed irrelevant to the much more democratic societies of North America; more probably it was because the Tory, while retaining his belief in a graded social order, realized that he was unlikely to get a favourable hearing for his views from the community at large. At any rate, any source which supplies an exposition of what the British American conservative meant by a phrase like "due subordination in society" is valuable.

The unpublished sermons of John Strachan contain some of the most illuminating expositions of conservative social thought available, perhaps because the Doctor in his pulpit, speaking to his parishioners, felt a freedom unknown to his pupils, on the hustings, in the legislature, or in the press. As an illustration, there is his sermon on I Timothy 4:8, "But Godliness is profitable unto all things." Strachan's notations show that it was first preached at sea September 24, 1824, and that he delivered it several more times in the 1820's and 1830's. His ostensible purpose was to comment upon the relationship between the enjoyment of the pleasures of this world and the prospect of salvation. Should religion "stalk abroad with all the rigour of Egyptian Taskmasters?"[33] He concluded (predictably enough) that when not carried to excess the pursuit of pleasure, wealth, and honours was natural, proper, and by no means out of keeping with the religious life.

But Strachan's purpose was not primarily to justify temporal happiness, but the existence and necessity of social inequality. His argument was immeasurably old, a kind of historical pastiche of the commonplaces of social conservatism, but with some quirks which are his alone. Just as in the natural world there is an ascending order of creation, and within each species there are both weak and strong individuals, so in human society are men given an infinite variety of capacities:

> One is formed to rule, another to obey. . . . Subordination in the Moral World is manifest and this appearance of nature indicates the intention of its Author. The beauty and advantages of this arrangement are obvious and universally acknowledged. . . . The various relations of individuals and Societies require a mutual exchange of good offices. . . . Hence it would appear that they who labour in the inferior departments of life are not on that account the slaves of their superiors. The Magistrate requires the aid of his people – the Master of his Servant. They are all dependent upon one another, as they subsist by an exchange of good offices. . . . The lowest order enjoys its peculiar comforts and privileges, and contributes equally with the highest to the support and dignity of Society.

Not only did the social order correspond to the different levels of ability given to men by God, but men were also allotted "different shares of sensibility," so that the pursuit of happiness became the pursuit of that degree of happiness one is capable of attaining. Because of this, only bitterness can come to the man who aspires to a place above his station. While "efforts to better our condition are laudable," the man who gets above himself will drink deeply of "Chagrin, Melancholy, Envy, Hatred and other wretched passions." Strachan offered as consolation for the inferiority of one's lot the perennial conservative cliché that the mighty of this world ought not to be envied their luxury and pomp; they pay for their splendours many times over with the heavy burden of care that attends high position:

> Let us not be dazzled by the opulence and splendour of the great. The delicacies of his Table would soon pall upon our sense, vitiate our taste, and perhaps enervate us by Sickness or disease. We may admire the pomp of his public appearance, when his pride, the duties of his station, the applause of a surrounding multitude, or the brilliancy of the whole scene may preserve an air of superior ease and happiness in his deportment, but let us follow him to his retirement during the season of reflexion and we may see him oppressed with cares, which neither the most delicate repast nor costly apparel nor a multitude of Friends and dependents nor all the glories of a crown can alleviate.

Not pausing to explain to his hearers how it was that the share of sensibility awarded the great did not bring them the kind of happiness commensurate with their rank, Strachan rushed on to provide a sovereign remedy for dissatisfaction with one's subordinate position in life (so long as one was not too subordinate). Instead of eating one's heart out with envy of those more fortunate, why not reverse the process?

> You compare your situation with that of your Superiors. This will turn your attention to the advantages you want rather than those you possess. . . . But compare it to the inferior stations of life, and the effect will be more favourable to your comfort. . . . You do not consider their blessings but plume yourselves as enjoying much superior. By thus contrasting your condition with those that are worse, you will see how much more unhappy you might be and thus derive satisfaction from your superiority. In this way learn to contract your desires and you will obtain all the happiness which others so anxiously pursue.

Strachan's recommendation is testimony to his sense of social psychology, if not to his grasp of Christian social ethics.

Stripped of its characteristic individual quixotries, this sermon is probably representative of early nineteenth-century conservative social thought. How relevant its categories were to the social and economic realities of British North America is quite another question. Deeply held social and political assumptions change when circumstances dictate, when they have clearly ceased to have any connection with the life they purport to explain. Perhaps it was such a change that explains the superscription scrawled upon this sermon by John Strachan in old age: "Read this Sermon on 12 March 1858 and found it very inferior to what I expected."

NOTES

1. See especially the two chapters entitled "The Elizabethan Assumptions."
2. S. D. Clark, *Church and Sect in Canada* (Toronto, 1948).
3. Charles Inglis, *A Sermon Preached in the Parish Church of St. Paul in Halifax on Friday, April 25, 1794. Being the day appointed by Proclamation for a General Fast and Humiliation in His Majesty's Province of Nova Scotia* (Halifax, 1794), 24.
4. See R. R. Palmer, *Age of the Democratic Revolution: A Political History of Europe and America, 1760-1800* (Princeton, 1959), ch. VII.
5. Charles Inglis, *Steadfastness in Religion and Loyalty Recommended, in a Sermon Preached before the Legislature of His Majesty's Province of Nova Scotia . . . Sunday, April 7, 1793* (Halifax, 1793), 22n.
6. Andrew Brown, *The Perils of the Time, and the Purposes for which they are Appointed. A Sermon Preached on the Last Sabbath of the Year 1794* (Halifax, 1795), 27.
7. *Ibid.*, 28.
8. Inglis, *Steadfastness*, 15, 16n.
9. Brown, *Perils*, 29-30.
10. *Ibid.*
11. Bishop William Warburton, *Alliance of Church and State* (London, 1766).
12. Inglis, *Steadfastness*, 9-12. The Rev. John Burns, Presbyterian minister of Stamford, Upper Canada, could find no other way to express this idea than by enunciating the doctrine of the Divine Right of Kings, in words virtually those of James I! "Kings are God's deputies, or vicegerents, here upon earth. They derive their power from him, and are the instruments, which his providence has made choice of, to govern and protect the world." *True Patriotism; A Sermon Preached in the Presbyterian Church in Stamford, Upper Canada, on the 3rd Day of June, 1814 . . .* (Montreal, 1814),

10. Upper Canada, the nursery of a variety of out-of-the-way political notions during these years, presents no more extraordinary spectacle than this revival of divine-rightism by a spiritual descendant of John Knox and the Melvilles.

13. Inglis, *Steadfastness*, 12-13.

14. Brown, *Perils*, 31. A representative Catholic development of similar themes is Rev. Edmund Burke, *Letter of Instruction to the Catholic Missionaries of Nova Scotia* (Halifax, 1804).

15. Brown, *Perils*, 31.

16. Inglis, *Steadfastness*, 17.

17. Mather Byles, *The Victory Ascribed to God* . . . (Saint John, N.B., 1798), 5.

18. Burns, *True Patriotism*, 15; Inglis, *Steadfastness*, 17, 22.

19. Jacob Mountain, *Sermon Preached at Quebec, January 10, 1799 . . . for General Thanksgiving* (Quebec, 1799), 29.

20. Brown, *Perils*, 34-5.

21. Inglis, *Steadfastness*, 18.

22. Brown, *Perils*, 19.

23. Inglis, *Sermon . . . for a General Fast*, 31, 23.

24. *Ibid*., 24-5; Brown, *Perils*, 24.

25. Byles, *Victory*, 9, 12.

26. Mountain, *Sermon . . . for General Thanksgiving*, 15-17.

27. *Ibid*., 25-30.

28. John Strachan, *Sermon Preached at York, Upper Canada, on the Third of June, being the Day Appointed for a General Thanksgiving* (Montreal, 1814), 5.

29. *Ibid*., 29-30.

30. *Ibid*., 8.

31. PAO, Strachan Papers, Sermon on text "And thy judgments are as the light that goeth forth," Hosea 6:5, delivered 14 December 1838.

32. Strachan, *Sermon . . . for a General Thanksgiving*, 38.

33. PAO, Strachan Papers, Sermon on text "But Godliness is profitable unto all things," I Timothy 4:8, first delivered 24 September 1824. All subsequent quotations are from this sermon.

III
The Working Class

The theme of working-class culture is central in Ruth Bleasdale's article. Disorders among working-class people often have been seen as irrational and brutal, and something to be deplored in the strongest terms. A major task of nineteenth-century society was to find ways to control this "animal" instinct among workers. Recently, however, historians have tried to understand such outbursts. Starting with George Rude's work on European crowds, they have discovered a logic to lower-class behaviour, or misbehaviour. They have found that violent disorders were of a kind with more peaceful expressions such as holiday activities, membership in social organizations, or the maintenance of distinctive patterns of domestic behaviour. They were all part of a lower-class lifestyle or culture, one that groups like the Irish canal-workers would fight to retain. Because of the long and persistent challenges to their culture, the Irish were the most pugnacious in its defence. However, French Canadians also responded in somewhat similar ways to challenges to their culture. So did Anglo-Irish and English who formed the militant Orange Order to express and protect their lifestyle. Contemporary Canadians who view the Third World attempts to develop while retaining their cultures, or who are concerned about the future of Canadian culture in North America, have a starting point for appreciating the struggles of the Irishmen on the pre-industrial canals.

FURTHER READING:
The classic article on the canals is H. C. Pentland, "The Lachine Strike of 1843," *Canadian Historical Review*, XXIX, 3 (1948),

255-77. The general context in which Pentland and Bleasdale see the canals is discussed in Pentland's *Labour and Capital in Canada 1650-1860* (Toronto, 1981). On the Irish in the 1840's, there is an excellent study, Kenneth Duncan, "Irish Famine Immigration and the Social Structure of Canada West," *Canadian Review of Sociology and Anthropology*, 2 (1965), 19-40, and reprinted in Michiel Horn and R. Sabourin, eds., *Studies in Canadian Social History* (Toronto, 1974), 140-63. Gregory Kealey has provided a good discussion of another cultural group, although that discussion ranges after 1849: "The Orange Order in Toronto: Religious Riot and the Working Class," in Kealey and Peter Warrian, eds., *Essays in Canadian Working Class History* (Toronto, 1976), 13-34. Bleasdale's account of the Irish should be compared with Michael Cross, "The Shiners' War: Social Violence in the Ottawa Valley in the 1830's," *Canadian Historical Review*, LIV, 1 (1973), 1-26. The works of Palmer and Fingard, suggested for Judith Fingard's "The Poor in Winter" printed above, obviously are relevant here as well.

Ruth Bleasdale is in the Department of History at Dalhousie University.

Class Conflict on the Canals of Upper Canada in the 1840's

by Ruth Bleasdale

Irish labourers on the St. Lawrence canal system in the 1840's appeared to confirm the stereotype of the Irish Celt – irrational, emotionally unstable, and lacking in self-control. Clustered around construction sites in almost exclusively Irish communities, they engaged in violent confrontations with each other, local inhabitants, employers, and law enforcement agencies. Observers of these confrontations accepted as axiomatic the stereotype of violent Paddy, irreconcilable to Anglo-Saxon norms of rational behaviour, and goverment reports, private letters, and newspaper articles characterized the canallers as "persons predisposed to tumult even without cause."[1] As one of the contractors on the Lachine Canal put it: "they are a turbulent and discontented people that nothing can satisfy for any length of time, and who never will be kept to work peaceably unless overawed by some force for which they have respect."[2]

Yet men attempting to control the disturbances along the canals perceived an economic basis to these disturbances which directly challenged ethnocentric interpretations of the canallers' behaviour. In the letters and reports of government officials and law enforcement agents on the canal works in Upper Canada the violence of the labourers appears not as the excesses of an unruly nationality clinging to old behaviour patterns, but as a rational response to economic conditions in the new world. The Irish

From *Labour/Le Travailleur*, 7 (1981), 9-39. Reprinted by permission of the editor. © Committee on Canadian Labour History.

labourers' common ethnoculture did play a part in shaping their response to these conditions, defining acceptable standards of behaviour and providing shared traditions and experiences which facilitated united protest. But the objective basis of the social disorder along the canals was, primarily, class conflict. With important exceptions, the canallers' collective action constituted a bitter resistance to the position they were forced to assume in the society of British North America.

Southern Irish immigrants flooding into the Canadas during the 1840's became part of a developing capitalist labour market, a reserve pool of unskilled labourers who had little choice but to enter and remain in the labour force.[3] Most Southern Irish arrived in the new world destitute. "Labouring paupers" was how the immigration agent at Quebec described them.[4] They had little hope of establishing themselves on the land. By the 1840's the land granting and settlement policies of government and private companies had combined to put land beyond the reach of such poor immigrants. Settlement even on free grants in the backwoods was "virtually impossible without capital."[5] The only option open to most Southern Irish was to accept whatever wage labour they could find.

Many found work in the lumbering, shipping, and ship-building industries, and in the developing urban centres, where they clustered in casual and manual occupations. But the British North American economy could not absorb the massive immigration of unskilled Irish.[6] Although the cholera epidemics of 1832 and 1834 and the commercial crisis of 1837 had led to a decline in immigration and a shortage of labour by 1838, a labour surplus rapidly developed in the opening years of the 1840's, as Southern Irish arrived in record numbers.[7] Added to this influx of labourers from across the Atlantic was a migration of Irish labourers north across the American border. During the 1840's the movement of labourers across the border had usually been in the opposite direction, a large proportion of Irish immigrants at Quebec proceeding to the United States in search of employment on public works projects. But the economic panic of 1837 had put a stop to "practically every form of public work" in that country, and further stoppages in 1842 sent thousands of Irish labourers into the Canadas looking for work. Some new immigrants at Quebec still travelled through to the United States despite the dismal prospects of employment in that country; Pentland concludes, however, that the net flow into Canada from the United

States in the years 1842-43 was 2,500.[8] Large-scale migration of the unskilled south across the American border revived in the latter half of the decade, but the labour market continued to be over-supplied by destitute Irish immigrants fleeing famine in their homeland.[9]

The public works in progress along the Welland Canal and the St. Lawrence River attracted a large proportion of the unemployed Irish throughout the decade. The Emigration Committee for the Niagara District Council complained that construction sites along the Welland operated "as beacon lights to the whole redundant and transient population of not only British America, but the United States."[10] From the St. Lawrence canals came similar reports of great numbers of "strange labourers" constantly descending on the canals. Even with little work left in the early months of 1847, labourers were still pouring into the area around the Williamsburg canals. Chief Engineer J. B. Mills asked the Board of Works what could be done with all the labourers.[11]

Many did secure work for a season or a few years. The massive canal construction program undertaken by the government of the Canadas during the 1840's created a demand for as many as 10,000 unskilled labourers at one time in Upper Canada alone. The work was labour-intensive, relying on the manpower of gangs of labourers. While mechanical inventions such as the steam-excavator in the Welland's Deep Cut played a small role in the construction process, unskilled labourers executed most aspects of the work, digging, puddling, hauling, and quarrying.[12] The Cornwall Canal needed 1,000 labourers during peak construction seasons in 1842 and 1843; the Williamsburg canals required as many as 2,000 between 1844 and 1847; while the improvements to the Welland employed between 3,000 and 4,000 labourers from 1842 to 1845, their numbers tapering off in the latter half of the decade.[13]

Despite this heavy demand, there were never enough jobs for the numbers who flocked to canal construction sites. Winter brought unemployment of desperate proportions. While some work continued on the Cornwall and Williamsburg canals and on the Welland to a greater extent, the number of labourers who could be employed profitably was severely limited. Of the 5,000 along the Welland in January 1844, over 3,000 could not find jobs, and those at work could put in but few days out of the month because of the weather.[14] Even during the spring and summer months, the number of unemployed in the area might exceed the number employed if work on one section came to an end or if work was suspended for the navigation season.[15]

Only a small number of those unable to get work on the canals appear to have found jobs on farms in the area. Despite the pressing demand for farm labourers and servants during the 1840's, the peasant background of the Southern Irish had not equipped them to meet this demand, and many farmers in Upper Canada consequently professed reluctance to employ Irish immigrants.[16] The Niagara District Council's 1843 enquiry into emigration and the labour needs of the district noted that farmers were not employing the labourers along the canal because they did not know "the improved system of British agriculture." Four years later the emigration committee for the same district gave a similar reason as to why farmers would not hire the immigrants squatting along the Welland Canal: "from the peculiar notions which they entertain, from the habits which they have formed, and from their ignorance of the manner in which the duties of farm labourers and servants are performed in this country, they are quite unprofitable in either capacity."[17] In the last half of the decade, fear that famine immigrants carried disease acted as a further barrier to employment of the Irish on farms.[18]

Despite their inability to find work the unemployed congregated along the canal banks. As construction commenced on the Welland, canal Superintendent Samuel Power endeavoured to explain why the surplus labourers would not move on: "the majority are so destitute that they are unable to go. The remainder are unwilling as there is not elsewhere any hope of employment." Four years later the situation had not changed. The Niagara District Council concluded that even if there had been somewhere for the unemployed to go, they were too indigent to travel.[19] Instead they squatted along the public works, throwing together shanties from pilfered materials – the fence rails of farmers and boards from abandoned properties.[20]

These shanties of the unemployed became a part of all construction sites. Their occupants maintained themselves by stealing from local merchants, farmers, and townspeople. According to government and newspaper reports, pilfering became the order of the day along public works projects, the unemployed stealing any portable commodity – food, fence rails, firewood, money, and livestock.[21] While reports deplored this criminal activity, observers agreed that it was their extreme poverty which "impelled these poor, unfortunate beings to criminal acts."[22] The

St. Catharines Journal, a newspaper generally unsympathetic to the canallers, described the condition of the unemployed in the winter of 1844:

> . . . the greatest distress imaginable has been, and still is, existing throughout the entire line of the Welland Canal, in consequence of the vast accumulation of unemployed labourers. . . . There are, at this moment, many hundreds of men, women, and children, apparently in the last stages of starvation; and instead . . . of any relief for them . . . in the spring, . . . more than one half of those who are now employed *must* be discharged. . . . This is no exaggeration statement; it falls below the reality, and which requires to be seen, in all its appalling features to entitle any description of it to belief.[23]

Such descriptions appear frequently enough in the letters of government officials to indicate that the *Journal* was not indulging in sensational reporting. The actual numbers of those on the verge of starvation might fluctuate–two years earlier 4,000 unemployed labourers, not a few hundred, had been "reduced to a state of absolute starvation."[24] But the threat of starvation was an ever-present part of life in the canal zones.

Upper Canada lacked a system of public relief which might have mitigated the suffering of the unemployed and their families. Only gradually between 1792 and 1867 was there a "piecemeal assumption of public responsibility for those in need" and not until the mid-1840's did the province begin to operate on the principle of public support.[25] Even had the principle of public relief been operative, the Niagara, Johnston, and Eastern Districts lacked the resources to provide a relief program such as that offered by Montreal to unemployed labourers on the Lachine Canal.[26] Nor was private charity a solution to the endemic poverty of the unemployed. When thousands of destitute immigrants first arrived in St. Catharines seeking employment on the Welland Canal in the spring of 1842, many citizens in the area came to their aid. But as the *St. Catharines Journal* pointed out in similar circumstances two years later:

> Those living in the vicinity of the Canal [had] not the means of supporting the famishing scores who [were] hourly thronging their dwellings, begging for a morsel to save the life of a starving child.[27]

The suffering of the unemployed shocked private individuals and government officials such as William Merritt, who led a fund-raising campaign for the starving and charged the Board of Works that it was "bound to provide provisions, in some way."[28] The crime of the unemployed became an even greater concern as desperate men violated private property in their attempts to stay alive. But for the Board of Works and its contractors the surplus labourers around the canals provided a readily exploitable pool of unskilled labour. From this pool, contractors drew labourers as they needed them–for a few days, weeks, or a season–always confident that the supply would exceed the demand. The men they set to work were often far from the brawny navvies celebrated in the folklore of the day. Weakened by days and months without adequate food, at times on the verge of starvation, labourers were reported to stagger under the weight of their shovels when first set to work.[29]

Contractors offered temporary relief from the threat of starvation; but they offered little more. The typical contractor paid wages which were consistently higher than those of farm labourers in the area of construction sites. But for their back-breaking, dangerous labour and a summer work day of fourteen hours, navvies received only the average or slightly above average daily wage for unskilled labour in the Canadas.[30] Since individual contractors set wage rates, wages varied from canal to canal and from section to section on the same canal; however, they usually hovered around the 2s.6d. daily, which Pentland suggests was the average rate for unskilled labour during the decade. On the Cornwall and Williamsburg canals wages fluctuated between 2s. and 3s., and if on the Welland Canal labourers in some seasons forced an increase to 4s., wages usually dropped back to 2s.6d. at the onset of winter, when contractors justified lower wages on the grounds that labourers worked fewer hours.[31]

These wage levels were barely adequate to sustain life, according to an 1842 government investigation into riots on the Beauharnois Canal. Many of those who testified at the hearings–foremen, engineers, magistrates, and clergymen–maintained that along the St. Lawrence labourers could not live on 2s.6d. per day. A conservative estimate gave the cost of food alone for a single labourer for one day at 1s.3d., suggesting that at the going rate a labourer could only feed himself and his wife, not to mention children, and then only on days when he was employed.[32] Under the best of circumstances, with work being pushed ahead during the summer months, this would only mean twenty days out of the month. In winter, if he was lucky enough to get work on the canals, he could not expect to put in more than ten days in a good month.[33]

Inadequate as his wages were, the labourer could not even be certain of receiving them. After a few months in a contractor's employ, labourers might discover that they had worked for nothing, the contractor running out of funds before he could pay his men. Other contractors, living under the threat of bankruptcy, forced labourers to wait months on end for their wages. These long intervals between paydays reduced labourers to desperate circumstances. Simply to stay alive, they entered into transactions with cutthroat speculators, running up long accounts at stores or "selling their time at a sacrifice," handing over the title to their wages in return for ready cash or credit. Such practices cost labourers as much as 13 per cent interest, pushing them steadily downward in a spiral of debt and dependency.[34]

Labourers might become indebted to one of the "petty hucksters who swarmed around public works, charging whatever they could get," or to one of the country store-keepers who took advantage of an influx of labourers to extract exorbitant prices.[35] Or frequently the contractor who could not find the money to pay wages found the means to stock a company store and make a profit by extending credit for grossly over-priced provisions. Although contractors claimed they set up their stores as a convenience to the labourers, a government investigation concluded that in actual fact stores were "known to be a source of great profit on which all the contractors calculated."[36] Many contractors ensured a profit from the sale of provisions by paying wages in credit tickets redeemable only at the company store. This system of truck payment was so widespread along the canals and so open to abuse[37] that the Board of Works introduced into the contracts a clause stipulating that wages must be paid in cash. The Board's real attitude toward truck, however, was more ambivalent than this clause suggests. Its 1843 Report to the Legislature argued that "truck payment" was in many cases "rather to be controlled than wholly put down."[38] It did not put a stop to store pay, and according to its officials on construction sites it did not control it very well either.[39] The result was that many canallers worked for nothing more than the provisions doled out by their employer. They did not see cash. Few could have left the public works with more than they had had when they arrived. Many were probably in debt to the company store when their term of work ended.

The combination of low wages, payment in truck, and long waits between paydays kept canallers in poverty and insecurity, barely able to secure necessities during seasons of steady employment, unable to fortify themselves against seasons of sporadic work and the inevitable long periods when there was no work at all. Government commissions and individual reports detailed the misery of the labourers' existence. Lewis Drummond, member of the Legislature for Quebec, had served on the Commission investigating conditions along the Beauharnois. During debate in the House, his anger at the "grinding oppression" which he had witnessed flared into a bitter denunciation of "sleek" contractors who had "risen into a state of great wealth by the labour, the sweat, the want and woe" of their labourers. He charged the government with having betrayed and abused the immigrant labourers:

> They were to have found continued employment, and been enabled to acquire means to purchase property of their own. They expected to meet with good treatment and what treatment had they met with? – With treatment worse than African slaves, with treatment against which no human being could bear up.[40]

Drummond was backed up by Richelieu MP Dr. Wolfred Nelson whose experience as medical attendant to the labourers on the Lachine prompted a less passionate but no less devastating appraisal:

> Their wants were of the direst kind. He [Dr. Nelson] had frequently to prescribe for them, not medicine, nor the ordinary nourishments recommended by the profession, but the commonest necessaries of life; he daily found them destitute of these necessaries, and he was, therefore, most strongly of opinion that the system under which they were employed, and which afforded them such a wretched existence ought to be fully enquired into.[41]

Conditions were equally bad on canals further up the St. Lawrence system. Work did not guarantee adequate food even on the Welland, which offered the highest wages.[42] David Thorburn, Magistrate for the Niagara District, wondered how the labourers could survive, as he watched them hit by a drop in wages and a simultaneous increase in food prices, struggling to feed their families, unable to provide " a sufficiency of food – even of potatoes."[43]

Work did not guarantee adequate housing either. A few contractors lived up to the commitment to provide reasonable and "suitable accommodation," constructing barrack-like shanties along the works for the labourers and their families.[44] But as Pentland has pointed out, the bunkhouse, "a sign of some responsibility of the employer for his men," was a development of the latter half of the nineteenth century.[45] The typical contractor of the 1840's left his employees to find whatever housing they could. Since only a very small percentage of canallers found room and board among the local inhabitants, most built their own temporary acccomodation, borrowing and stealing materials in the neighbourhood to construct huts and shacks, similar to the shanties thrown up by the unemployed.[46] A canaller usually shared accommodation with other canallers either in the barrack-like structures provided by contractors or in the huts they erected themselves. Of the 163 shanties built by labourers at Broad Creek on the Welland, only twenty-nine were single family dwellings. The rest were occupied by one, two, or three families with their various numbers of boarders. These dwellings formed a congested shanty town typical of the shanty towns that sprang up along the canals, and reminiscent of squalid Corktown, home of labourers on the Rideau Canal in the 1820's and 1830's.[47]

For the brief period of their existence, these shanty towns along the canals became close-knit, homogeneous working-class communities, in which the bonds of living together reinforced and overlapped with bonds formed in the workplace. Canallers shared day-to-day social interaction and leisure activities, drinking together at the "grog" shops that sprang up to service the labourers, and lying out on the hillsides on summer nights.[48] And they shared the daily struggle to subsist, the material poverty and insecurity, the wretched conditions, and the threat of starvation.

Bound together by their experiences along the canals, the Irish labourers were also united by what they brought from Ireland – a common culture shaped by ethnicity. Canaller communities were not simply homogeneous working-class communities but Irish working-class communities, ethnic enclaves in which the values, norms, traditions, and practices of the Southern Irish ethno-culture thrived. Central to this culture was a communal organization which emphasized mutuality and fraternity, primarily within family and kinship networks.[49] While the persistence of kinship relationships among the canallers cannot be measured, many labourers lived with women and children in family units. Thirteen hundred "diggers" brought seven hundred women and twelve hundred children to live along the Welland between Dalhousie and Allanburgh in the winter of 1844; and at Broad Creek in the summer of 1842, the Board of Works enumerated 250 families among the 797 men and 561 women and children. Shanty towns around the Cornwall and Williamsburg canals also housed many women and children who had followed the labourers from Ireland or across the Canadian-American border, maintaining the strong family structure characteristic of Southern Ireland.[50]

Given the Irish pattern of migrating and emigrating in extended families, kinship networks may also have been reproduced on the canals. The fact that both newly arrived immigrants and labourers from the United States were from the limited region of Munster and Connaught increases the probability that canallers were bound together by strong, persisting kinship ties. But whether or not the labourers were bound by blood they brought to the construction sites traditions of co-operation and mutual aid in the work place. As peasants in Munster and Connaught, they had held land individually, but had worked it co-operatively. When forced into wage labour to supplement the yields from their tiny holdings, the pattern of work again had been co-operative, friends, relatives, and neighbours forming harvesting or construction gangs which travelled and worked together throughout the British Isles.[51]

The clearest evidence of cultural unity and continuity along the canals was the labourers' commitment to the Roman Catholic faith. In contrast with the Irish Catholic labourers in the Ottawa Valley lumbering industry, whom Michael Cross found to be irreligious, canal labourers took their religion seriously enough to build shanty chapels for worship along the canals and to contribute to the construction of a new cathedral in St. Catharines. A stone tablet on the St. Catharines' cathedral commemorates "the Irish working on the Welland Canal [who] built this monument of faith and piety" but who, in the eagerness to be part of the opening services, crowded into the church yard 2,000 strong, destroying graves and markers in the process.[52]

Canallers were prepared to defend their faith in active conflict with Orangemen. Each July 12th brought the threat or reality of violent clashes between Orangemen commemorating the triumph of William of Orange at the Battle of Boyne, and Roman Catholic labourers infuriated at the celebration of an event which had produced the hated penal code. The entire canaller community rallied to participate in anti-Orange demonstrations. In 1844 all the canallers along the Welland, organized under leaders and joined by friends from public works projects in Buffalo, marched to confront Toronto Orangemen and their families on an excursion to Niagara Falls.[53] Similarly, all labourers on the Welland were encouraged to participate in an 1849 demonstration. A labourer with a large family who was reluctant to march on the Orangemen at Slabtown was ordered to join his fellows or leave the canal. He should have left the canal. Instead he went along to Slabtown and was shot in the head.[54]

The canallers also demonstrated a continued identification with the cause of Irish nationalism and the struggle for Repeal of the legislative union of Britain and Ireland. They participated in the agitation for Repeal which spread throughout the British Isles and North America in 1843.[55] Lachine Canal labourers joined Irishmen in Montreal to call for an end to Ireland's colonial status; and labourers on the Welland met at Thorold to offer "their sympathy and assistance to their brethren at home in their struggle for the attainment of their just rights."[56] On the Williamsburg canals, labourers also met together in support of Irish nationalism and Daniel O'Connell, the "Liberator" of Ireland. A local tavernkeeper, who interrupted a pro-O'Connell celebration by asking the canallers to move their bonfire away from his tavern, lived in fear they would be back to burn the tavern down.[57]

Strong, persisting ethnocultural bonds united the canallers, at times in active conflict with the dominant Protestant Anglo-Saxon culture. But their ethnoculture was also a source of bitter division. A long-standing feud between natives of Cork and those from Connaught divided the labourers into two hostile factions. The origin of the feud is obscure. It may have developed during confrontations in the eighteenth and nineteenth centuries between striking agricultural labourers of one county and black leg labourers transported across county lines. or possibly it dated as far back as the rivalries of the old kingdoms of mediaeval Ireland.[58] Whatever its origin, the feud had become an integral part of the culture which Southern Irish labourers carried to construction projects throughout Britain and North America.[59]

The feud did not simply flare up now and then over an insult or dispute between men who otherwise mingled freely. Feuding was part of the way in which canallers organized their lives, membership in a faction dictating both working and living arrangements. Men of one faction usually worked with members of the same faction. At times Cork and Connaught did work together under one contractor on the same section of the work, particularly during the first few seasons of construction on the Welland when contractors hired labourers regardless of faction. But contractors quickly learned to honour the workers' preference to work with members of their faction, if only for the peace of the work.[60] Members of the same faction usually lived together also, cut off from the other faction in their separate Cork or Connaught community. Members of these communities offered each other material assistance in weathering difficult times. During the summer and fall of 1842, when half the Connaughtmen along the Broad Creek were ill with malaria, those Connaughtmen who were able to work "shared their miserable pittance" and provided necessities and medicine for the sick labourers and their dependents.[61] During the same season, the Connaughtmen also pooled their resources to retain a lawyer to defend seventeen faction members in prison awaiting trial.[62]

The other side of this communal help and support, however, was suspicion of outsiders and intense hostility toward members of the rival faction. Hostility frequently erupted into violent confrontations beween the factions. These confrontations were not a ritualized reminder of past skirmishes, but battles in deadly earnest, involving severe beatings and loss of life. The brutality of the encounters between Cork and Connaught led the *St. Catharines Journal* to denounce the participants as "strange and mad belligerant factions – brothers and countrymen, thirsting like savages for each other's blood – horribly infatuated."[63] Most participants in these skirmishes were heavily armed with "guns, pistols, swords, pikes, or poles, pitch forks, scyths," many of which were procured from local inhabitants or the militia stores. In preparation for their revenge on the Corkmen, in one of their more spectacular thefts, Connaughtmen on the Welland actually took possession of blacksmith shops and materials to manufacture pikes and halberds.[64] Usually they simply accosted citizens in the streets or raided them at night.[65]

Armed conflict between the factions could reduce the canal zones to virtual war zones for weeks on end, "parties of armed men, 200 or 300 in number constantly assembling and parading," planning attack and counter-attack, at times fighting it out on the streets of St. Catharines and smaller centres around the Williamsburg canals.[66] As Power explained to military authorities in the Niagara District: "one riot is the parent of many others, for after one of their factional fights the friends of the worsted party rally from all quarters to avenge the defeat."[67]

The fighting of two drunken men might precipitate a clash between the factions.[68] But men who reported to the Board of Works concerning factional fights were unanimous in concluding that the underlying cause of feuding was the massive and chronic unemployment in the canal areas. David Thorburn, magistrate for the Niagara District, explained:

> The first moving cause that excites to the trouble is the want of work, if not employed they are devising schemes to procure it, such as driving away the party who are fewest in number who are not of their country. . . .[69]

Another magistrate for the Niagara District agreed that "the want of employment to procure bread" was the "principal root" of all the troubles; and Captain Wetherall, appointed to investigate the unrest along the canals, reached the same conclusion: "Strife to obtain work takes place between the two great sectional parties of Cork and Connaught. . . . The sole object of these combinations is to obtain work for themselves, by driving off the other party."[70] These observers appreciated the fact that the feud was a deep-seated hostility rooted in the Southern Irish culture. They also believed that the Irish were given to letting their hostilities erupt into open conflict. Nonetheless, they were convinced that the problems associated with the feud, the open conflict and disruption of the work, would disappear if the problem of unemployment were solved.

This was the argument put forward by the labourers themselves at a meeting called by James Buchanan, ex-consul at New York and a respected member of the Irish community in North America. Buchanan posted notices along the Welland in 1844 asking the "Sons of Erin" to meet with him to "reconcile and heal the divisions of [his] countrymen in Canada."[71] Corkmen refused to attend since the Connaughtmen's priest was helping to organize the meeting. But the Connaughtmen sent delegates to meet privately with Buchanan and assembled for a public meeting at Thorold. After listening to patriotic speeches and admonitions to peace and order, the Connaughtmen laid down their terms for an end to factional fights: "give us work to earn a living, we cannot starve, the Corkmen have all the work, give us a share of it."[72]

Thus, along the canals the feud of Cork and Connaught became the vehicle through which an excess of labourers fought for a limited number of jobs. In this respect, the feud was similar to other conflicts between hostile subgroups of workers competing in an over-stocked labour market. In the unskilled labour market of the Canadas, competition was frequently between French Canadians and Irish labourers. Along the canals, in the dockyards, and particularly in the Ottawa Valley lumbering industry, the two ethnic groups engaged in a violent conflict for work, at times as intense and brutal as the conflict of Cork and Connaught.[73]

Similar ethnic clashes occurred between Anglo-Saxon and Irish Celtic labourers competing in the unskilled labour market in Britain. Long-standing animosities between these two groups have led historians to emphasize the xenophobic nature of such confrontations.[74] But in an analysis of navvies on the railways of northern England, J. B. Treble argues that these superficially ethnic clashes were actually rooted in economic conditions, which fostered fears that one group was undercutting or taking the jobs of the other group. Treble concludes that however deep the racial or cultural animosities between groups of labourers, "the historian would ignore at his peril economic motivation, admittedly narrowly conceived in terms of personal advantage, but for that very reason immensely strong."[75] Like the conflict between Irish and French and Irish and Anglo-Saxon labourers, the factional fights became part of a general process of fragmentation and subgrouping, which John Foster sees developing during the nineteenth century in response to industrialization. By bringing hostile groups into competition with each other, the process militated against united action and the growth of a broad working-class consciousness.[76] The feud was one variation in this broader pattern of division and conflict among workers.

Yet the feud and the bitter fight for work did not preclude united action in pursuit of common economic goals. In a few instances the factions joined together to demand the creation of jobs. During the first summer of construction in 1842, on the Welland thousands of labourers and their families repeatedly paraded the streets of St. Catharines with placards demanding "Bread or Work," at one point breaking into stores, mills, and a schooner. In a petition to the people of Upper Canada, they warned that they would not "fall sacrifice to starvation": "we were encouraged by contractors to build cantees [sic] on said work; now can't even afford 1 meals victuals . . . we all Irishmen; employment or devastation."[77] Setting aside their sectional differences and uniting as "Irish labourers," Cork and Connaught co-operated to ensure that no one took the few hundred jobs offered by the Board of Works. Posters along the canal threatened "death and vengeance to any who should dare to work until employment was given to the whole." Bands of labourers patrolled the works driving off any who tried to take a job.[78]

By bringing all construction to a halt the labourers forced the Superintendent of the Welland to create more work. Going beyond the limits of his authority, Power immediately let the contract for locks three to six to George Barnett and began pressuring contractors to increase their manpower.[79] But as construction expanded the canallers began a scramble for the available jobs until the struggle for work was no longer a conflict between labourers and the Board of Works, but a conflict between Cork and Connaught, each faction attempting to secure employment for its members.[80]

The following summer unemployed labourers on the Welland again united to demand the creation of jobs. This was a season of particularly high and prolonged unemployment. In addition to the usual numbers of unemployed flooding into the area, 3,000 labourers discharged from the feeder and the Broad Creek branches in the early spring had to wait over three months for work to commence on the section from Allanburgh to Port Colborne. Incensed by the Board of Works' apparent indifference to their plight, the unemployed pressured on-the-spot officials until in mid-July Power again acted independently of the Board, authorizing contractors to begin work immediately.[81] Anticipating the Board's censure, Power justified his actions as necessary to the protection of the work and the preservation of the peace:

However easy it may be for those who are at a distance to speculate on the propriety of delaying the work until precise instructions may arrive, it is very difficult for me, surrounded by men infuriated by hunger, to persist in a course which must drive them to despair.[82]

The jobs opened up by Power could employ only half of those seeking work, but that was sufficient to crack the canallers' united front and revive the sectional conflict.[83] In general, Cork and Connaught appear to have united to demand jobs only during periods when there was virtually no work available, and consequently no advantage to competing among themselves.

It was in their attempts to secure adequate wages that the canallers most clearly demonstrated their ability to unite around economic issues. During frequent strikes along the canals the antagonistic relationship between the two factions was subordinated to the labourers' common hostility toward their employers, so that in relation to the contractors the canallers stood united. A Board of Works investigation into one of the larger strikes on the Welland Canal found Cork and Connaught peacefully united in a work stoppage. Concerning the strike of 1,000 labourers below Marshville, the Board's agent, Dr. Jarrow, reported that the labourers at the Junction had gone along the line and found both factions "generally ready and willing" to join in an attempt to get higher wages:

> No breach of the peace took place, nor can I find a tangible threat to have been issued. . . . Several men have been at work for the last two days on many of the jobs. . . . Those who have returned to work are not interfered with in the least degree. Contractors do not seem to apprehend the least breach of the peace. . . . The workmen seem well organized and determined not to render themselves liable to justice–. . . . Both the Cork and Connaught men are at work on different jobs below Marshville, and they seem to have joined in the Strick [sic] and I have not been able to find that their party feelings have the least connection with it.[84]

This was not an isolated instance of unity between the factions. Many strikes were small, involving only the men under one contractor, who usually belonged to the same faction; however, on the Welland in particular, Cork and Connaught joined in large strikes. Unity may have been fragile, but the overriding pattern that emerges during strikes is one of co-operation between the factions.[85] Not only did the factions unite in large strikes, but during a small strike involving only members of one faction, the other faction usually did not act as strike-breakers, taking the jobs abandoned by the strikers. What little information there is on strike-breaking concerns striking labourers confronting members of their own faction who tried to continue work, suggesting that the decision to work during a strike was not based on factional loyalties or hostilities.[86] Thus, most strikes did not become extensions of the bitter conflict for work. Rather, strikes brought labourers together to pursue common economic interests. The instances in which Cork and Connaught united provide dramatic evidence of the ability of these economic interests to overcome an antipathy deeply rooted in the canallers' culture.

Canallers frequently combined in work stoppages demanding the payment of overdue wages. More often their strikes centred on the issue of wage rates. In a report concerning labour unrest on the canals of Upper and Lower Canada, Captain Wetherall concluded: "the question of what constitutes a fair wage is the chief cause from which all the bitter fruit comes." The priest among labourers on the Williamsburg agreed with Wetherall, going so far as to suggest that if the rate of wages could be settled once and for all troops and police would not be required for the canal areas. Similarly, Thorburn ranked wage rates with unemployment as a major cause of labour disturbances on the Welland.[87]

Since officials often reported "many" or "a few" strikes without indicating how many, the level of strike activity can only be suggested. Contractors expected, and usually faced, strikes in the late fall when they tried to impose the seasonal reduction in wage rates.[88] Strikes demanding an increase in wages were harder to predict, but more frequent. Each spring and summer on the Cornwall, Welland, and Williamsburg canals work stoppages disrupted construction. Even in winter those labourers fortunate enough to continue working attempted to push up wages through strikes.[89] The degree of success canallers enjoyed in their strikes cannot be determined from the fragmentary and scattered references to work stoppages. It is clear, however, they forced contractors to pay wages above the level for unskilled, manual labour in general, and above the 2s. or 2s.6d. the Board of Works considered the most labourers on public works could expect.[90] On the Cornwall and Williamsburg canals, strikes secured and maintained modest increases to as high as 3s. and 3.6d.[91] Gains were much greater on the Welland. As early as the winter of 1843 labourers had driven wages to what Power claimed was the highest rate being offered on the continent.[92] While Power's statement cannot be accepted at face value, wages on the Welland may well have been the highest for manual labour in the Canadas and in the northeastern United States, where jobs were scarce and wages depressed. Strikes on the Welland forced wages even higher during 1843 and 1844, until the Board of Works calculated that labourers on the Welland were receiving at least 30 per cent more than the men on all the other works under its superintendence.[93]

How did the canallers, a fluid labour force engaged in casual, seasonal labour, achieve the solidarity and commitment necessary to successful strike action during a period of massive unemployment? Work stoppages protesting non-payment of wages may have been simply spontaneous reactions to a highly visible injustice, requiring little formal organization, more in the nature of protests than organized strikes. But the strikes through which canallers aggressively forced up wages or prevented contractors from lowering wages required a greater degree of organization and long-term commitment. Labourers might be on strike for weeks, during which time they would become desperate for food.

In a variety of ways, the canallers' nationality contributed to their successful strike action. Strikers found unity in the fact that they were "all Irishmen," in the same way that the unemployed identified with each other as "Irishmen" in their united demands for work. In the only well-documented strike by canallers, the Lachine strike of 1843, the labourers themselves stated this clearly. Corkmen and Connaughtmen issued joint petitions warning employers and would-be strike-breakers that they were not simply all canallers, they were "all Irishmen" whose purpose and solidarity would not be subverted.[94]

Membership in a common ethnic community provided concrete aid in organizing united action. At least in the summer of 1844 on the Welland, leadership in anti-Orange demonstrations overlapped with leadership in labour organization. During this season of frequent strikes, as many as 1,000 labourers assembled for mass meetings.[95] The authorities could not discover exactly what transpired at these meetings, since admittance was restricted to those who knew the password; a military officer, however, was able to observe one meeting at a distance. Ensign Gaele reported witnessing a collective decision-making process in which those present discussed, voted on, and passed resolutions. He drew particular attention to the participation of a man "who appeared to be their leader," a well-spoken individual of great influence, the same individual who had ridden at the head of the canallers on their march to intercept the Orangemen at Niagara Falls.[96] The situation on one canal during one season cannot support generalizations concerning organization on all canals throughout the 1840's. It does, however, suggest one way in which unity around ethnocultural issues facilitated unity in economic struggles by providing an established leadership.

Of more significance to the canallers' strike activity was the vehicle of organization provided by their ethnicity. Like other groups of Irish labourers, most notably the Molly Maguires of the Pennsylvania coal fields, canallers found that the secret societies which flourished in nineteenth-century Ireland were well-adapted to labour organization in the new world.[97] At a time when those most active in strikes were subject to prosecution and immediate dismissal, oath-bound societies offered protection from the law and the reprisals of employers. The government investigation into disturbances on the Beauharnois found sufficient evidence to conclude that secret societies were the means by which the canallers organized their strikes. But it was unable to break through the labourers' secrecy and uncover details concerning the actual operation of the societies.[98] Similarly, the Catholic priest, Rev. McDonagh, despite his intimate knowledge of the canallers' personal lives, could only offer the authorities the names of two societies operating along the Welland, the Shamrock and Hibernian Societies. He could provide no information as to how they functioned, whether there were a number of small societies or a few large ones, whether all labourers or only a segment of the canallers belonged to them. And he "couldn't break them."[99]

The oaths which swore labourers to secrecy also bound them to be faithful to each other, ensuring solidarity and commitment in united action and enforcing sanctions against any who betrayed his fellows. In addition, societies operated through an efficient chain of communication and command, which allowed for tactics to be carefully formulated and executed.[100] Navvies did not develop a formal trade union. Consequently, in comparison with the activities of workers in the few trade unions of the 1820's, 1830's, 1840's in British North America, the direct action of the

Irish labourers appears "ad hoc."[101] But the fact that the navvies' organization was impenetrable to authorities and remains invisible to historians should not lead to the error of an "ad hoc" categorization. Although clandestine, secret societies were noted for the efficiency, even sophistication, of their organization.[102] And although not institutionalized within the formal, structured labour movement, they were the means of organizing sustained resistance, not spontaneous outbreaks of protest.

Organization within secret societies rather than within a formal trade union also meant that canallers did not reach out to establish formal ties with other segments of the working class. As a result, they have left no concrete evidence of having identified the interests of their group with the interests of the larger working class, no clear demonstration that they perceived of themselves as participating in a broader working-class struggle. But while their method of organization ruled out formal linking and expression of solidarity with the protest of other groups of workers, secret societies testified to the Irish labourers' link with a long tradition of militant opposition to employers in the old world. The secret societies which flourished in Dublin throughout the first half of the nineteenth century were feared by moderates in the Irish nationalist movement because of their aggressive pursuit of working-class interests. During the same period, the agrarian secret societies of the Southern Irish countryside primarily organized agricultural labourers and cottiers around issues such as rising conacre rents and potato prices. Although the ruling class of Britain and Ireland insisted that agrarian societies were essentially sectarian, these societies were, in fact, the instruments of class action, class action which at times united Protestant and Catholic labourers in a common cause.[103]

This cultural legacy of united opposition was invaluable to the canal labourers in their attempts to achieve higher wages. During their years of conflict with landlords and employers, the peasant labourers of Southern Ireland acquired a belief system and values necessary to effective united action in the workplace. Their belief system probably did not include a political critique of society which called for fundamental change in the relationship between capital and labour. Although Chartist and Irish nationalist leaders worked closely in the mid-nineteenth century, none of the varied radical strains of Chartism made significant advances in Ireland, which suggests that Irish labourers may not have seen themselves as members of a broader class whose interests were irreconcilable to the interests of capital.[104] But if theory had not given them a framework within which to understand the conflict of capital and labour, experience had created in them a deep-seated suspicion of employers and a sensitivity to exploitation. They brought to the new world the belief that their interests were in conflict with the employers' interest. Wetherall tried to explain their outlook to the Board of Works:

> They look on a Contractor as they view the "Middle Man" of their own Country, as a grasping, money making person, who has made a good bargain with the Board of Works for labour to be performed; and they see, or imagine they see, an attempt to improve that bargain at their expense . . . such is the feeling of the people, that they cannot divest themselves of the feeling that they are being imposed on if the contractor has an interest in the transaction.[105]

In the labourers' own words, posted along the works during the Lachine strike: "Are we to be tyrannized by Contractors . . . sur-render/To No Contractors who wants to live by the sweat of our Brow."[106]

Irish labourers also brought to the new world a willingness to defy the law and, if necessary, to use force to achieve their ends. Years of repression and discrimination had fostered what Kenneth Duncan has characterized as "a tradition of violence and terrorism, outside the law and in defiance of all authority."[107] In Britain the Irish labourers' willingness to challenge the law and the authorities had earned them a reputation for militance in the union movements at the same time that it had infused a revolutionary impulse into Chartism.[108] In the Canadas, this same willingness marked their strike activity.

Newspapers and government officials usually reported the strikes along the canals as "rioting" or "riotous conduct," the uncontrollable excesses of an ethnic group addicted to senseless violence.[109] Yet far from being excessive and indiscriminate, the canallers' use of violence was restrained and calculated. Force or the threat of force was a legitimate tactic to be used if necessary. Some strikes involved little, if any, violence. Although he claimed to have looked very hard, Dr. Jarrow could find no instances of "outrage" during the first week of the Marshville strike of 1843, a strike involving 1,500 labourers along the Welland. In another large strike on the Welland the following summer, the *St. Catharines Journal* reported that there were no riotous disturbances.[110] When strikers did use force it was calculated to achieve a specific end. Organized bands of strikers patrolling the canal with bludgeons were effective in keeping strikebreakers at home.[111] Similarly, when labourers turned their violence on contractors and foremen, the result was not only the winning of a strike but also a remarkable degree of job control.[112] After only one season on the Williamsburg canals, labourers had thoroughly intimidated contractors. One did not dare go near his work. Another, the labourers "set at defiance" and worked as they pleased.[113] Canallers also attacked the canals, but these were not instances of senseless vandalism. Power viewed what he called "extraordinary accidents" as one way in which labourers pressured for redress of specific grievances.[114] On the Welland a related pressure tactic was interfering with the navigation. During the strike of approximately 1,500 labourers in the summer of 1844, captains of boats were afraid to pass through because they feared rude attacks on their passengers. Such fears appear to have been well-founded. The previous winter, 200 canallers had attacked an American schooner, broken open the hatches, and driven the crew from the vessel, seriously injuring the captain and a crew member. Soldiers were required to keep "at bay the bloodthirsty assailants" while the crew reboarded their vessel.[115]

The canallers' willingness to resort to violence and defy authority antagonized large segments of the population, who lamented the transplanting to the new world of outrages "characteristic only of Tipperary."[116] But despite the protestations of newspapers and private individuals that the canallers' use of force was inappropriate to the new world, the Irish labourers' militant tradition was in reality well-suited to labour relations and power relations in the Canadas. The canallers' experience with the government and law enforcement agencies could only have reinforced what the past had taught – that the laws and the authorities did not operate in the interests of workers, particularly Irish Catholic workers. In their strikes, canallers confronted not just their employers but the united opposition of the government, courts, and state law enforcement officers.

The government's opposition to strikes was based on the conviction that labourers should not attempt to influence wage rates. To government officials such as J. B. Mills of the Williamsburg Canal, the repeated strikes along the canals added up to a general "state of insubordination among the labourers," an "evil" which jeopardized the entire Public Works program. Reports of the Board of Works condemned strikers for throwing construction schedules and cost estimates into chaos and applauded contractors for their "indefatigable and praiseworthy exertions" in meeting turnouts and other difficulties with their labourers.[117] Leaving no doubt as to its attitude toward demands for higher wages, the Board worked closely with contractors in their attempts to prevent and break strikes. On their own initiative, contractors met together to determine joint strategies for handling turnouts and holding the line against wage increases.[118] The Board of Works went one step further, bringing contractors and law enforcement officers together to devise stratagems for labour control and assuming the responsibility for co-ordinating and funding these stratagems.[119] Contractors and the Board joined forces in a comprehensive system of blacklisting which threatened participants in strikes. Operating on the assumption that the majority of the "well-disposed" were being provoked by a few rabble-rousers, contractors immediately dismissed ringleaders. Even during a peaceful strike such as the one at Marshville, in the winter of 1843, contractors discharged "those most active."[120] For its part the Board of Works collected and circulated along the canals descriptions of men like "Patrick Mitchell, a troublesome character" who "created insubordination amongst labourers" wherever he went.[121] Once blacklisted, men like Mitchell had little hope of employment on the public works in Canada.

Many labourers thus barred from public works projects also spent time in jail as part of the Board's attempt to suppress disturbances. Although British law gave workers the right to combine to withdraw their services in disputes over wages and hours, employers and the courts did not always honour this right. When the Board of Works' chief adviser on labour unrest argued that the Board should suppress the "illegal" combinations on the Welland and Williamsburg canals, he was expressing an opinion widely held in British North America and an opinion shared by many officials involved in controlling labour unrest on the Public Works.[122]

While opinion was divided over the rights of workers, there was general agreement that employers had the right to continue their operations during a strike, the course of action usually chosen by contractors, who seldom opted to negotiate with strikers. Workers who interfered with this right, by intimidating strike-breakers or contractors or generally obstructing the work, invited criminal charges. Since the charge of intimidation and obstruction was capable of broad interpretation, including anything from bludgeoning a contractor to talking to strike-breakers, this provision of the law gave contractors and the Board considerable scope for prosecuting strikers.[123]

To supplement existing labour laws, the Board of Works secured passage of the 1845 Act for the Preservation of the Peace near Public Works, the first in a long series of regulatory acts directed solely at controlling canal and railway labourers throughout the nineteenth century.[124] The Act provided for the registration of all firearms on branches of the Public Works specified by the Executive. The Board of Works had already failed in earlier attempts to disarm labourers on projects under its supervision. An 1843 plan to induce canallers on the Beauharnois to surrender their weapons was discarded "partly because there [was] no legal basis for keeping them." The following year a similar system on the Welland was also abandoned as illegal. Magistrates who had asked labourers to give up their weapons and to "swear on the Holy Evangelist that they had no gun, firearm, or offensive weapon" were indicted.[125] The 1845 Public Works Act put the force of the law and the power of the state behind gun control.

Most members of the Assembly accepted the registration of firearms along the canals as unavoidable under circumstances which "the existing law was not sufficient to meet."[126] A few members joined Aylwin of Quebec City in denouncing the measure as a dangerous over-reaction to a situation of the government's own making, "an Act of proscription, an Act which brought back the violent times of the word Annals of Ireland."[127] A more sizable group shared LaFontaine's reservations that the bill might be used as a general disarming measure against any citizen residing near the canals. But the Attorney General's assurances that the disarming clause would apply "only to actual labourers on the public works" secured for the Bill an easy passage.[128] Even a member like Drummond, one of the few to defend canallers in the House, ended up supporting the disarming clause on the grounds that it would contribute to the canallers' welfare by preventing them from committing the acts of violence to which contractors and hunger drove them. Drummond managed to convince himself that disarming the labourers would not infringe on their rights. He believed that all men had the right to keep arms for the protection of their property. But the canallers had no property to protect – "they were too poor to acquire any." Therefore they had neither the need nor the right to possess weapons.[129]

In addition to disarming the labourers, the Public Works Act empowered the Executive to station mounted police forces on the public works.[130] Under the Act, Captain Wetherall secured an armed constabulary of twenty-two officers to preserve order among the labourers on the Williamsburg canals. The Board of Works had already established its own constabulary on the Welland, two years prior to the legislation of 1845. Throughout 1843 and 1844 the Welland force fluctuated between ten and twenty, diminishing after 1845 as the number of labourers on the canals decreased. At a time when even the larger communities in Upper Canada, along with most communities in North America, still relied on only a few constables working under the direction of a magistrate, the size of these police forces testifies to the Board's commitment to labour control.[131] While the forces fulfilled various functions, in the eyes of the Board of Works their primary purpose was to ensure completion of the works within the scheduled time. Even protection of contractors from higher wages was not in itself sufficient reason for increasing the size of one of the forces. When Power asked for accommodation for a Superintendent of Police at the Junction, the Board answered that the old entrance lock was the only place where a strong force was necessary, since no combination of labourers for wages on the other works could delay the opening of the navigation, "the paramount object in view." A later communication expressed more forcefully the Board's general approach to funding police forces, stating that the only circumstances under which the expense of keeping the peace could be justified were that if it were not kept up the canals would not be "available to the trade."[132]

Despite this apparently strict criterion for funding police, the Board usually intervened to protect strike-breakers, probably because any strike threatened to delay opening of the navigation in the long, if not the short, term. Indeed, in their 1843 Report to the legislature, the Commissioners argued that it was part of their responsibility to help contractors meet deadlines by providing adequate protection to those labourers willing to work during a strike.[133] In meeting this responsibility the Board at times hired as many as sixteen extra men on a temporary basis. When it was a question of getting the canals open for navigation the government appears to have been willing to go to almost any lengths to continue the work. In the winter of 1845, the Governor-General gave Power the authority to hire whatever number of constables it would take to ensure completion of construction by spring.[134]

Canal police forces worked closely with existing law enforcement agencies, since the common law required the magistrates to give direction in matters "relating to the arrest of suspected or guilty persons," and generally to ensure that the police acted within the law.[135] But Wetherall's investigation into the conduct of the Welland Canal force revealed that magistrates did not always keep constables from abusing their powers: "The constables oft exceed their authority, cause irritation, and receive violent opposition, by their illegal and ill-judged manner of attempting to make arrests." In one instance, the constables' behaviour had resulted in a member of the force being wounded. In another, an action had been commenced for false imprisonment. Wetherall also drew attention to complaints that the police force was composed of Orangemen, at least one of whom had acted improperly in "publicly abusing the Roman Catholic Religion – damning the Pope – etc., etc."[136]

The Williamsburg Canal force also came under attack for its provocative behaviour. Inhabitants of Williamsburg Township petitioned the Governor-General concerning the conduct of Captain James Macdonald and his men during a circus at Mariatown:

> The police attended on said day where in course of the evening through the misconduct of the police on their duty two persons have been maltreated and abused cut with swords and stabbed, taken prisoners and escorted to the police office that all this abuse was committed by having the constables in a state of intoxication on their duty when the Magistrate who commanded them was so drunk that he fell out of a cart. A pretty representative is Mr. MacDonald.[137]

The Roman Catholic priest on the Williamsburg canals joined in denouncing the police force, warning the labourers: "They are like a parcel of wolves and roaring mad lions seeking the opportunity of shooting you like dogs and all they want is the chance, in the name of God leave those public works."[138]

Of invaluable assistance to the constables and magistrates were the Roman Catholic priests, hired by the Board of Works as part of the police establishment and stationed among canallers. Referred to as "moral" or "spiritual" agents, they were in reality police agents, paid out of the Board's police budget and commissioned to preserve "peace and order" by employing the ultimate threat – hell.[139] They were of limited value in controlling Orange/ Green confrontations. They were actually suspected of encouraging them.[140] Their effectiveness in stopping factional fights was also limited, at least on the Welland where the Reverend McDonagh was suspected of harbouring sectional sentiments.[141] Their most important function was to prevent or break strikes. Intimate involvement in the canallers' daily lives equipped them as informers concerning possible labour unrest.[142] When canallers struck, authorities could rely on priests to admonish labourers to give up their "illegal" combinations and return to work, to show "that the Gospel has a more salutary effect than bayonets."[143] Priests were not insensitive to the suffering of their charges and to its immediate cause. McDonagh repeatedly argued the canallers' case with government officials, contractors, and civil and military authorities.[144] On the Williamsburg canals, the Reverend Clarke's criticism of the treatment of labourers became such an embarrassment to the government that he was shipped back to Ireland, supposedly for health reasons.[145] But at the same time that priests were protesting conditions along the canals, they were devoting most of their energy to subverting the protest of their parishioners. McDonagh fulfilled this function so successfully that the Superintendent on the Welland Canal told the Board he knew of "no one whose services could have been so efficient."[146]

By supplementing existing laws and enforcement agencies, the government was able to bring an extraordinary degree of civil power against the canal labourers. Even an expanded civil power, however, was inadequate to control the canallers; hence, the military became the real defenders of the peace in the canal areas. As early as the first summer of construction on the Welland, the Governor-General asked the Commander of the Forces to station the Royal Canadian Rifles in three locations along the Welland, sixty men at St. Catharines, sixty at Thorold, and thirty at Port Maitland. In addition, a detachment of the coloured Incorporated Militia attached to the Fifth Lincoln Militia was stationed at Port Robinson. Aid was also available from the Fifth Canadian Rifles permanently stationed at Chippewa.[147] From these headquarters, troops marched to trouble spots for a few hours, days, or weeks. Longer postings necessitated temporary barracks such as those constructed at Broad Creek and Marshville in the fall of 1842.[148] No troops were posted on either the Cornwall or Williamsburg canals, despite the requests of contractors and inhabitants. Detachments in the vicinity, however, were readily available for temporary postings.[149]

With a long tradition of military intervention in civil disturbances both in Great Britain and British North America, the use of troops was a natural response to the inadequacies of the civil powers.[150] Troops were important for quickly ending disturbances and stopping the escalation of dangerous situations such as an Orange/Green clash or a confrontation between labourers and contractors.[151] The use of troops carried the risk that men might be shot needlessly. As Aylwin told the Legislature:

> If the constable exceed his duty there is a certain remedy; he may perhaps throw a man in prison; but if that man be innocent he will afterwards be restored to his family; when, however, the military are called out the soldier is obliged to do his duty, and men are shot down who perhaps . . . are quite as unwilling to break the peace as any man in the world.

Such had been the case during a confrontation on the Beauharnois Canal. Troops were called in and "bloody murders were committed." Labourers were "shot, and cut down, and driven into the water and drowned."[152] On the canals of Upper Canada, however, the military does not appear to have charged or opened fire on canallers. No matter how great their numbers or how well they were armed, canallers usually disbanded with the arrival of troops and the reading of the Riot Act.

Detachments were even more valuable as a preventive force. Before special detachments were posted along the Welland, the Governor-General explicitly instructed magistrates to use the troops in a preventive capacity, calling them out if "there should be any reason to fear a breach of the Peace, with which the civil power would be inadequate to deal."[153] Magistrates gave the broadest possible interpretation to the phrase "any reason to fear" and repeatedly called in the military when there had been merely verbal threats of trouble. When a large number of unemployed labourers appeared "ripe for mischief," when strikers seemed likely to harrass strike-breakers, magistrates requisitioned troops.[154]

Magistrates used the troops to such an extent that they provoked the only real opposition to military intervention in civil affairs–opposition from the military itself. Both on-the-spot commanders and high-ranking military officials complained that troops were being "harrassed" by the magistrates, that the requisitions for aid were "extremely irregular," and that the troops were marching about the frontier on the whim of alarmists.[155] The expense of keeping four or five detachments on the march does not appear to have been a factor in the dispute over the use of troops, since the civil authorities met the cost of deploying troops in civil disturbances. The British treasury continued to pay for salaries, provisions, and stores, but the Board of Works accepted responsibility for constructing barracks and for providing transportation and temporary accommodation at trouble spots when necessary.[156] The only point at issue appears to have been the unorthodox and unnecessary use of detachments.

This dispute was the only disharmony in the co-operation between civil and military authorities and even it had little effect on the actual operation of the system of control. At the height of the dispute, commanding officers still answered virtually all requisitions, although in a few instances they withdrew their men immediately if they felt their services were not required.[157] After the Provincial Secretary ruled that commanders must respond to all requisitions, whatever the circumstances, even the grumbling stopped.[158] Particularly on the Welland, regular troops were kept constantly patrolling the canal areas in apprehension of disturbances, "looking for trouble," as Colonel Elliott put it.[159]

With special laws, special police forces, and a military willing if not eager to help, the government of the Canadas marshalled the coercive power of the state against labourers on the public works. Yet the government failed to suppress labour unrest and prevent successful strike action. Many officials and contractors accepted this failure as proof of the Celt's ungovernable disposition. Invoking the Irish stereotype to explain the disorder along the canals, they ignored their own role in promoting unrest and obscured the class dimension of the canallers' behaviour. They also misinterpreted the nature of the relationship between the canallers' ethnoculture and their collective action. What the Southern Irish brought to the new world was not a propensity for violence and rioting, but a culture shaped by class relations in the old world. Class tensions, inseparably interwoven with racial hatred and discrimination, had created in the Southern Irish suspicion and hatred of employers, distrust of the laws and the authorities, and a willingness to violate the law to achieve their ends. This bitter cultural legacy shaped the Irish labourers' resistance to conditions in the Canadas and gave a distinctive form to class conflict on the canals.

NOTES

I would like to thank Don Avery and Wayne Roberts for their comments on earlier drafts of this paper.

1. PAC, Record Group 11, Department of Public Works, 5, Canals [RG11-5], Welland Canal Letterbook, [WCLB] Samuel Power to Thomas Begly, Chairman of Board of Works, 12 August 1842.

2. PAC, RG 8, British Military and Navy Records, I, C Series, 60, Canals [C 60], Bethune to MacDonald, 31 March 1843.

3. H. C. Pentland, "Development of a Capitalistic Labour Market in Canada," *Canadian Journal of Economics and Political Science*, XXV, 4 (1959), 450-61.

4. A. C. Buchanan, *Parliamentary Papers* (1842), 373; cited in W. F. Adams, *Ireland and the Irish Emigration to the New World* (Connecticut, 1932).

5. Gary Teeple, "Land, Labour, and Capital in Pre-Confederation Canada," in Teeple, ed., *Capitalism and the National Question in Canada* (Toronto, 1972); Leo A. Johnson, "Land Policy, Population Growth and Social Structure in the Home District, 1793-1851," *OH*, LXIII, 1 (1971), 41-60. Both Teeple and Johnson attach particular significance to the ideas of Edward Gibbon Wakefield, who advocated a prohibitive price on land to force immigrants into the labour force. V. C. Fowke, "The Myth of the Self Sufficient Canadian Pioneer," *Transactions of the Royal Society of Canada*, LVI, Series III (1962).

6. R. T. Naylor, "The Rise and Fall of the Third Commercial Empire of the St. Lawrence," in Teeple, *Capitalism and the National Question*, 1-13; Teeple, "Land, Labour, and Capital," *ibid.*, 57-62.

7. H. C. Pentland, "Labour and the Development of Industrial Capitalism in Canada" (Ph.D. thesis, University of Toronto, 1960), 239. In the fall of 1840 contractors on the Chambly Canal could not procure labourers even at what the government considered "most extravagant rates." Canada, *Journals* of the Legislative Assembly [*Journals*] (1841), Appendix D; Adams, *Ireland and Irish Emigration*; Helen I. Cowan, *British Emigration to British North America: The First Hundred Years* (Toronto, 1961).

8. Pentland, "Labour and Industrial Capitalism," 273. See also: Frances Morehouse, "The Irish Migration of the 'Forties,' " *American Historical Review*, XXXIII, 3 (1927-8), 579-92.

9. The best treatment of famine immigrants in British North America is Kenneth Duncan, "Irish Famine Immigration and the Social Structure of Canada West," *Canadian Review of Sociology and Anthropology*, II, 2 (1965), 19-40.

10. Report of the Niagara District Council, in *Niagara Chronicle*, 4 August 1847.

11. PAC, RG11-5, 390, file 93, Williamsburg Canals, Estimates and Returns, 1844-58, Public Notice of the Board of Works issued by Begly, 26 February 1844; PAC, RG11-5, 390, file 94, Police Protection and the Williamsburg Canals, Mills to Begly, 16 February 1847.

12. J. P. Merritt, *Biography of the Hon. W. H. Merritt* (St. Catharines, 1875), 310. Concerning the construction industry in Britain, Gosta E. Sandstrom has argued that the very existence of an easily exploitable labour pool deferred mechanization, relieving state and private management "of the need for constructive thinking." See Sandstrom, *The History of Tunnelling* (London, 1963). For a discussion of the relationship between labour supply and mechanization at mid-century, see: Raphael Samuel, "The Workshop of the World: Steam Power and Hand Technology in Mid-Victorian Britain," *History Workshop*, 3 (1977), 6-72. Labourers on North American canals were still performing basically the same tasks their counterparts had performed half a century earlier in Europe. See: Anthony Burton, *The Canal Builders* (London, 1972). There was a variety of new inventions used on the Erie Canal, some of which might have come to Canada, from a sharp-edged shovel for cutting roots to a stump-puller operated by seven men and a team of horses or oxen: Alvin Marlow, *Old Towpaths: The Story of the American Canal Era* (New York, 1964), 53.

13. John P. Heisler, *The Canals of Canada*, National Historic Sites Service, Manuscript Report 64 (Ottawa, 1971), 220-1, 224-5, 226-7.

14. PAC, RG11-5, 407, file 113, Thorburn to Daly, 10 January 1844.

15. *Ibid.*, Thorburn to Murdoch, 18 August 1842; PAC, RG11-5, WCLB, Power to Begly, 20 March, 17 July 1843.

16. Duncan, "Irish Famine Migration," 26. For a discussion of the application of the improved system of British agriculture, see: Kenneth Kelly, "The Transfer of British Ideas on Improved Farming to Ontario During the First Half of the Nineteenth Century," *OH*, LXIII, 2 (1971), 103-12.

17. *St. Catharines Journal*, 31 August 1843; *Niagara Chronicle*, 4 August 1847.

18. Duncan, "Irish Famine Migration," 26.

19. PAC, RG11-5, WCLB, Power to Begly, 8 April 1843; *Niagara Chronicle*, 4 August 1847.

20. PAC, RG11-5, 390, file 94, Hiel to Begly, 16 February 1844.

21. *Ibid.*, file 93, Public Notice of the Board of Works, 26 February 1844; *Journals* (1844-5), Appendix Y, Report of Mills, 20 January

1845; *ibid.*, Mills to Begly, 21 January 1845; *ibid.,* Jarvis to Daly, 28 October 1845.

22. *Niagara Chronicle*, 4 August 1847.
23. *St. Catharines Journal*, 16 February 1844.
24. Petition of Constantine Lee and John William Baynes to Sir Charles Bagot, cited in Dean Harris, *The Catholic Church in the Niagara Peninsula* (Toronto, 1895), 255. Lee was the Roman Catholic priest for St. Catharines, Baynes the community's Presbyterian minister. See also: PAC, RG11-5, 389, file 89, Correspondence of Samuel Keefer, 1843-51, Superintendent of Welland Canal, 1848-52, Keefer to Begly, 1 February 1843; PAC, RG11-5, 407, file 114, McDonagh to Killaly, 2 May 1843; 407, file 113, Thorburn to Daly, 10 January 1844; 381, file 56, John Rigney, Superintendent, Cornwall Canal, 1841-44, Godfrey to Begly, 22 April, 8 June 1843.
25. Richard B. Splane, *Social Welfare in Ontario, 1791-1893* (Toronto, 1965), 68-9, 74.
26. *St. Catharines Journal*, 26 January 1844.
27. *Ibid.*, 16 February 1844.
28. Harris, *Catholic Church*, 255; PAC, RG11-5, 388, file 87, Correspondence of Hamilton Killaly, 1841-55, Welland Canal, Merritt to Killaly, 12 August 1842.
29. PAC, RG11-5, 389, file 89, Keefer to Begly, 1 February 1843. Terry Coleman discusses the stereotype of the navvy on construction sites in Britain in *The Railway Navvies: A History of the Men Who Made the Railways* (London, 1965), ch. 12.
30. Farm labourers' wages appear in PAC, RG5, B21, Emigration Records, 1840-4, Information to Emigrants, April 1843, for Brockville, Chippewa, Cornwall, Fort Erie, Indiana, Niagara, Port Colborne, Prescott, Queenston, Smith's Falls; *ibid.*, For the Information of Emigrants of the Labouring Class, December 1840, the Johnstown District. Wages were not consistently higher around any one of the canals. Newspapers also contain references to wage levels. Only newspapers paid much attention to the serious accidents on construction sites. Work on these canals did not involve tunnelling, the most hazardous aspect of the work. But the malaria mosquito, which thrived on many canal sites, made up for this. In October 1842, Dr. John Jarrow reported to the Board of Works that "scarcely an individual" of over 800 men on the Broad Creek works would escape the "lake fever." Three-quarters of the labourers' wives and children already were sick. Very few of those under two would recover: PAC, RG11-5, 407, file 104, Welland Canal Protection, 1842-50, Memorandum of Dr. John Jarrow to the Board of Works, 1 October 1842.
31. Pentland, "Labour and Development of Industrial Capitalism," 232. Pentland underlines the difficulty in making valid generalizations because of "considerable variation from time to

time and from place to place." All wages have been translated into sterling, using the conversion rate of 22s. 2¾d. currency per £ sterling, as published in PAC, RG5, B21, Quarterly Return of Prices in the Province of Canada in the Quarter Ending 31 October 1844. The variation in wages along the canals was determined through the frequent references to wage levels in the records of the Department of Public Works and newspaper articles. Wages fluctuated within the same range on the Lachine and Beauharnois Canals in Canada East: H. C. Pentland, "The Lachine Strike of 1843," *CHR*, XXIX, 3 (1948), 255-77; *Journals* (1843), App. T, Report of the Commissioners appointed to inquire into the Disturbances upon the line of the Beauharnois Canal; *Journals* (1843), App. Q; *ibid.* (1845), App. AA.

32. Given that labourers at Beauharnois used company stores and received store pay, as did many canallers in Upper Canada, and considering the fairly constant price of foodstuffs along the St. Lawrence system, the findings of the Beauharnois Commission can be applied to labourers on the Cornwall, Welland, and Williamsburg canals: *Journals* (1843), App. T; PAC, RG5, B21. Information to Immigrants, April 1843; *ibid.*, For the Information of Emigrants, December 1840, the Johnstown District; *ibid.*, Quarterly Return of Prices for the City of Montreal in the Quarter ended 31st October 1844.

33. These figures represent averages of the estimated number of days worked during each month on the Cornwall, Welland, and Williamsburg canals.

34. PAC, RG11-5, WCLB, Power to Begly, April 1842, 10 March 1843; PAC, RG11-5, Welland Canal Commission [WCC], folder 8, Begly to Power, 24 January 1844; RG11-5, 390, file 94, Killaly to Begly, 26 March 1846; 381, file 56, Godfrey to Begly, 8 June 1843; 389, file 89, Keefer to Begly, 2 May 1848; 388, file 88, Keefer to Begly, 14 March 1849. Frequently the government withheld money from contractors, making it impossible for them to pay their labourers. The government also took its time paying labourers employed directly by the Board of Works.

35. *Journals* (1843), App. Q; PAC, RG11-5, WLCB, Power to Begly, 1 October 1842.

36. PAC, RG8,C60, Memorandum of Captain Wetherall, 3 April 1843.

37. *Journals* (1843), App. Q; PAC, RG11-5, WCLB, Power to Begly, 1 February 1844. Power draws attention to the public outcry but does not elaborate.

38. *Journals* (1843), App. Q.

39. PAC, RG11-5, 388, file 87, McDonagh to Killaly, 25 January 1843; *ibid.*, WCLB, Power to Sherwood and Company, 1 February 1844; *ibid.*, 390, file 94, Wetherall to Killaly, 2 March 1844.

40. Elizabeth Gibbs, ed., *Debates of the Legislative Assembly of*

United Canada (Montreal, 1973), IV/2, 1844-5, Lewis Drummond, 1460.

41. *Ibid*., Wolfred Nelson, 1511.
42. The cost of living does not appear to have fluctuated significantly from canal to canal. See note 32.
43. PAC, RG11-5, 407, file 113, Thorburn to Daly, 19 January 1844.
44. *Ibid*., 388, file 87, Articles of Agreement between the Board of Works and Lewis Schielaw, 1 April 1845. See: Ruth Bleasdale, "Irish Labourers on the Canals of Upper Canada in the 1840's" (M.A. thesis, University of Western Ontario, 1975), 34-7.
45. Pentland, "Lachine Strike," 259.
46. Bleasdale, "Irish Labourers," 36-7.
47. PAC, RG11-5, 407, file 104, Memorandum of Dr. Jarrow, 1 October 1842; A. H. Ross, *Ottawa Past and Present* (Toronto, 1927), 109.
48. PAC, RG11-5, WCLB, Power to Begly, 17 January 1845; *ibid*., 390, file 93, Mills to Begly, 26 June 1845; 389, file 90, Miscellaneous, 1842-51, Keefer to Robinson, 1 March 1842.
49. Conrad Arensberg, *The Irish Countryman* (New York, 1950), 66-8.
50. *St. Catharines Journal*, 16 February 1844; PAC, RG11-5, 407, file 104, Memorandum of Dr. Jarrow, 1 October 1844.
51. T. C. Foster, *Letters on the Condition of the People of Ireland* (London, 1847); J. G. Kohl, *Travels in Ireland* (London, 1844); K. H. Connell, *The Population of Ireland, 1760-1845* (Oxford, 1950).
52. Michael S. Cross, "The Dark Druidical Groves: The Lumber Community and the Commercial Frontier" (Ph.D. thesis, University of Toronto, 1968), 470; Harris, *Catholic Church*, 262-4; *St. Catharines Journal*, 25 August 1843; Harris, *Catholic Church*.
53. PAC, RG8, C60, Merritt to Daly, 21 September 1844; *ibid*., Elliott to Young, 23 July 1844.
54. *Ibid*., C317, MacDonald to Daly, 14 July 1849.
55. Adams, *Ireland and Irish Emigration*, 89.
56. *St. Catharines Journal*, 24 August 1843.
57. *Journals* (1844-5), App. Y, Gibbs to Higginson, 6 January 1845.
58. T. D. Williams, *Secret Societies in Ireland* (Dublin, 1973), 31.
59. E. P. Thompson, *The Making of the English Working Class* (Middlesex, 1972).
60. By commencement of the second season of construction, employers followed Merritt's suggestion to employ only Corkmen on the upper section and only Connaughtmen on the lower section of the Welland Canal. On the Williamsburg canals the factions laboured on different sections of the work.
61. PAC, RG11-5, WCLB, Power to Begly, 25 August 1843.
62. *Ibid*., 407, file 104, Robinson to Begly, 19 October 1842.
63. *St. Catharines Journal*, 7 July 1842.
64. PAC, RG11-5, 407, file 113, Thorburn to Daly, 10 January 1844;

407, file 104, Hobson to Daly, 20 January 1844; 407, file 113, Thorburn to Daly, 17 January 1844.

65. *Ibid.*, Thorburn to Daly, 10 January 1844; *Journals* (1844-5), App. Y, Jarvis to Daly, 28 October 1844.

66. *Journals* (1844-5), App. Y, Killaly to Daly, 5 November 1844; PAC, RG11-5, 389, file 89, Power to Begly, 17 January 1845; 407, file 113, Thorburn to Daly, 10 January 1844; *St. Catharines Journal*, 7 July 1843; *Brockville Recorder*, 8 August 1844.

67. PAC, RG11-5, WCLB, Power to Elliott, 28 December 1843.

68. *Ibid.*, 407, file 113, Thorburn to Daly, 10 January 1844.

69. *Ibid.*

70. *Ibid.*, 407, file 104, Hobson to Daly, 20 January 1844; *ibid.*, Wetherall to Killaly, 26 March 1844.

71. *Ibid.*, 407, file 113, Public Notice to the Sons of Erin, Engaged on the Welland Canal, who are known as Corkmen and Connaughtmen, 12 January 1844.

72. PAC, RG11-5, WCC-6, Thorburn to Daly, 19 January 1844.

73. Pentland, "Lachine Strike"; J. I. Cooper, "The Quebec Ship Labourers' Benevolent Society," *CHR*, XXX, 4 (1949), 336-43; Cross, "Dark Druidical Groves"; Michael S. Cross, "The Shiners' War: Social Violence in the Ottawa Valley in the 1830's," *CHR*, LIV, 1 (1973), 1-26.

74. E. L. Tapin, *Liverpool Dockers and Seamen, 1870-1890* (Hull, 1974).

75. J. H. Treble, "Irish Navvies in the North of England, 1830-50," *Transport History*, 6 (1973), 227-47.

76. Foster's comparative study of class consciousness in three nineteenth-century towns rests on an analysis of varying degrees of fragmentation and sub-group identification: John Foster, "Nineteenth-Century Towns – A Class Dimension," in H. J. Dyos, ed., *The Study of Urban History* (London, 1968), 281-9; Foster, *Class Struggle and the Industrial Revolution: Early Industrial Capitalism in Three English Towns* (London, 1974); Neville Kirk, "Class and Fragmentation: Some Aspects of Working-Class Life in South East Lancashire and North-East Cheshire, 1850-1870" (Ph.D. thesis, University of Pittsburgh, 1974). Kirk explains the decline of class consciousness in terms of the fragmentation of the working class into subgroups, emphasizing the widening gap between "respectable" and "non-respectable" workers and the bitter conflict between Roman Catholic Irish and other segments of the work force.

77. Petition of Lee and Baynes cited in Harris, *Catholic Church*, 255; PAC, RG11-5, 407, file 113, Thorburn to Murdoch, 18 August 1842; *St. Catharines Journal*, 11 August 1842; PAC, RG11-5, 388, file 87, Petition presented to Reverend Lee, 1 August 1842.

78. *St. Catharines Journal*, 11 August 1842.

79. PAC, RG11-5, WCLB, Power to Begly, 12 August 1842.

80. *St. Catharines Journal*, 11 August 1842; PAC, RG11-5, WCLB, Power to Begly, 15 August 1842.

81. PAC, RG11-5, WCC-6, Power to Begly, 14 February 1843; *ibid.*, WCLB, Power to Begly, 20 March, 17 July 1843.

82. *Ibid.*, Power to Begly, 1 August 1843. The following winter Thorburn praised Power for his attempt to ease unemployment by ensuring that contractors hired as many labourers as possible: *ibid.*, 407, file 113, Thorburn to Daly, 19 January 1844. Of course, Power may have been motivated equally by a desire to push the work ahead.

83. *Ibid.*, WCLB, Power to Begly, 25 August 1843.

84. *Ibid.*, 407, file 104, Jarrow to Merritt, 6 January 1843.

85. Pentland describes the betrayal of one faction by the other in one of the large strikes on the Lachine: Pentland, "Lachine Strike."

86. For example: PAC, RG11-5, 407, file 104, Cotton and Row to Wheeler, 26 August 1846.

87. PAC, RG8, C60, Memorandum of Wetherall to the Board of Works, 3 April 1843; PAC, RG11-5, 90, file 94, Clarke to Killaly, 6 March 1845; 407, file 113, Thorburn to Daly, 10 January 1844.

88. *Journals* (1844-5), App. Y, Jarvis to Begly; PAC, RG11-5, 390, file 93, Mills to Killaly, November 1844; *ibid.*, 29 November 1844.

89. *Journals* (1843), App. Q, (1844-5), App. AA; PAC, RG11-5, 381, file 56, Godfrey to Begly, 26 March 1844; 390, file 94, Wetherall to Killaly, 2 March 1844; 389, file 89, Power to Begly, 4 March 1845.

90. *Journals* (1843), App. Q, (1844-5), App. AA.

91. *St. Catharines Journal*, 7 June 1844; PAC, RG11-5, 381, file 56, Godfrey to Begly, 9 April 1844.

92. *Ibid.*, WCLB, Power to Begly, 10 March 1843.

93. *Ibid.*, Power to Begly, 17 July 1843; *St. Catharines Journal*, 16 November 1844; PAC, RG11-5, WCC-7, Power to Begly, 7 December 1843; *Journals* (1844-5), App. AA.

94. *Montreal Transcript*, 28 March 1843, cited in Pentland, "Lachine Strike," 266.

95. According to the *St. Catharines Journal*, 20 September 1844, there were four major strikes between 1 April and 20 July.

96. PAC, RG8, C60, Gaele to Elliott, 23 July 1844, Elliott to Young, 23 July 1844.

97. For an analysis of secret societies in Ireland, see: Williams, *Secret Societies*. On the Molly Maguires: Anthony Bimba, *The Molly Maguires* (New York, 1932).

98. *Journals* (1843), App. T.

99. PAC, RG11-5, 407, file 113, Thorburn to Daly, 10 January 1844.

100. Williams, *Secret Societies*, 31.

101. Stephen Langdon, "The Emergence of the Canadian Working Class Movement, 1845-75," *Journal of Canadian Studies*, VIII, 2 (1973), 3-4.

102. Williams, *Secret Societies*, 31.

103. *Ibid.*, 7, 25-7.
104. Rachel O'Higgins, "The Irish Influence in the Chartist Movement," *Past and Present*, 20 (1961), 83-96.
105. PAC, RG8, C60, Wetherall to Board of Works, 3 April 1843.
106. *Montreal Transcript*, 28 March 1843.
107. Duncan, "Irish Famine Migration."
108. O'Higgins, "Irish in Chartist Movement," 83-6.
109. *St. Catharines Journal*, 31 August 1843; *Niagara Chronicle*, 10 July 1844. For further examples of the sensational manner in which newspapers reported labour disturbances, see: *St. Catharines Journal*, 16 November, 14 December, 21 December 1843, 17 May, 2 August, 16 August, 20 September 1844; *Niagara Chronicle*, 20 February 1845; *Brockville Recorder*, 7 September, 21 December 1843, 21 March, 8 August 1844; *Cornwall Observer*, 8 December 1842, 9 January 1845.
110. PAC, RG11-5, 407, file 104, Jarrow to Merritt, 6 January 1843; *St. Catharines Journal*, 28 June 1844.
111. PAC, RG11-5, 407, file 113, Thorburn to Daly, 10 January 1844; PAC, RG8,C60, testimony of James McCloud, sworn before Justices Kerr and Turney, 14 September 1844.
112. *Journals* (1844-5), App. Y, Jarvis to Daly, 28 October 1844; PAC, RG11-5, WCLB, Power to Begly, 3 January 1844.
113. *Journals* (1844-5), App. Y, Jarvis to Daly, 28 October 1844.
114. PAC, RG11-5, WCLB, Power to Begly, 14 February 1843.
115. PAC, RG11-5, 407, file 113, Thorburn to Begly, 1 July 1844; *Cornwall Observer*, 8 December 1842. Also: PAC, RG11-5, WCLB, Power to Begly, April 1842.
116. *Cornwall Observer*, 9 January 1845.
117. PAC, RG11-5, 390, file 93, Mills to Killaly, 29 November 1845, November 1844; *Journals* (1844-5), App. AA.
118. PAC, RG11-5, 407, file 113. Thorburn to Daly, 10 January 1844, 17 January 1844.
119. *Ibid.*, 10 January 1844.
120. *Ibid.*, file 104, Jarrow to Merritt, 6 January 1844.
121. PAC, RG11-5, WCC-7, Power to Begly, 10 February 1843; *ibid.*, Begly to Power, 8 April 1843; PAC, RG11-5, WCC-8, Begly to Power, 3 September 1845.
122. A. W. R. Carrothers, *Collective Bargaining Law in Canada* (Toronto, 1965), 13-15; PAC, RG8, C60, Wetherall to Board of Works, 3 April 1843; *Journals* (1843), App. T. See also: Pentland, "Lachine Strike," for a discussion of the conflicting opinions concerning combinations and strikes.
123. Carrothers, *Collective Bargaining Law*, 14; Henry Pelling, *A History of British Trade Unions* (Middlesex, 1973), 31-2.
124. An Act for the better preservation of the Peace and the prevention of riots and violent outrages at and near public works while in progress of construction, 8 Vic. c. 6.

125. Pentland, "Labour and Development of Industrial Capitalism," 413; PAC, RG11-5, 407, file 113, Thorburn to Daly, 17 January 1844; PAC, RG11-5, WCC-6, Thorburn to Daly, 19 January 1844; *ibid.*, WCLB, Power to contractors, 16 January 1844; *ibid.*, 407, file 104, Wetherall to Killaly, 26 March 1844.

126. Gibbs, *Debates*, IV/2, 1844-5, Attorney General James Smith, 1443.

127. *Ibid.*, T. C. Aylwin, 1459.

128. *Ibid.*, L.-H. LaFontaine, 1505, James Smith, 1515-17.

129. *Ibid.*, Lewis Thomas Drummond, 1516-17.

130. *Ibid.*, Drummond, 1515.

131. PAC, RG11-5, WCLB, Bonnalie to Begly, 12 March 1844; PAC, RG11-5, 388, file 89, Power to Begly, 11 February 1846, 17 January 1847; PAC, RG8, C60, Daly to Taylor, 17 May 1845; PAC, RG11-5, 390, file 94, Hill to Begly, 16 February, 21 June 1847. Both forces continued until the great bulk of the work on their respective canals was finished, the Welland Canal constabulary until 31 December 1849, that on the Williamsburg canals until 31 October 1847, the month that the last of the canals was opened.

132. PAC, RG11-5, WCC-8, Begly to Power, 2 December, 27 December 1845.

133. *Journals* (1843), App. Q.

134. PAC, RG11-5, WCLB, Power to Begly, 3 March, 14 February 1845.

135. Leon Radzinowicz, *A History of the Criminal Law and its Administration from 1750* (London, 1948), III, 284.

136. PAC, RG11-5, 407, file 104, Wetherall to Killaly, 26 March 1844.

137. PAC, RG5, C1, Provincial Secretary's Office, Canada West, 161, #11,362, Memorial of Inhabitants of Mariatown to Lord Metcalfe.

138. *Ibid.*, 164, #11,611, MacDonald to Daly, 12 September 1845.

139. Report of a Committee of the Executive Council, 13 July 1844, cited in Pentland, "Labour and Industrial Capitalism," 432. The Board of Works also employed moral agents on the Beauharnois and Lachine canals in Lower Canada: Pentland, "Labour and Industrial Capitalism," 414. Rev. McDonagh received £200 per annum for his services on the Welland Canal.

140. PAC, RG8, C317, MacDonald to Begly, 14 July 1849.

141. PAC, RG-11, 407, file 104, Wetherall to Killaly, 26 March 1844.

142. *Ibid.*, 279, #2195, Extract from Report of the Committee of the Executive Council, 25 October 1849; 407, file 114, McDonagh to Killaly, 2 May 1843; 407, file 104, Hobson to Daly, 20 January 1844.

143. *Ibid.*, 407, file 114, McDonagh to Killaly, 2 May 1843; 90, file 94, Clarke to Killaly, 6 March 1845, Wetherall to Killaly, 2 March 1844; 388, file 87, McDonagh to Killaly, 25 January 1843; 407, file 113, Thorburn to Daly, 10 January 1844; 407, file 104, Killaly to Begly, 10 October 1849.

144. *Ibid.*, McDonagh to Killaly, 25 January 1843; 407, file 114,

McDonagh to Killaly, 2 May 1843; 407, file 104, Wetherall to Killaly, 26 March 1844.

145. PAC, RG5, C1, Provincial Secretary, 164, #11,611, MacDonald to Daly, 12 September 1845.
146. PAC, RG11-5, 407, file 104, Killaly to Begly, 10 October 1849.
147. PAC, RG8, C60, Daly to Armstrong, 19 August 1842; *ibid.*, Morris to Taylor, 19 August 1842; PAC, RG11-5, WCLB, MacDonald to Begly, 18 April 1843; PAC, RG8, C60, requisition to Fitzwilliam, 12 July 1844.
148. PAC, RG11-5, 407, file 104, Robinson to Begly, 1 October 1842.
149. *Ibid.*, 379, file 44, Magistrates of the Eastern District to Begly, 31 August 1842; *Journals* (1844-5), App. Y, 8 January 1845; *ibid.*, Petition of the Justices of the Peace and other Inhabitants of the County of Dundas; PAC, RG11-5, 407, file 113, Thorburn to Murdoch, 18 August 1842.
150. Radzinowicz, *History of Criminal Law*, IV, 115-39.
151. See, for example: PAC, RG11-5, WCLB, Power to Begly, 3 January 1844; 407, file 104, Hobson to Daly, 20 January 1844.
152. Gibbs, *Debates*, IV/2, 1844-5, T. C. Aylwin, 1456.
153. PAC, RG11-5, 407, file 113, Thorburn to Murdoch, 18 August 1842.
154. *Ibid.*, WCLB, Power to Elliott, 5 January 1844; PAC, RG8, C60, MacDonald to Col. Elliott, 2 April 1844, Merritt to Daly, 21 September 1844; PAC, RG5, C1, Provincial Secretary, 100, #4956, Milne to Bagot, 21 December 1842.
155. PAC, RG8, C60, Armstrong to Browning, Military Secretary, 11 January 1844; *ibid.*, Temporary Commander of Canada West to Elliott, 16 July 1844.
156. *Ibid.*, William Fieder to Taylor, 8 September 1843; PAC, RG11-5, 379, file 44, Harvey to Killaly, 30 August 1842.
157. PAC, RG11-5, 379, file 44, Tuscore to Killaly, 5 September 1842; *ibid.*, WCLB, Power to Elliott, 28 December 1843, 3 January 1844.
158. PAC, RG8, C60, Elliott to Cox and Geale, 30 September 1844.
159. *Ibid.*, Temporary Commander of Canada West to Elliott, 16 July 1844.

IV
Violence and Protest

Violence touched most people in the emerging society of pre-industrial Canada. One ongoing study has identified over 400 riots in the four mainland colonies during the first half of the nineteenth century. In at least fifty of these riots, one or more people lost their lives. Canadians fought over religious differences, ethnic differences, economic differences, political differences. If they were Irish labourers, they rioted to improve their situation; if they were Tory gentlemen, as in the Montreal troubles of 1849, they rioted to hold on to their situation. Without creating some Wild West myth, it is necessary to consider this pervasive element in Canadian society and attempt to determine how it helped to shape that society. At the simplest level, violence was a major factor in the Nova Scotia election of 1830, in Lower Canada in 1834 and Upper Canada in 1836, and in the Province of Canada in 1841 and 1844. Violence between Protestant Orangemen and Irish Catholics in New Brunswick and Upper Canada influenced the shape of social institutions and even residential patterns, encouraging ghettoization for self-defence.

Political protest, often accompanied by violence, was present from the beginning of the colonies. The conservative political system, imposed by Britain, placed power in the hands of appointed governors and colonial elites. Almost inevitably, those blocked from power by this tight system and those dissatisfied with elite politics organized to protest. Before a responsible parliamentary regime was established in all the colonies in the

139

1840's, the opposition was driven to radicalism and violence by governors who were beyond the reach of local politics, irresponsible executives and legislative councils–which were colonial senates– all of which could veto legislation from the popularly elected assemblies.

As the Cross article suggests, there has been controversy over the necessity for the major acts of political violence, the rebellions in the two Canadas. Similarly, the results of the rebellions have produced disagreement. Of some things there can be no doubt. British North America was thrown into upheaval for a period of two years by war and rumour of war. Many suffered grievously: those on both sides who were killed or wounded or had their homes destroyed; those transported to the prison colonies in Australia; those who lived in exile, until 1849 in the case of W. L. Mackenzie.

FURTHER READING:

On the Lower-Canadian rising: Joseph Schull, *Rebellion: the Rising in French Canada, 1837* (Toronto, 1971); Fernand Ouellet, *Lower Canada, 1791-1840* (Toronto, 1980); and Ouellet, "Les insurrections de 1837-8: un phénomène sociale," *Histoire sociale/Social History*, 2 (1968), 54-82.

There has been little specialized work on the rebellion in Upper Canada. Among valuable general works, however, are Gerald M. Craig, *Upper Canada, The Formative Years* (Toronto, 1963), and S. D. Clark, *Movements of Political Protest in Canada* (Toronto, 1959). On other types of violence, see, for example: M. S. Cross, "The Shiners' War: Social Violence in the Ottawa Valley in the 1830's," *Canadian Historical Review*, LIII, 1 (1973), 1-26; and F. H. Armstrong, "The York Riots of March 23, 1832," *Ontario History*, LV, 2 (1963), 61-72.

The Cross excerpt in this section originally appeared as the "Afterword" to the republication of the letters of one of the rebels transported to a penal colony in Van Diemen's Land. His exciting story is told in Benjamin Wait, *The Wait Letters* (Erin, Ont., 1976).

1837: The Necessary Failure

by Michael S. Cross

It was dark as the steamer *Red Jacket* eased into the Upper-Canadian shore. Twenty-six men, carrying fifty stand of arms, disappeared silently into the woods. It was the night of Monday, June 11, 1838; the place was opposite the head of Navy Island in the Niagara River; the men were Upper-Canadian refugees and their American sympathizers, come to liberate the province from its British overlords. Their target was the Short Hills, that perpetually disaffected region in the interior of the Niagara Peninsula. Setting up base in the Long Swamp, the invaders avoided the loyalist patrols searching for them, made contact with potential rebels in the Short Hills, and gradually built up their force. By June 20, they were ready to strike.

As with so many of the military actions of 1837-1838, their attack was inglorious, an insignificant incursion. But this reality obscures a greater reality – the seriousness of their purpose, the tragedy of their failure. They had recruited an army of from 100 to 200 rebels and, on June 20, they marched the twelve miles from their base in the swamp to St. John's, the major village in the Short Hills. There a party of mounted troops, the Lancers, sent to investigate rumours of a Patriot invasion, had stopped for the night at Overholt's tavern. Leaving a sentry outside, the sergeant and nine men of the patrol settled down to sleep. It was two o'clock on the morning of June 21 when shadowy figures sur-

From Michael S. Cross, "Afterword," in Benjamin Wait, *The Wait Letters* (Erin, Ont., 1976), 145-59.

rounded the tavern and its sleeping soldiers, figures wearing an improvised Patriot uniform – white ribbons on one side of their hats, cloth cut-outs of an eagle on the other. A startled young sentry spied the intruders, challenged them, and was fired upon for his trouble. Beating a hasty retreat into the tavern, the sentry awakened his commander, Sergeant Bailey, and roused the soldiers to defence.

Barricaded inside the building, the tiny contingent of Lancers held the rebels at bay. In a half hour of erratic shooting, one defender and two attackers were wounded. Neither side, it appeared, could do the other much damage: stalemate. James Morreau, the Patriot leader, ordered his men to gather straw and to pile it around the inn. They would burn the building and the soldiers with it. Bailey, recognizing the reasonable limits of heroism, surrendered. The Patriots marched their prisoners into the woods, stripped them of their food, arms, equipment, and horses, and then released them.

This tiny triumph was the rebels' last. As was typical in the fevered atmosphere of beleaguered Upper Canada, the handful of invaders grew in rumour to a great army. Fifteen hundred Americans, it was reported, had poured over the border into the Short Hills to launch the long-feared, full-scale invasion. The lieutenant governor of Upper Canada, Sir George Arthur, hurried from Toronto to Hamilton, where he called out the militia. The citizen-soldiers marched into the disaffected area, Pelham and Gainsborough townships, ready to resist the Yankee invasion. They found, instead of the major battle they expected, that their job was simply to hunt down Morreau and his band of refugees. The Patriots, aware they could not resist overwhelming force, attempted to slip back across the border to American safety, but the militia controlled the crossing points. By June 22, the day after the fight at Overholt's tavern, sixteen rebels had been captured. Among them, Arthur reported to the commander-in-chief, Sir John Colborne, was rumoured to be Colonel Morreau. Arthur did not believe the rumour. "This man is a Canadian of the name of Wait a remarkably *(blank in manuscript)* person, bold and intelligent."[1]

Both Morreau and Wait, as it developed, fell into the net. Within a week about thirty-six rebels had been arrested in a manhunt that went on for a month and eventually rounded up seventy-five suspects. In the Niagara gaol were all of the leaders. The commander of the invaders had been Colonel James Mor-

reau, or Morrow, a thirty-two-year-old tanner from Pennsylvania. His chief compatriots were Jacob Beamer, Samuel
Chandler, Alexander McLeod, and Benjamin Wait, that "bold
and intelligent" man. Beamer, as Wait's narrative pictures him,
was a crude and brutal man, a twenty-nine-year-old innkeeper
and carpenter from Oakland township near London, Upper
Canada. Chandler was a key figure, a man with local contacts
who could encourage the residents of the Short Hills to join their
liberators; American-born, Chandler was forty-eight, a wagon-
maker, and a resident of Thorold. From East Gwillimbury
township, north of Toronto, Alexander McLeod was a twenty-
four-year-old carpenter who had joined William Lyon Mackenzie in the attack on Toronto in December 1837.[2]

And Benjamin Wait. He was captured during his escape, taken
at Navy Island, and imprisoned on June 25. A native of
Markham township near Toronto, Wait was then two months
short of twenty-five years of age. He had lived with his family in
Haldimand township, on the Grand River, and operated a sawmill. By the summer of 1837, he was a clerk at Port Colborne. His
personal movements from that point are shadowy, his story sufficiently contradictory that one unsympathetic historian has called
him "a boisterous and prevaricating Upper Canadian agitator."[3]

The best guess is that he fled Upper Canada that summer of
1837, running to the United States to avoid imprisonment for
debt; just another of the many victims of the depression which
wracked the province that year. Certainly, well before his depar-
ture, Wait had a reputation as an agitator, as an "advanced"
Reformer. That tendency was reinforced by family ties. His wife,
Maria, who would play such a heroic role in saving his life from
execution, was the principal heir of Robert Randall, long-time
radical member of the provincial legislature. Randall carried a
heavier load of official disapproval than most radicals for he had
run afoul of some leading members of the provincial elite in a
dispute over ownership of some land. It must have been especially chilling for Benjamin Wait, on trial for his life in August
1838, to see on the bench one of Randall's old enemies in the land
dispute, Judge Jonas Jones.

Wait may have re-crossed the border in December 1837 to join
the western uprising in the London district. That would account
for his rapid rise to a position of importance in the Patriot forces
which mustered in the United States to liberate Upper Canada
after the failure of the domestic risings. The uncertainty about

his activity remains, however. He claimed to be second in command of the unsuccessful invasion at Pelee Island in February 1838, but some historians have disputed the claim. He was certainly an organizer of the Short Hills incursion, nevertheless, and he certainly languished in gaol after June 25, his life in the balance.

Those captured in the Short Hills raid were tried in a series of hearings between July 18 and August 18. Their fates were decided more by politics than by the judicial process, which was as well for Benjamin Wait, given the bias against him of the sitting magistrate, Judge Jones. The situation was one of total confusion for a period of months. The legality of Upper-Canadian legislation on the punishment of foreigners – and some of the Short Hills raiders were Americans – was uncertain. The provincial Executive Council was dubious whether the political situation called for severity or leniency. And the governor-general, Lord Durham, did not help by shifting his position rapidly and erratically. In the immediate aftermath of the incursion, Durham disapproved of Arthur's actions in turning the rebels over to civilian tribunals instead of taking "summary measures," drumhead executions, against them.[4] Later, presumably assessing the political climate, "Radical Jack" took a more liberal stance and urged clemency for the convicted invaders.

In the result, the politics of leniency prevailed. Although eighteen men were sentenced to death, only one – Colonel Morreau – was executed, hanged at Niagara on July 30. As the Wait memoir discusses so eloquently, the others were saved after the representations of Maria Wait and Miss Chandler, daughter of the condemned Samuel Chandler, and after a public outcry. Of the rebels who had crossed over from the United States, fourteen had their death sentences altered to transportation for life to the penal colony in Van Diemen's Land, two were commuted to three years' imprisonment in Kingston Penitentiary, one received a fourteen-year sentence, five were freed without trial, and two were acquitted. Again for political reasons, those who joined the rebellion in Upper Canada were dealt with more leniently. One was transported, one sent to prison for three years, six absconded and escaped punishment, seven freed without trial, and six acquitted. Another twenty-six, accused of complicity on shaky evidence, were released.

As the legal tangle continued, the fate of those condemned to transportation hung in the balance. It was a delicate issue, for

Lord Durham's action in banishing Lower-Canadian rebels to Bermuda, and threatening them with death should they return, was held by Britain to be beyond his authority. The dispute led to Durham's resignation and his return to England in the autumn of 1838. The unhappy Short Hills prisoners were shunted about as their cases were argued. On October 6, 1838, those whose sentences had been commuted to transportation were transferred by ship from Niagara to Toronto. Disembarking at the Toronto wharf, they were greeted by a large and hostile crowd which shouted abuse at the men as they were led through the streets to the city gaol. The next day they were on the move again, to Kingston and incarceration in military cells at Fort Henry. On November 9, they were herded aboard the steamer *Cobourg*, to be carried to Prescott, where they were chained on the deck of another ship, the *Dolphin*, for movement to Cornwall. The nervous government, fearful of new invasions to free the prisoners, continued to shift them east. After a stay in the Cornwall gaol, they were sent to Coteau du Lac, to the Cascades, Lachine, and, on November 17, to Montreal. The next day the weary rebels were moved by steamer to Quebec, where they languished in the decrepit gaol until November 22, when they were hauled on sleds, handcuffed and chained, to the docks to board the *Captain Ross*, the ship which would take them to Britain where the imperial authorities would decide their disposition.

Benjamin Wait was one of the most active in attempting to convince the British courts and British government to free the prisoners. Writing from the Liverpool gaol, where they were incarcerated, to the British radical Joseph Hume, Wait contended that their removal from Upper Canada had been illegal and unconstitutional, that his trial had been irregular and the introduction of evidence improper.[5] The letters and petitions were to no avail; on January 4, 1839, their chains refastened, Wait and ten companions were put aboard the *Meteor* for transportation to Australia. This peculiar drama still had twists. The *Meteor* was driven back by bad weather, the prisoners were held in dilapidated prison ships off Portsmouth until, finally, on March 17 the *Marquis of Hastings* bore them off into exile.

Wait would escape from Van Diemen's Land and make his way back to the United States in 1842. He was reunited with his wife Maria in Niagara Falls, New York, where she had been teaching school. Their new life together was short-lived; Maria died in May, 1843, after giving birth to twins. Benjamin moved to

Michigan and re-entered the timber business at Grand Rapids. He remained a well-known public figure, for the *Letters from Van Diemen's Land*, which he had written with Maria and published in 1843, was the first of the Patriot narratives to appear. Active in timbering and a founder of the journal which spoke for the business, the *Northwestern Lumberman*, Wait was for many years a prominent citizen of Michigan. He died, aged eighty-two, at Grand Rapids on November 9, 1895.

Why had Benjamin Wait and his compatriots risked their lives and fortunes? Conventional historical wisdom would suggest they did so because they were fools and agitators, because they were misguided and misled. The rebellion in Upper Canada, so this interpretation has run, was an unnecessary event in the political history of the country, a political history which was working itself towards responsible government and eventual democracy. The uprising had a negligible effect upon that political history, beyond the disorder and suffering it caused for those involved. It was, then, the logical culmination of the career of the mad demagogue, William Lyon Mackenzie, who was chiefly responsible for all the trouble. The simultaneous rebellion in Lower Canada was similarly unnecessary and misdirected. It was, in the older interpretation which springs from Lord Durham's views in his famous Report of 1839, a struggle of races. The backward French Canadians, unable to compete economically or politically with the progressive English, lashed out in rebellion. Or it was, in more recent interpretation, a conspiracy by a professional elite in French Canada to secure their own economic and political advancement by stirring the ignorant people into revolt.

Clearly Benjamin Wait and men like him would have rejected such arguments. Their view of the cause was summed up by their reaction to the punishment they received. They felt that their sentences, of whatever severity, were unjust. They were unjust almost by definition, because these men felt that they were fighting for liberty and progress and justice. By what rationale should they be punished for waging such a good fight? The relative leniency with which most were treated, the public support which began to emerge for them, the rapid pardons granted to most rebels by 1843: these suggest that much of the Canadian population and even, guiltily, the government shared in some measure the rebels' self-evaluation.

The rebellions in the Canadas might well have been seen as

struggles for liberty for they were part of the wave of "liberal" rebellion which swept across the Western world in this period. From the Decembrist revolt in Russia in 1825, to the revolutions of 1830 in western and central Europe, to the Chartist movement in Britain, to the revolutions of 1848 across Europe, people everywhere were striking against outworn autocracies, striking for liberty. Why should Canada have avoided the contagion of freedom, why should the Canadian rebellions be evaluated so much more harshly?

To compare the Canadian rebellions with their European counterparts puts them in context, but does not explain them. The troubles of 1837-1838 in British North America grew out of local conditions and local problems; the rebellion movements developed with their own logic.

The rebellions in the two Canadas were quite separate but interrelated explosions. On the political level, it was hard for many contemporaries to share the rosy view of colonial development that hindsight has given historians. In Lower Canada, politics had become polarized between a popular assembly, dominated by French-speaking members, and the appointive branches of government, which were overwhelmingly English. The legislative council, appointed by the governor, the executive council, also appointed, and the governor himself, could check any attempt by the assembly to liberalize institutions, to make the tax system more fair, or to expand the responsibilities of the elected branch of government. The fact that this political division corresponded to ethnic divisions between English and French made the conflict more bitter but did not cause it, for similar conflicts arose in Upper Canada, where the assembly as well as the executive was English-speaking. There the Reformers had gained control of the assembly between 1828 and 1830 and between 1834 and 1836. On each occasion they found their attempts to reform provincial institutions blocked from above, the business of the province brought to a halt by an intransigent executive which checked and vetoed the legislation brought forth by the Reform assemblies.

It was hard to believe, then, that patience would bring political progress, that Canadians ought to wait quietly to receive the blessings of the British constitution. Indeed, one of the triggers for the rebellions was the political regression which marked the years 1836 and 1837. In Lower Canada, the situation had deteriorated rapidly since the French-Canadian radicals had presented a series of demands for fundamental democratic reforms, the Ninety-two Resolutions, in 1834–demands ignored by the English authorities. By 1836 the fight between assembly and executive had reached a deadlock and the assembly followed the only course of action open to it. It went on strike, refusing to pass the money bills which would provide the executive the funds it needed to operate. The response of England, in the spring of 1837, was astonishing in its arbitrary violation of the supposed principles of British government. The governor in Lower Canada was given the authority to seize provincial funds without requiring the normal approval by the legislature. Like the Bourbons, it appeared, the imperial government learned nothing from history, for it was taxation without representation which had been the rallying abuse urging Americans into revolution sixty years earlier. A British government which would not honour even the most hallowed principles of its own constitution could hardly be expected to be the agent of political progress. Canadians would have to make that progress themselves.

Upper-Canadian Reformers were equally shocked and outraged by the course of politics there. In 1836 a new lieutenant governor had arrived. Francis Bond Head, acting on British orders (for the British were always more willing to make concessions to English colonists than to *Canadiens*), took a group of Reformers into his executive council. The naive Reformers thought a great new day had dawned, that there was to be popular influence over executive decisions. They were soon disillusioned and the Reformers resigned from the council. Head, a vain and undiplomatic blunderer, proceeded to pick fight after fight with the Reform-dominated assembly and finally, in 1836, to dissolve it and call an election. He then used the full power of patronage and coercion which rested with a colonial governor to swing the election to the compliant Tories. Under the full weight of executive interference, most leading Reformers were defeated, including the chief radical spokesman, William Lyon Mackenzie. Their complaints about the election, including substantial evidence of serious electoral irregularities perpetrated by the provincial government, were carried to England in September 1836 by Charles Duncombe, radical member of the assembly. But the colonial secretary, Lord Glenelg, would not even see the Canadian delegate. It was a devastating experience for Upper-Canadian Reformers. Against all evidence, they had held a naive faith in British justice; they had been convinced that the troubles of Canada stemmed from domestic misrule by colonial aristocrats and that Britain, if made aware of the true situation, would rectify it. In Duncombe's reaction to his failed mission, in his bitter disillusionment, can be read one cause of the rebellions. As he wrote to fellow Reformer Robert Baldwin, he now felt that the people of Canada, "if ever they have good government . . . must look among themselves for the means of producing it, for they [British authorities] care very little for the people of Canada other than as a source of patronage to the Colonial Office. That must be changed."[6]

This mood of disillusionment, this sense of betrayal, was heightened by the coercion of Lower Canada. Radicals in the upper province had the last vestiges of their faith in Britain shattered; if fundamental rights could be stripped from French Canadians, they could be stripped as well from English Canadians. A powerful feeling of political desperation had seized radicals in both colonies.

Economic distress added to this feeling. Lower Canada had been troubled throughout the 1830's by agricultural depression, the attacks of insects on crops, and crop failures. Upper Canada was plunged into depression in 1836 by the stoppage of all public works in the province as the result of cutting off of government funds in the dispute between Bond Head and the assembly. To these domestic problems was added the impact of a general international depression in 1837. Benjamin Wait was far from alone in having to flee Upper Canada to escape from his debts.

Economic causes went deeper than the immediate depression. The rebellions in the Canadas, as with all revolutions, were rooted in the economic relationships of their societies. Colonial economies were by their nature exploitive – that was their purpose. This was most strikingly so in Lower Canada where, in addition to the usual exploitation involved in an imperial economy devoted to the export of raw materials, one group had been systematically excluded from the higher levels of economic activity. French Canadians were not part of the dominant economic élite, and the system effectively prevented them from becoming so. Cut off from their contacts in France by the Conquest, unable to develop new contacts, new sources of capital, in England, French-Canadian businessmen had inevitably given way to English-speaking ones. By the nineteenth century big business was not an arena ambitious *Canadiens* would even consider attempting to enter. That situation helped add bite to political controversies. Young French Canadians of ambition, business closed to them, entered the liberal professions, law, medicine. And politics. Politics became a surrogate for business, a way of climbing in society, the power and patronage of politics replacing the status and economic rewards of business success. To find the higher reaches of politics closed off by the English as well was frustrating and enraging.

To the degree that this is an accurate picture of the French-Canadian political élite, their agitation was selfish, their movement toward rebellion *was* a "conspiracy" to improve their own positions, not a liberal attempt to improve the lot of the people. Some of the so-called "popular" leaders had little interest in or regard for the people. Louis-Joseph Papineau, the dominant figure in the opposition movement, was a seigneur, a man who owned a great estate on the Ottawa River and whose primary concern was not to help his peasants progress but, rather, to extract the highest possible income from them. Haughty, filled with aristocratic pretensions, Papineau used the rhetoric of democracy but shared few of its basic assumptions.

Yet the rebellion movement in Lower Canada won widespread support; it won the adherence of perhaps 5,000 men who were willing to risk their lives for the cause. Unless we are to assume that so large a number were simply gullible and misled, it is clear that the masses who joined the rebellion had their own reasons, their own frustrations, their own goals. The system blocked them as it blocked the professional élite. The seigneurial lands were full and had been farmed for too many generations. The one accessible area of new land in Lower Canada, the Eastern Townships, had been handed over by the government for exploitation to a group of capitalists, the British American Land Company. *Habitants* could see the dismal prospects for their sons–life on seigneurial lands which would be divided into even smaller and less viable farms, or emigration to the United States. The agricultural difficulties of the 1830's increased the frustration and increased the readiness to take extreme measures in the search for a solution.

This frustration would have been most pointed for established and ambitious farmers with families, for they would see most clearly the potential problems of the future. This is borne out by the ages of rebels. Among identified leaders of the movement, those in business and the professions tended to be young, 40 per cent of them under thirty years of age. They were the young men on the way up, blocked by the English domination of business and the executive government. Among rural leaders, however, the pattern was reversed; 76 per cent were over thirty. They were the established *habitants*, unable to expand their farms, unable to provide for their sons.[7]

That the rebellion was not simply a race war is shown by the heavy involvement of Lower-Canadian Irish. At the level of leadership there were men such as Dr. Edmund Bailey O'Callaghan, one of the major organizers and theoreticians of the movement. And among the shock troops were Irish workers from Montreal, men with a traditional hatred of England, men frustrated by the discrimination and exploitation they faced in their working lives. They, as with the French-Canadian masses, had their own reasons for rebellion, reasons quite distinct from those of the middle-class élites who led the revolution.

There were similar political frustrations for middle-class men in Upper Canada, their ambitions thwarted by the local élite at Toronto, the Family Compact. But the frustrations did not have the added edge of ethnic tensions and the economic system was far more open to them than it was to their French-Canadian counterparts. They might be driven to more extreme political positions by the intransigence of the Compact, but they would not be driven to the extreme of rebellion.

The leadership of the Upper-Canadian movement came from outside the mainstream of the Reform party, from the radical fringe that had for years been at odds with that respectable mainstream. Mackenzie was no Papineau: he had no landed interest to protect; he had no peasants to exploit. Raised in Scottish poverty, William Lyon Mackenzie rejected the economic system which had exploited him and his kind. In the process he developed a romanticized view of independent agrarians, people who operated outside the system of exploitation. This group, the "honest yeomen," was the group he spoke to, rather than the middle-class professionals and businessmen. It was characteristic that, in his draft constitution for the independent "State of Upper Canada," which he published in November 1837, Mackenzie decreed "There shall never be created within this State any incorporated trading companies, or incorporated companies with banking powers. Labor is the only means of creating wealth."[8]

Mackenzie's conception of a rural utopia, with no chartered banks, no large businesses, no factories, with direct democracy and easy civil rights, was naive and unreachable. Upper Canada could not cut itself off from the advance of industrial capitalism, from the influence of finance capitalism. Nor was his conception one that was likely to win ready acceptance from the middle-class men-on-the-make who made up the Reform party. It could speak, however, to many frustrated farmers in the province. There was a clear geographical and economic pattern to the rebellion movement, a pattern of agrarian frustration. The chief areas of support for the uprising were: the Midland district in the east, the backcountry behind Kingston; the Home district above Toronto; the Niagara district and its backcountry, the Gore district; and the London district in central-west Upper Canada. All were well-settled agricultural areas, areas beyond the struggling stage of frontier development. All, too, were areas where farmers faced difficulty in expanding and fulfilling their ambitions and in finding land for their sons. They were debtor regions, in debt to pay for land and for implements, in debt to the merchants who supported the Family Compact, in debt to the banks that Mackenzie promised to abolish. As in Lower Canada, they were angered by the land system. Most good land in Upper Canada had been granted away by 1830, to government officials, Loyalists, the Anglican church, and that great speculator, the Canada Land Company, which held a million acres of land in western Upper Canada. Along with their compatriots in the lower province, many Upper-Canadian farmers were ready to change the land system by whatever means proved to be necessary.

Mackenzie's ideas were not shared by all those involved in the movement. The Upper-Canadian radical cause had its sprinkling of businessmen, lawyers, and doctors who sought to better themselves by disrupting the status quo. It also had significant support from the landless, from agricultural labourers and some Toronto workers, notably those in the iron trade and the breweries. These men faced directly the exploitation inherent in the economic structures. The existing land system assured that they would never have their own property; it doomed them, in this age before trade unions, to low wages and bad working conditions. There were other characteristics which marked rebels, as well. They were more likely to be of American or Scottish origin, than to be English. They were more likely to be Presbyterians or Baptists than to be Anglicans.

The rebels in both provinces were far from a homogeneous group, coming from different ethnic, religious, and economic backgrounds. But they shared certain characteristics. They were men who found themselves blocked from achieving the promise of the New World by a closed and oppressive economic system. They were men who found the levers of political power jammed by a time-worn constitutional structure. They were men who found that, to gain the liberty, economic and political, that they claimed by right, they had to take up guns.

If their backgrounds differed, so did their ideas about what would emerge from rebellion. The middle-class leaders foresaw a liberal, laissez-faire society–much like the United States–in which their ambitions would have free rein. Mackenzie, and some of his rural supporters, expected an agrarian utopia of small farms and educated, honest yeomen. Most, perhaps, had no clear vision of the future. Indeed, most probably had no desire to engage in a full-scale revolution. Many rebels later reflected that their goals were much more limited. In Lower Canada it was fighting between the Tory Doric Club and *patriote* organizations which escalated into the rebellion in November 1837. The chief organizer of the Sons of Liberty, the reform society, was Thomas Storrow Brown. Brown claimed that the Sons of Liberty was not created to foment revolution but "merely to complete an organization that would enable us to act effectively in election or other riots against the Tory Party who were already combined in clubs."[9] Similarly, after his arrest, the Upper-Canadian rebel leader, Samuel Lount, contended that his purposes had been quite limited: "he did not know of any intention to rise in rebellion for more than 2 weeks previous to the Monday on which the Assemblage took place at Montgomery's. . . . I had no idea it was to be a rebellion. I was informed and led to believe that what we wanted could be obtained easily – without bloodshed. . . ."[10]

Such declarations could be taken as the rationalizations after the fact of losers, especially in the case of Lount, who was pleading for his life. Yet the claims were repeated often enough by enough rebels to be convincing. And they have the force of logic. Few men are willing to risk everything; few men are willing to contemplate treason. But there were enough men, angry enough, to take up arms in a demonstration of force. They hoped to overawe the government, compel it to make fundamental concessions. If they had had time to think about it, they would have realized that their actions did constitute rebellion, and they might have pulled back. But there was no time to think; events, their own anger, and desperation bore them along, plunged them over the edge into revolution.

It all moved with hectic rapidity. In the summer of 1837,

furious radicals in both provinces organized protests. Attacked by Tory mobs, they armed in self-defence. Government inaction, the frequent physical conflicts with Tories, these created an atmosphere of near-explosive tension. Then, in the late fall, the explosions came. Fighting between radicals and Tories in Montreal brought government action, orders for the arrest of radical leaders. The *patriotes* fled the city, mustered their forces, and prepared to resist. It was mid-November 1837. Major battles between the *patriotes* and British troops in the Richelieu Valley followed but, after early victories, the rebel army was soon scattered. News of the Lower-Canadian rising triggered the rebellion in Upper Canada. Badly planned and worse led, the attack on Toronto in the first week of December was a disaster, easily repulsed by a hastily assembled militia. An uprising in the London district, planned to complement the assault on the capital, was a similar fiasco. By the middle of December, the internal risings were crushed, their leaders in flight to the United States.

The fight went on for a year, however. The rebels found a ready hearing in the United States where hatred of Britain had deep roots, and where an adventure in the interests of liberty was attractive to many. American support groups sprang up, most notably the Hunters Lodges, which claimed to have 100,000 members at their height in 1838. Frequent invasions, such as the Short Hills incursion, were undertaken, all marked by poor planning and incompetent leadership. Nor were sufficient men available. Americans enjoyed the excitement of drilling and sabre-rattling at the British but few were willing to risk their lives in actual invasions.

The Patriot cause in the United States was further weakened by conflict within the leadership. From the time they crossed the border, the rebel chieftains were divided over the tactics and the goals of the movement. Among the Upper Canadians, the split was seen most dramatically between Mackenzie and Charles Duncombe. Duncombe, the American-born leader of the rising in the London district, was prepared to integrate the Canadian refugees into the American support groups, for he saw the proper goal of the liberation of Canada to be its annexation to the United States. This Mackenzie vigorously and angrily rejected. He was prepared to accept American aid, but insisted that the movement must be Canadian-directed, and with independent Canadian purposes. Mackenzie went so far as to charge Duncombe with being a paid agent of the United States government.

Divided, dispirited by defeats, lacking effective military leadership, the Patriot movement could only fail. It never succeeded in tapping the large body of support which clearly existed within the Canadas, which needed encouragement and the hope of success before it would join the cause. By the end of 1838, the rebellion movement was dead.

Was it a comic and foolish episode, irrelevant to the real political progress of the Canadas? That is certainly the usual view. The standard history of Upper Canada, by Gerald Craig, for example, is harsh in its final judgement of the rebellion:

> Mackenzie and his associates managed to dupe only a few hundred farm lads and other rather simple people, many of whom paid a bitter price for their adventure, into believing that an armed uprising would cure the province's ills. The vigour with which people from one end of Upper Canada to the other rose to support the government showed that in no sense was Mackenzie the leader of a popular movement. His later admission that resort to force had been a mistake was cold comfort to the men and their families whose lives he had helped to ruin and to the reform cause which he had greatly injured.[11]

Such an interpretation rests on a whole set of dubious assumptions. One is that the rebellion movement had no wide popular support. Given the rapid defeat of the internal rising, thanks to its poor execution, it is an assumption which cannot be tested, for only the foolhardy would have rallied to a losing cause. One could argue with equal plausibility that a body of support existed which could not be mobilized because of the fiasco on Yonge Street in December 1837; certainly government observers of the time feared that such support for rebellion existed and might emerge to the surface under certain circumstances. Even the lieutenant governor, Sir George Arthur, shared such fears. In an interview with a captured Patriot leader, Edward Theller, Arthur revealed his anxieties. As Theller reported the conversation, Arthur told him "that they were disposed at first to use every means they could, to have me executed and that they would right or wrong have done my business, had they not fears of the Irish who were encouraged by some of those who would not wish the government to know that they had any hand in it."[12] One can do no more than speculate on the potential size of the rebellion, based on a reading of the social and political history of the province.

The interpretation assumes, as well, that the rebels were "simple people," people incapable of making political judgements. However, as we have seen, they in fact tended to be men of substance, established agrarians: the only close study of Upper-Canadian rebels, of those in the Duncombe rising in the west, demonstrates that rebels on average held more property than their neighbours, were more prosperous than the norm.[13] Whether or not those involved thought they were engaged in full-scale revolution, they were aware they had undertaken armed resistance to the government. And they knew why they were resisting: they knew they were trying to change an oppressive and unjust society.

The argument suggests that the "reform cause" was damaged by rebellion. In 1838 that appeared to be true, with the radicals gone into exile, the moderates tarred by association. But a public reaction soon became apparent, a reaction against the Family Compact and against its Tory allies. They were blamed for the persecutions of innocents which marked the suppression of the rebellion and, more importantly, for creating the conditions which caused the rebellion in the first place. In this climate the Reform party re-emerged with new strength, combining French and English liberals into a political force which would win responsible government in the 1840's.

That was one accomplishment of the rebellions. They broke the political stalemate in the Canadas, the stalemate which had left the opposition parties powerless, for the rebellions compelled Britain to recognize the failures of existing colonial governments. The Durham Report, the union of the two Canadas in 1841, the extension of the power of the elected branch of government and, eventually, responsible government – all flowed directly from the shock provided by the rebellions. The rebellions greatly accelerated the pace of political change and in the process hurried along the development of Canada's modern forms of self-government.

Which is not to suggest that rebellion meant the ideas of Papineau or Mackenzie were triumphant. The real victors of 1837-1838 were the men who were uninvolved, the men who supported neither side. The suppression of the rebellions destroyed the radicals, the political factions of Papineau and Mackenzie. The revulsion which followed destroyed the executive élites, the Chateau Clique and the Family Compact. In the 1840's, new forces filled this created vacuum. New business-minded men came to the forefront, modern men, men devoted to the interests of a new capitalist order. On the Reform side, the stereotypical figure was Francis Hincks, on the Conservative side, John A. Macdonald. Partially in reaction to the emotional politics which had produced the rebellions, partially in service of self-interest, they developed a different style of politics, a different sort of state, a different Canada. In this new order, what was good for business was good for the country. Roads, canals, railroads, factories, these were the preoccupations of the industrial capitalist Canada that Hincks, Macdonald and their kind erected.

There was a nice irony in it all. Mackenzie and the members of the Compact had fought and destroyed each other. They had done so in the interests of their conceptions of the good society, conceptions which differed greatly yet touched at a key point; both sides envisaged a Canadian that was agrarian, that was devoted to values that were non-capitalist. In destroying each other, they left the field to men whose conception of society was very different, men whose only goal was rapid industrial capitalist development.

While in exile, William Lyon Mackenzie was horrified by what the United States had become. He wondered whether the American-style democracy that the rebellion attempted to create would not have ended up sharing the evil future he saw looming in the United States. He wrote to a friend in Upper Canada despairingly:

> It is very fortunate that we rebels of Toronto failed. It has given some of the constitution makers, that would have been, a taste of the working of free institutions, so called, where they are in practice – and has convinced me that the weak part of the American Constitution lies here. The Fathers of this republic are famous for hav'g estab'd constitutions nearly on this plan suggested by Paine – they provided ag't a nobility – a state church – primogeniture & half blood laws – monarch & so on, but corporations, monopolies, banks of issue, they either left untouched, or, if they did not, the judges have so expounded their acts. And this inlet to knavery is unsettling every'g, & giving a mercinary [*sic*] character to a people formed to be an example to the world.[14]

What Mackenzie could not foresee, in his despair, was that the defeat of the rebellions had unleashed these same forces in Canada. The fall of the radicals and their aristocratic opponents left Canada to the mercies of the "corporations, monopolies, banks of issue," to the men of "mercinary character." That was the ultimate tragedy of the failure of the rebellions of 1837.

NOTES

1. C. R. Sanderson, ed., *The Arthur Papers* (Toronto, 1943), I, Arthur to Colborne, 26 June 1838, 209.
2. For biographical details on the rebels, see: Colin Read. "The Short Hills Raid of June, 1838, and its Aftermath," *OH*, LXVIII, 2 (1976), 93-109.
3. J. P. Martyn, "The Patriot Invasion of Pelee Island," *OH*, LVI, 3 (1964), 161.
4. PAC, Lord Grey of Howick, 2, Charles Grey to Lord Grey, 8 July 1838, 62.
5. PAC, Roebuck Papers, 4, file XXII, Wait to Hume, 22 December 1838, 7-12; Wait to Hume, 26 December 1838, 32-5.
6. TPL, Robert Baldwin Papers, I, A42/69, Duncombe to Baldwin, 15 September 1836.
7. The figures come from Fernand Ouellet, "Les insurrections du 1837-8: un phénomène social," *Histoire sociale/Social History*, 2 (1968), 81.
8. Charles Lindsey, *The Life and Times of Wm. Lyon Mackenzie* (Toronto, 1862), II, 354.
9. PAC, T. S. Brown, mss. by T. S. Brown, n.d., 2.
10. PAC, John Rolph, 2, deposition of Samuel Lount, 18 January 1838, 105.
11. Gerald M. Craig, *Upper Canada: The Formative Years, 1784-1841* (Toronto, 1963), 249.
12. PAC, Edward Theller, Theller to "Garry," 19 June 1838, 5. Anxious reports from government members and their agents are to be found in the *Arthur Papers* and in such manuscript collections as the Durham Papers at PAC.
13. Colin F. Read, "The Rising in Western Upper Canada, 1837-38" (Ph.D. thesis, University of Toronto, 1974).
14. PAC, William and Andrew Buell, W. L. Mackenzie to Andrew Buell, 12 October 1839, 24-5.

V
Social Control

By mid-century, Victorian Canadians had grasped eagerly the dogma of progress and development. With it came a certain confidence that they could change, for the better, not only the physical environment but men as well. In a variety of ways they set out to reshape men and create good citizens. The school was the most important institution for accomplishing this goal. As a result, the school system received much attention, was a frequent and controversial subject of political debate, and changed rapidly itself. From a loose structure which reached a small proportion of the population in the 1830's, the school system in all of the colonies moved quickly towards its modern form – publicly funded, accessible to all, compulsory. Many thought the public school system to be the greatest and most important product of the nineteenth century. It may well have been. For historians, however, it is necessary to determine why the school system developed in the form it did, what it was intended to accomplish, and how well it functioned as an instrument of social control.

FURTHER READING:
The literature on schools is voluminous. The standard text is J. D. Wilson, R. M. Stamp, and L.-P. Audet, eds., *Canadian Education: A History* (Scarborough, 1970). An intelligent selection of documents is to be found in Alison L. Prentice and Susan E. Houston, eds., *Family, School and Society in Nineteenth-Century Canada* (Toronto, 1975). Some of the best of new ap-

proaches are represented in Michael B. Katz and Paul Mattingly, eds., *Education and Social History: Themes from Ontario's Past* (New York, 1975). Some articles of special value are: Judith Fingard, "Attitudes Towards the Education of the Poor in Colonial Halifax," *Acadiensis*, II, 2 (1973), 15-42; R. D. Gidney, "Elementary Education in Upper Canada: A Reassessment," *Ontario History*, LVX, 3 (1973), 169-85; Allan Greer, "The Sunday Schools of Upper Canada," *Ontario History*, LXVII, 3 (1975), 169-84. R. B. Splane, *Social Welfare in Ontario, 1791-1893* (Toronto, 1965), gives an overview of other institutions of social control.

Susan E. Houston is chairman of the History Department at York University.

Politics, Schools, and Social Change in Upper Canada

by Susan E. Houston

The educational debate in Upper Canada in the 1830's and 1840's mirrored the tensions of two decades of crucial social, economic, and political ferment. Why was the issue of tax-supported, publicly controlled elementary schooling so contentious at this time? Was it because public schooling was so "in the air" internationally that Upper Canadians could not remain detached? Was this debate merely another chapter in the ongoing church-state issue?[1] Partially; but most importantly the foundation of the provincial school system between 1846 and 1850 was the deliberate creation of Upper Canadians who shared a common outlook and common aspirations. In a society overwhelmingly rural and agricultural, the dominant orientation of this shared outlook was urban. Moderately conservative in social philosophy, the middle classes met the problems of rapid social change at mid-century with solutions appropriate to an urban commercial society.

Until very recently, Canadian historians have confined their interest in education almost exclusively to school controversies touching on issues of biculturalism and church-state relations. Commonly their treatment of the development of educational institutions has relied on an analogy to democracy; thus the advance from log school-house to compulsory secondary education for all in Ontario has been enshrined in textbooks and popular

Reprinted from *Canadian Historical Review*, LIII (1972), 249-71, by permission of the author and University of Toronto Press. © University of Toronto Press, 1972.

literature alongside Canada's march to nationhood. The myth of progress, enlightenment, and humanitarian concern, which evolved originally as an account of the history of American education, spilled over to fill the vacuum in Canadian educational historiography. In the mythology, the movement for free public education is part of the larger struggle of the lower classes for participation in the democratic process, and the classic alignment of interests shows the "conservatives" in opposition to public school establishment.[2] Accordingly, in Upper Canada John Strachan and his rival Egerton Ryerson, the ascendency of whose influence in educational matters parallels the decline of Strachan's, have traditionally represented the contending forces. Unfortunately, both too much and too little has been made of the North American and international cast of Canadian school provision. The current renaissance in educational history in the United States has so seriously challenged the traditional interpretation that Canadian historians can no longer rely on facile analogies to Jacksonians and Whigs in the school debate. At the same time, faith in the potentiality of education has been associated too narrowly with the United States. As one tenet of Liberalism, the ideology of educational advance was an international phenomenon. "The schoolmaster was abroad": Sir James Kay-Shuttleworth in England, Victor Cousin in France, Thomas Dick in Scotland, Horace Mann and Henry Barnard in the United States, and Egerton Ryerson in Upper Canada. These men, and their counterparts in virtually every European country, formed a community of articulate and self-conscious educational innovators.

The pace and direction of the educational advance in Upper Canada in these two decades was intimately linked to the changes being wrought in virtually every facet of colonial life. As the immigration of the late 1820's and early 1830's filled in empty townships, the primitive spirit-breaking struggle of the pioneer increasingly became a memory. Settlement meant an end to the physical isolation of frontier life and an increasing concentration of population at numerous local centres. While, by 1851, roughly 15 per cent of the population lived in incorporated places,[3] the model of society provided by larger commercial centres such as Toronto and Kingston clearly exercised a commanding influence. The newspaper, with incalculable effect, bridged the distance from farmhouse to county town, to provincial capital, to London and New York.[4] Indeed, Toronto's commercial dominance of her southwestern Ontario hinterland matched a cultural and intellectual influence which contributed significantly to the educational debate.[5]

Growing crime in cities provided early educational critics with a persistent issue. By the 1830's the special problems of urban youth and juvenile criminality became distinguished from the general morass of crime. As one writer observed, "at Toronto great incentives to vice in the very young exist."[6] As early as 1835, legislators saw in the possibility of preventing the children of Toronto's poor from "growing up in idleness and vice, the pupils of old proficients in crime" a telling argument in support of free schooling for poor but promising youngsters.[7] Moreover, there were those who glimpsed a "spirit of insubordination" abroad threatening the honest independence of the working and labouring classes, particularly servants.[8] This fear of violence and civil unrest and suspicion of the danger of the uneducated mind in the relative freedom of Upper-Canadian society were to provide fertile ground for educational promoters. The equation of ignorance and vice, schooling and virtue, would appear in the arguments of spokesmen of various political hues throughout this period, for despite its overwhelmingly rural economy and setting, Upper-Canadian society was something of an anomoly. The emotional and intellectual tie of a preponderance of adult settlers with Britain contributed to a sophistication in social attitude which belied the homely setting. It is possible to identify a new state of mind in the colony in the 1830's and 1840's: in socio-economic terms, this new outlook could be attributed to a "middle class," in towns and cities defined occupationally in the range from artisan to professional, in the countryside more by prosperity.[9] However, occupational categories drawn from the twentieth century may not be particularly relevant to Upper Canada in the nineteenth century when the distinction between "blue collar" and "white collar," so critical today, was much less clear.[10] More suggestive, perhaps, are the pervasive images of commercial prosperity and expansiveness, which bound rural and urban settler alike in a commitment to "improvement." This commonality of sentiment, expressive of shared aspirations and anxieties, had its symbolic roots in the city, whose very vitality simultaneously exhilarated and appalled earnest Victorians. As the cause of a publicly supported, universal system of education gained momentum in Upper Canada after 1841, this "urban outlook" provided sufficient ground for a consensus favouring common school promotion to secure bipartisan support for school legislation by 1850.[11]

The problem of government support for common schools had reached crisis proportions by the mid 1830's mainly because it remained very much as it had in 1820. The inadequacy of the schools had become a commonplace. The basic administrative structure of elementary education had been established by the Common School Act of 1816 (56 George III, c. XXVI) and its amended versions in 1820 (I George IV, c. VII) and 1824 (4 George IV, c. VIII). While legislative pressure raised the government grant to £5,650 in 1833, there was no further revision of the school law until 1841. Finance and control were critical issues which, in the politically self-conscious 1830's, caused division both among and between Reformers and Tories, Assembly and Council. The financial basis for public education touched such questions as the possible misapplication by Strachan of the 1798 School Land Grant and the division of the clergy reserves, and was thus mired deeply in the main political conflict of the period. With the abolition of Strachan's Board of Education in 1833, control over common school affairs continued to be exercised informally, but practically, by the Council of King's College.[12] Again, political lines were drawn as the issue of appointment *v* election in school affairs provided a test case for the general principle of democratic participation and local responsibility. Thus throughout the 1830's the reports of the legislative select committees on education mirrored the dominant political complexion of the Assembly. The repeated efforts of Tory-weighted committees, ably chaired by the moderate Mahlon Burwell, to augment government grants, voluntary subscriptions, and fees by property assessment were conscientiously resisted by the Reformers, whose wariness of taxation caused them to press for a grant of 1,000,000 acres from the Crown Reserves. Such was the strength of Reform hopes that even farsighted Ryerson, perhaps to his subsequent embarrassment, could only give a nodding acknowledgment to the equitableness of property taxation before asking whether there might not be a sufficient quantity of school lands and, if it came to that, might not bank stock be taxed as well.[13] The goal of Reform administrative proposals was to place "the direction of education in the hands of those who are personally interested."[14] Consequently, a proposal such as Burwell's to give the appointment of a general board and district boards of education to the governor was "radically objectionable. It makes the system of education in theory a mere engine of the Executive, and liable to all the abuse, suspicion, jealousy and opposition of despotism; and withholds from the system of Common School education in its first and prominent feature that character of common interest and harmonious cooperation which . . . are essential to its success, and even to its acceptance with the province."[15] Most of the annual efforts in aid of education in these years were lost in Assembly wrangling. However, when in March 1835 a bill to promote education finally passed the Assembly, the Legislative Council rejected its democratic features on the grounds that a town meeting was not "a proper place to select those who are to preside over the morals and intellectual improvement of the rising generation; such superintendents ought to be persons of competent education and moral worth, or they cannot discharge the duties of their office."[16]

As the pressure for a solution to the educational stalemate mounted, the Reform Assembly in April 1835 authorized three commissioners to "obtain information respecting the system and government of schools and colleges." Dr. Charles Duncombe, on behalf of the commissioners, went to the United States and reported his findings, along with a draft bill for the regulation of the common schools, in February 1836. As a member of select committees on education, 1831-6, Duncombe was representative of the men whose interest and concern had led the Assembly efforts in the cause of education in these years. He has traditionally been portrayed as particularly typical of Reform interest in education, especially in his study of American practices. It is frequently maintained that in contrast to Strachan, who knew only too well what he wanted in an educational system, the Reform party was indecisive, united only in opposition and in having an attachment to such American features as elected trustees.[17]

In point of fact Duncombe was not particularly impressed by what he saw on his visit to the United States: in his view the Americans were "equally destitute of a system of National Education."[18] Furthermore, the radicalism of his political views, expressed especially in his support of Mackenzie up to and including the rebellion, has tended to obscure the conservatism inherent in his blueprint for social policy. Indeed, his enthusiasms reveal a model educational promoter. The overriding justification for government support for a common school system, Duncombe argued, lay in the necessity for "ensuring the welfare and safety of the Government": "the great crisis is hastening on when it shall be decided whether disenthralled intellect and liberty shall voluntarily submit to the laws of virtue and of Heaven, or run wild to insubordination, anarchy and crime." Preoccupied with the consequences, for the individual and society, of the new political and economic conditions in Upper Canada and throughout the world, Duncombe saw relief in the disciplining potential of public education: "whatever may have been the state of things heretofore, it is criminal to acquire knowledge merely for the sake of knowledge. The man must be disciplined and furnished according to the duties that lie before him."

Now Charles Duncombe was very likely what Hodgins and history have made him out to be, illustrative of Reform interest in education. However, there are two dangers in generalizing about proposals such as he offered in terms of American models. One can be tempted to make an analogy to a dubious interpretation of American educational development in this period in terms of a democratic impulse.[19] Moreover, one can overlook the extent to which Duncombe's commission, his preoccupation and recommendations, both continued and extended the argument for public education.

The fact that Duncombe not only reported on schools in the United States separately, but also on lunatic asylums and on prisons and penitentiaries is immensely suggestive, not only of the analogies drawn by legislative minds circa 1835, but of the kinds of concerns which public education might be expected to meet.[20] Ignorance, vice, crime, poverty, drunkenness, and lunacy comprised the staples of nineteenth-century social reform. The possible combinations and progressions of these elements – ignorance and crime; ignorance, vice, lunacy; crime, drunkenness, poverty (but not so commonly, poverty, ignorance, crime) – contributed to a "package" approach to social problems. Thus the century abounded with new theories and practices in penal discipline, more imaginative efforts in the treatment of mental illness, rational schemes for the support of the indigent and dependent population, and plans for public educational systems. Duncombe's three reports together detail the current state of American opinion and practice in crucial areas of reform effort. Further, what their very coexistence suggests, their arguments and recommendations make explicit: Duncombe saw in Upper-Canadian society the same social problems which in a more urbanized milieu, such as the northeastern United States, were critical. The undoubted discrepancy in the stages of development of the two societies lends to Duncombe's reports, in hindsight, the air of a preview, for much of their concern would be repeated over the next half century as Canadian society caught up with where New England and New York had been. But for Duncombe, his recommendations were not a preview: he saw, or thought he saw, the problems already, although they were not the kind which would reach serious proportions in a rural and agricultural society.

Juvenile delinquents, for example: "a class whose increasing numbers and deplorable situation loudly calls for more effective interposition, and the benevolent interference of the legislature."[21] This was not the inevitable lawlessness of a sparsely settled, highly mobile society. This was a problem endemic to town and city life, the product in large part of the state of landless poverty upon which urban society perched. "Every person that frequents the streets of this city [Toronto] must be forcibly struck with the ragged and uncleanly appearance, the vile language, and the idle and miserable habits of numbers of children, most of whom are of an age suitable for schools, or for some useful employment. The parents of these children are, in all probability, too poor, or too degenerate to provide them with clothing fit for them to be seen in at school; and know not where to place them in order that they may find employment, or be better cared for." The plight of these children undermined popularly held theories of moral culpability. "Accustomed, in many instances, to witness at home nothing in the way of example, but what is degrading; early taught to observe intemperance, and to hear obscene and profane language without disgust; obliged to beg, and even encouraged to acts of dishonesty to satisfy the wants induced by the indolence of their parents—what can be expected, but that such children will in due time, become responsible to the laws for crimes, which have thus, in a manner, been forced upon them?" As convicted offenders, juveniles presented a test case to penal critics, like Duncombe, who would advocate the centrality of reformation in penal discipline. Such children, "pitiable victims of neglect and wretchedness," should be placed under special guardianship, and rescued "from the melancholy fate which almost inevitably results from an apprenticeship in our common prisons." And most importantly, the vicious cycle of ignorance and crime, the awful progression from youthful to adult criminality, provided proof of the urgent need for a common school system.[22] With his statistics from Sing Sing prison, Duncombe started a fashion for quoting jail statistics which would flourish among educational promoters in Upper Canada for generations. This emphasis on the relation of public schooling to crime prevention, so useful in gaining the support of property owners reluctant to bear a tax burden, also communicates a value judgement implicit in the common school movement: the public school as a moral agency. Moreover, one particularly directed toward a class of persons who need the ministering of the school, particularly as compensation for the inadequacies of their "natural" family. Thus, in its beginnings at least, a common school system was an institution established and supported by one group of people, not for their own children, but for the children of others. The Tory image of public schooling as a philanthropy was one which liberal-minded nineteenth-century educational promoters worked hard to dispel by the rhetorical use of "common" school in the sense of "universal." The reasons they gave for supporting a school system, however, suggest their sensitivity to social distinctions as well as to semantic niceties.

In the light of his conviction of the uses of public education, and his well-informed acquaintance with American practices, Duncombe's particular pedagogical proposals are straightforward. He emphasizes the moral and religious aspects of the curriculum (to the point of preferring sectarian separate schools to the exclusion of religion), the inductive method, and the establishment of normal schools – the whole to be improved by a greater stringency in inspection to bolster the "responsible *profession* of teaching." On the issue of finance, the need was overriding: "our schools want in character, they want respectability, they want permanency in their character and in their support; their funds should be sufficient to interest all classes of the community in endeavouring to avail themselves of them; but whatever the amount should be, it should not be subject to any contingency as an annual vote of the Legislature."[23] By an accompanying bill, Duncombe proposed, by dividing the School Grant, to use it as an incentive to local tax support: one half would be paid to each district in proportion to the number of school-age children; the other on the basis of money collected by voluntary assessment, not exceeding one penny in the pound. In the matter of control, the bill's provisions very much expressed the democratic sentiment of Buell's bill of 1831: three commissioners were to be elected at the annual town meeting and would exert effective control over examining and hiring teachers and choosing school sites. In all, as a solution to the educational stalemate, Duncombe proposed to advance Reform efforts to democratize the administration of public affairs at the same time as he breached their resistance to taxation with a compromise of grant and assessment support.

Duncombe's bill passed the Assembly, but was rejected by a select committee of the Legislative Council on the pretext of lateness in the session. In giving a brief statement of their objections, concerned primarily with the "too complicated machinery" for administration, the committee did endorse the principle of an "assessment levied upon each District in support of the schools within the same, equal to the allowance given by the Government."[24] After the summer election of 1836, Mahlon Burwell renewed his proposals for a permanent Common School Fund based on matching grant and assessment revenues. In 1838, very much the same bill passed the Assembly, only to be rejected by the Legislative Council primarily on the point of taxation. This defeat of a principle to which they had lent support previously does not necessarily represent a change of attitude on the part of the Tory councillors. Quite probably, with economic depression and post-Rebellion feelings running high, their point about the burden of education taxes at this particular moment was well-taken. In 1839, the first combined assault on the problem of finance saw the Assembly and Council join forces to petition for an appropriation of 1,000,000 acres of waste land for the support of Common schools. The bill passed in the Assembly, but apparently at such a late point that the Council could not act. The Assembly considered a bill authorizing an annual assessment; but perhaps as the land appropriation bill had failed, the matter was not pursued. Thus by 1839 the rigidity of political positions on the common school question appeared to have softened. The rebellion catastrophe and growing disapproval of government reprisals may well have contributed support to efforts to devise an educational system in terms broadly acceptable to an increasingly vocal element urging its provision.

Sir George Arthur's commission of inquiry into the state of affairs in the colony in 1839 included the state of education and its possible improvement. The three education commissioners–the Rev. John McCaul, the Rev. H. J. Grasett, and S. B. Harrison–form a curious trio: the headmaster of Upper Canada College and future president of the University of Toronto; a prominent evangelical cleric and dean of St. James; and an influential moderate reformer and Sydenham's provincial secretary. Two were members of Ryerson's first Board of Education in 1846 and all three members of its successor, the Council of Public Instruction. That they appear to have shared decidedly Tory views on education should caution against a too facile importing of political categories to the educational debate.[25] In many ways the commission's report was out of date before it was tabled in February 1840.[26] Lord Durham had already roundly, if briefly, denounced the educational provisions in Upper Canada. Moreover, Sydenham's style would end the reign of Tory interests which the commission report assumed. Nevertheless, despite its impotence in initiating a policy, the report does illustrate widely held opinions about a common school system, many of which, slightly modified, would shape the legislation of the 1840's.

Although they deplored the state of education, the commissioners found no fault worthy of mention in the basic design of the school system established in 1816. What was wanting in their view was an efficient application of Strachan's blueprint: a monolithic, government-controlled system would ensure uniform provision, proper teacher training, and sound financial support. A government-appointed Board of Commissioners for common schools would license teachers, choose textbooks, and generally regulate; the salaried inspector-general would oversee the daily operations of both common and grammar schools. District trustees, nominated by the governor, would co-ordinate boards of township directors of schools elected by the shareholders of each school who were to have formed a joint stock association to build and maintain the schools. As the Rev. Robert Murray, soon to be the first assistant superintendent of education, Canada West (1842-4), observed to the commission, teachers were to be rescued from the present "system of gross oppression" by uneducated local trustees.

An improvement in the quality and condition of teachers appeared the first step in improving the state of the common schools. It was thought rather unfortunate that the wages of the working classes were so high, for "the income of the schoolmaster should at least be equal to that of a common labourer." However, teachers' wages could be stabilized if a tax of three farthings in the pound complemented the annual parliamentary grant to provide a school fund sufficient to assure a fixed allowance to teachers of £15 per annum. This would then be supplemented by tuition fees. In the debate over finance by endowment or assessment, a third source of revenue – the direct fees of children attending school – appeared insignificant by comparison. Traditionally devoted to teachers' wages, the propriety of tuition fees had never been seriously questioned. Very much in the tradition of the poor laws, the commission would exempt indigent householders and even whole townships from the assessment regulations, and a selected number of pauper children, registered as such, were to be accepted at school free of charge. However, for the rest, the commission was very impressed by the importance of a charge for the education "even of the humblest classes of society"; their suggested fee, however, was "two dollars per quarter." Mahlon Burwell, although no longer representing London in the Assembly, had briefed the commission on his views on tuition fees: "charges of tuition fee . . . are absolutely necessary to arrest and keep enduring the attention of parents to the interests and well working of Common Schools, and should never be dispensed with, but in such cases of indigent parents as the Trustees of Common Schools might, on account of indigence alone, direct that their children should be taught gratuitously." The moderateness of Burwell's conservatism is striking; apparently his support for a common school system of education soundly financed and reasonably controlled (although with a substantial edge in favour of the governor) made him appear to his friends as "too democratic." It is of some interest in a reassessment of Strachan's position that he regarded Burwell's bill to be "on the whole, by far the best measure for the establishment of Common Schools which I have yet seen."[27] That Burwell's attitude on taxation and fees was as moderate as any in the legislature at this time illustrates the distance the debate would travel under Union.

Up to 1841, both the administrative and financial basis for the common school system depended on the increasingly inadequate working of the machinery of local government. The 1841 Common School Act, based largely on Duncombe's Report, applied to the united province. Despite the advantage of the 1841 District Municipal Act, it floundered in Upper Canada partly because the new councils were hampered by existing limitations of an assessment of two pence in the pound. The assessment provisions of the Act were comparable to what had been proposed in the late 1830's; however, the procedure proved to be too complicated. The general inadequacy of the 1841 Act meant a temporary continuation of chaos; but a systemization of education was in the air once the administrative and financial super-structure had been built. Francis Hincks' Act of 1843 (7 Vict. c. XXIX) was a major test of the Reform position. While Murray, the incumbent superintendent, deplored his lack of power to effect any measure of uniformity, he quite rightly sensed his position would not be improved by the Reformers, for there existed "in certain quarters a deep-rooted jealousy of such power being committed to one man."[28] Although the 1843 Act substituted assistant superintendents for each section of the province, for the unified superintendency it abolished, it gave the power of supervision to County Superintendents appointed by the court of Wardens for the county. Commenting on his bill, Hincks noted, "in framing this system . . . you will observe that, as in all other instances, the late Ministry have divested the grant of all local patronage. Everything has been left to the people themselves; and I feel perfectly convinced that they will prove themselves capable of managing their own affairs in a more satisfactory manner than any Government Boards of Education or visiting Superintendents could do for them."[29] With the principle of property assessment, Hincks and the reformers were on less sure ground than in their "democratization" of control. Hincks acknowledged that opposition to taxation was widespread and popular: "I know that a prejudice exists against the tax; but it is merely from prejudice and ignorance of its effect. The tax is for the benefit of the resident settlers. The higher the tax, the lower will be the Rate-Bill on the parents. A portion of the tax falls on the non-Residents, on the rich, on those who have no children; therefore, it is for the interest of the people to have the tax as high as the law allows."

The question of the nature of the opposition to property taxation for school support is particularly confused because the contemporary rhetoric of school promotion stereotyped certain sources of opposition and minimized others. Since the issue was not fully resolved until compulsory free elementary schooling was enacted in 1871, debate continued throughout most of Ryerson's superintendency. Unfortunately, the historian's task has not been helped by the assiduous efforts of Hodgins in the *Documentary History* to ensure an interpretation consistent with Ryerson's "achievement." Clearly, opposition to and support for the assessment principle appears sufficiently heterogeneous to preclude simple economic or political polarities, such as Reform *v* Conservative, rich *v* poor. As the 1843 Act shows, the Reform leadership had swung firmly behind the taxation clause.[30] Both John Roblin and Baldwin argued on the second reading that the rich man must be made to see that although he was taxed the most, he benefited the most from an "intelligent, orderly population around him."[31] The emphasis placed on the rich man in the stock arguments over taxation suggests that these pleas are intended to persuade the rich to stop objecting – certainly that is Hodgins' gloss. However, Hincks' remarks indicate the opposition was popular: emphasis on the rich bearing the tax burden could as well be interpreted as aimed at placating protesting middle and lower-middle income groups with visions of the groaning rich. Certainly it would be illuminating to know just how far down the income scale identification with the expression "rich man" stopped – where the point of perceived benefit met a sense of burden.

What seems clear is that support for taxation was allied with a held conviction of the value of education. The apathy toward schooling characteristic of the back townships had been confirmed by years of nothing but local initiative in school maintenance. But settlement, and fears of republicanism and the undesirable influence American teachers could exercise over the youth of the colony, increased interest in education and provided a common theme to the literature of petitions and local school reports. The urgency with which those concerned with fostering loyalty to Britain, especially after 1837, sought to resolve the problem of alien teachers and American textbooks displays a willingness on the part of the more prosperous element in society, rural and urban, to turn to public education as a means of social control. It is this fear of a motley of Americanism, civil disorder, ignorance, and the lower classes generally in an increasingly socially differentiated society which provided the mainspring of middle-class support for education and willingness to assume the burden of taxation for something with which it felt personally unconnected, other people's children. The alternatives were clearly drawn: "unless the provision for the support of education is made certain and permanent, this great country must rapidly sink deeper and deeper in ignorance and vice. No man possessed of property in this Province, who attends for a little to the state of ignorance which pervades the great mass of the many thousands who are annually settled among us, and the ignorance in which our native youth are growing up around us could hesitate for a moment to pay any reasonable tax for the support of education, as he would thereby be increasing the value of his estate, and securing himself and his posterity in the possession of it."[32] In values and attitudes, prosperity brought a common conservatism to those Upper Canadians who benefited from it; and a common fear of the undisciplined and uneducated mind. Egerton Ryerson, as a member of that group and spokesman for its attitudes, argued for a common school system in precisely the terms which would ensure its general acceptance.

Ryerson's various roles as Methodist, educator, and polemicist bear the stamp of his essentially conservative social and political philosophy.[33] Moreover, as he made disarmingly clear to Sydenham, he very much regarded his own opinions, "superficial or well-considered," to be "such as any common sense practical man, whose connections and associations and feelings are involved in the happiness and well being of the middle classes of society, might be expected to entertain."[34] An early and strong commitment to "Canadianism" was one of Ryerson's most remarkable traits, with significance for both church and educational history. His preoccupation with adapting educational practices to the "civil and social institutions, and society and essential interest" of Upper Canada counterpoints struggles within Methodism.[35] Hodgins described the chief outlines of the school system to an American audience in 1855 as "identical with those of other countries, but in its adaptation to the wants of the country and the genius of the people, it is essentially Canadian."[36] The undue emphasis since placed on the identity of common features has somewhat obscured the seriousness of Ryerson's intention. Certainly the search for American models for the origins of aspects of Canadian education has been encouraged by the widespread tendency of nineteenth-century Canadian writers to build their case on quotations. Ryerson was no exception; his annual reports as chief superintendent are larded with excerpts from American and European educators and detailed explanations of their practices. Horace Mann, secretary of the Massachusetts Board of Education, 1837-48, was a favourite to whom he acknowledged, "you will perceive from my Report how largely I have availed myself of your observations on European schools, and how fully I concur with you in opinions as to the merits of the Government authorized methods of teaching."[37] As he admits, in regard to teacher training as with so much of his educational thinking, Ryerson shows a striking similarity to Mann. *The Journal of Education*, tours of school conventions, and the very rhetoric of his argument seem to reveal his debt. However, much of the quotation at least was calculated effect. As Ryerson confided to Draper, "in pointing out *defects* in systems of instruction and modes of teaching I have almost invariably quoted *American* authors – and have thus *incidentally* exposed the defects of almost every part of the American system, and have *practically* shown that every redeeming feature of the American School System has been, or is being borrowed from European Governments. I have also quoted the same authorities on almost every point most likely to be objected to by radical writers or partisans."[38] The broad similarity in tactic and argument derives from a similarity in roles: Ryerson, Mann, Henry Barnard of Connecticut – all were self-conscious educational promoters. They agreed on many features of a public school system because they shared much the same social philosophy and, as a consequence, a similar belief that for a school system to be effective as an instrument of social policy, a concept of public education must be woven into the fabric of a society.

To see in the common school system an instrument for forging a national identity was almost commonplace in the nineteenth century. Ryerson's "Canadianism" was a qualified one, however; he saw the school system rendering "this Country British in domestic feeling, as I think it now is intentionally at least in loyalty."[39] His role in defence of Metcalfe in 1844 accentuated his sense of mission. As he reminded Higginson from France in 1845, his "leading idea" was "not only to impart to the public mind the greatest amount of useful knowledge based upon, and interwoven throughout, with sound Christian principle, but to render the Educational System, in its various ramifications and applications, the indirect, but powerful instrument of British Constitutional Government."[40] This enthusiasm, fed by the events of the intervening decades, had carried Ryerson far from his youthful suspicion of the danger involved in a "system of education in theory a mere engine of the Executive."[41] Now he saw "much of importance in respect to Canada" in how Louis Philippe solved the problem "of governing a restless people upon ever popular principles and yet strengthening the Throne." His interest in the French system was absorbed by "the peculiar connection of the whole system with, and its influence upon, the thinkings and feelings of the public mind and the other various parts of its Governmental machinery, combining to produce the general results, and the connection of these with other branches of public policy."[42] Ryerson's professed "leading idea" explains the particular vigour with which he assailed American textbooks in the first months of his appointment. "Anti-British in every sense of the word," such books were "one element of powerful influence against the established Government of the Country."[43] Because he believed there to be a correlation, geographically, between the heavy use of American textbooks and support for the 1837 rebellion, their sinister influence, "silent and imperceptible in its operation," was to be countered by the immediate and widespread adoption of Irish National textbooks.[44] American teachers were not as dangerous, although they had been proscribed by the alien clauses of the 1843 and 1846 Acts.[45] Sensing public opinion against repeal, Ryerson waited until 1848 to drop the restriction on alien teachers.[46]

Non-denominational Protestantism could provide a common faith on which to rest the shared loyalty basic to a national consciousness.[47] Certainly Ryerson's commitment to a belief in the non-sectarian character of Christianity in the common schools was both consistent and firm: "Christianity – the Christianity of the Bible – regardless of the peculiarities of Sects, or Parties is to be the basis of our System of Public Instruction, as it is of our Civil Constitution."[48] Ironically, Ryerson's innumerable public hassles with various political and religious critics complemented an attempt to isolate the school and the very subject of education from religious sectarianism and political debate. The key word was *harmony*. In the field, district wardens were to be alert to the possibility that controversy might "disturb the harmony, or weaken the energy of united action in the work of educational instruction."[49] Centrally, the Education Office would operate "in such a way as will contribute most to the harmony and wishes of the community."[50] Thus, not only would neighbours find common cause in local school affairs, but, hopefully, a shared recognition of the value of the school system as a whole would span the gulfs of nationality, religion, location, occupation – and class – which divided Upper Canadians.[51] Finally, the school experience itself would contribute by its "commonness" – that elusive ideal of universality to which educational promoters clung while never dreaming of sending their own children to the public school. Something of this lies behind Ryerson's growing disapproval of the separate school idea.[52] He sincerely believed that "all that is essential to the moral interests of youth may be taught in what are termed Mixed Schools."[53] As the issue of Roman Catholic schools blossomed from a protection for minority rights to a full-scale challenge to the public system, Ryerson feared the consequences of the social isolation of Irish Catholic urban poor who by and large comprised the separate school population. The inferiority of their schools could well perpetuate their position of social inferiority: "it is to be feared that many children set off and assigned to the separate school suffer serious disadvantages in comparison with other children residing in the same neighbourhoods;–apart from the disadvantage of their isolation, the salutary influence of the emulation and energy which arises from pursuing the same studies in connection with the youths of other classes in the community, and with whom they are to act and associate in future life."[54] Similarly, with "the masses" generally. The main system once established, Ryerson directed his campaigns against parental apathy and neglect of children's schooling at points progressively lower on the social scale. His comprehensive view of public education provided the mainspring: "not the mere acquisition of certain arts or of certain branches of knowledge, but that instruction and discipline which qualify and dispose the subjects of it for their appropriate duties and employments of life, as Christians, as persons for business and also as members of the civil community in which they live." Such a view offered no contradiction to an implicit acceptance of a hierarchically ordered society. Education, like the Bible, should be universal property; but although he would extend its reach, even by compulsion, to the lowest levels of society, Ryerson very much regarded the organization of the school system as adapting to "the wants of the several classes of the community . . . their respective employments or professions."[55]

The common school system was clearly for the poorer classes who "need the assistance of the Government, and . . . are the proper subjects of their special solicitude and care"; the rich, with grammar schools and more, "can take care of themselves."[56] It seemed not to matter to men such as Ryerson that the story they repeated of the sons of the manufacturer and the door keeper sitting side by side was apocryphal, for neither they nor their friends sent their boys to the common school.[57] The idea of harmony between social classes, not of an end to social classes, provided the story's appeal. Thus, with a mid-Victorian's strong sense of property, Ryerson promoted public education to accomplish the tasks for which the social conservative would instinctively use it: to prevent pauperism, crime, vice, ignorance and to contribute to the increased productivity of the labour force.[58] The fear and concern of the middle class for the consequences of the transformation the colony was experiencing were to be answered by an educational system which would neutralize its potential for social disruption. The heavy influx of famine Irish in 1847 merely made the position of the common school system unassailable. Estimating an addition, in one year, of destitute immigrants equal to nearly one-sixth of the total resident population, Ryerson could warn Upper Canadians that "the physical disease and death which have accompanied their influx among us may be the precursor of the worse pestilence of social insubordination and disorder." Congregations of ignorant, poverty-stricken immigrants in towns and cities animated the pictures of slums and pauperism which educational promoters had been painting; it appeared obvious that, without schools, Irish children would perpetuate racial behaviour patterns and grow up "in the idleness and pauperism, not to say mendicity and vices of their forefathers."[59]

There seemed no doubt in 1846 that a province-wide common school system would have to be imposed on Upper Canada. Certainly Ryerson was resigned to spending much of the next two or three years promoting it in the districts, "in many cases again and again."[60] However, his basic conviction "that a system of public instruction should be in harmony with the views and feelings of the great body of the people, especially of the better educated classes,"[61] elicited increasing response from the urban and rural middle classes. The debate on the proper financial support for the common school system is indicative of this growing support. That the debate had advanced significantly in the five years since the Union is clear when one contrasts the Hincks' Bill (7 Vict., c. XXIX, 1843) with that which Draper introduced three years later. The 1843 Act provided for the government grant to be at least matched, but not more than doubled, by district, city, and town councils authorizing an assessment on all rateable property, the balance of the teachers' salaries to be supplied by an additional rate bill imposed on all parents of school children by the local school trustees. The Act made optional provision for "free" schools in cities or towns only. Ryerson suggested the rate bill be abolished entirely. In the draft of the 1846 Common School bill presented to the Assembly, the obligations of district councils to levy an assessment to equal the government grant were similar to those of 1843. In addition, however, local school trustees had the duty of levying rates on the property of all inhabitants equal to the aggregate sum received from the legislative grant and the district levy, in the place of the rate bill against the parents.[62] In Ryerson's opinion these provisions were crucial. The rate bill was a form of discrimination; it meant that poor parents withdrew their children from the school so as not to be billed for its support. He felt the case was incontestable: "Education is a public good; ignorance is a public evil. What affects the public ought to be binding upon each individual composing it. In every good government, and in every good system, the interests of the whole society are obligatory upon each member of it."[63] At the same time, however, he forecast the opposition of "the rich, and the childless, and the selfish." Draper stoutly defended the proposed section in committee on the principle that "all should possess every facility of education, and that those who possess property should assist and pay for the education of the children of their poorer neighbours; and thus raise the lower classes in the scale of moral and intellectual beings."[64] But despite the frankness of his appeal, he "was well beaten"; the rate bill was reintroduced.[65]

Ryerson thought he saw the villain. Writing to urge Draper not to give up the assessment clause, "above all others . . . the *poor man's* clause, and at the very foundation of a system of public education," Ryerson complained of objections

by precisely the class of persons – or rather by the individuals that I expected. I have heard one rich *man* objecting to it – a Methodist – a magistrate – a man who educates his own children at College and in Ladies' Seminaries – but who looks not beyond his own family. He says, I am told, "he does not wish to be compelled to educate *all the brats* in the neighbourhood." Now to educate "all the brats" in every neighbourhood is the very object of this clause of the bill; and in order to do so, it is proposed to *compel* selfish rich men to do what they ought to do, but what they will not do voluntarily.[66]

By November he was more specific: "Mr. Robert Baldwin and his friends, and some Members on the opposite side of the House of Assembly, united to oppose this clause of the Bill, and it was lost."[67]

In trying to assess the significance of Baldwin's opposition to the extension of the very principle which he had supported since 1841, one is involved in the question of the degree to which antipathy to Ryerson personally influenced the educational debate. Political feeling ran high in the debate on the school bill. Price challenged Draper as to whether Ryerson, rumoured to be attempting to introduce the "Prussian system of education" into Canada, had really drafted the bill.[68] Ryerson's salary and his close working relationship with Draper provided Reform spokesmen with easy targets.[69] But even Ryerson felt he "could not have imagined that so much party feeling would be brought to the consideration of such a subject."[70] Significantly, Baldwin justified his opposition to the free school idea on the grounds that "it was better to make the parents pay something for the benefit they receive, and then they would be more interested in the school."[71] The class implications of the "incentive" argument appealed particularly to those well established in prosperity who, convinced of their social responsibilities, nevertheless distrusted the intelligence and morality of their charges. Baldwin's personal reservations on this point may well have been such as to combine easily with the general Reform politicking over the bill. Behind the formal legislative opposition of such Reform leaders as Baldwin and J. H. Price, Ryerson perceived real resistance: "it is from the class of the community which they represent, or are identified with, that the only difficulties in carrying into effect an efficient system emanate."[72] The anticipated objections of the "independent yeomanry of the country" suggest part of this opposition. "Many individuals desire to give their children a better education than can be obtained in common schools, who can ill afford it."[73] To those straining for a foot in the door of a grammar or private school, a common school tax added to such school fees would be "very oppressive." Here was Ryerson's mission field: some could be placated by a common school sufficiently improved by trained teachers and "systematization" to which they could send their own children free; "the more affluent," "the intelligent portion of the people," could be convinced of the wisdom of educating other people's children.[74]

The Reformers diligently stirred up opposition to Ryerson, the school system, and free schools when the 1847 school bill made free schooling compulsory in cities and towns. Obviously urban mechanics and artisans were thought to be sympathetic to arguments about the infringement by compulsory taxation of their parental right to pay for their own children's schooling. Editorials goaded the parents of common school youngsters with taunts of "pauper education" now that they no longer paid for themselves.[75] But the opposition was short-lived. In 1849 Malcolm Cameron's attempt to reverse the trend of systematization succeeded with a curiously garbled common school bill which actually received royal assent. However, at Ryerson's urging, Baldwin suspended the offending legislation before it could take effect, thus clearing the way for the major school legislation of 1850. As a gesture to the opposition of various district councils and the city of Toronto especially, where the schools were closed for the year 1848-9, Ryerson compromised on the parental rate bill. But while free schools remained optional until 1871, the cities and towns quickly capitulated, led by Toronto in 1851. Suspicion lingered, apparently, among the mechanics of Yorkville in 1852; but by then the Rev. John Roaf, whose extreme voluntaryism would keep resistance alive, was a minor voice.[76] Most of the Reformers – especially the Toronto leaders – had become free school supporters and educational promoters in their own right.[77]

There is no doubt that Ryerson was committed to the end of the rate bill for humanitarian as well as strategic reasons; he was conscious of the desire for schooling as well as of the need. However, his public arguments suggest something less than his full interest in the principle. He saw abolishing the rate bill as a step toward the goal of greater systematization. A trustee's rate bill, or assessment, upon all the inhabitants of a school section would be "a second edition of the school tax imposed by the District Council." "After a year or two," the whole school tax would be consolidated into a "District Fund to pay teach [*sic*] quarterly, the same as all public officers. You can then have a District Board – a gradation of teachers salaries – independence of teachers of local trustees, their appointment by and accountability to a more efficient tribunal – the whole receiving a common direction and a common stamp from the Government."[78] The draft bill which Draper introduced was designed to ensure the "common stamp" much as the McCaul Commission had envisaged. Ryerson was critical of the 1843 Act, and the fragmenting of authority among local superintendents so jealously urged by Reformers, on the grounds it contravened the principle of responsible government: one responsibility, one authority.[79] His design balanced local and central control. District superintendents had considerable power to raise money and manage local operations; but the superintendent, advised by an appointed Board of Education, controlled the distribution of government grants, authorized textbooks, established the much sought-after normal school for training teachers, and devised regulations on general matters of school policy. The appointment of district superintendents by the Crown would ensure the vital link in communication. On this, however, Ryerson was defeated, and the existing provisions for appointment by district municipal councils remained in effect. That Ryerson did "not attach much importance to the clause" is indicative of the extent to which he had sufficient forces on his side.[80] Pressures for centralization came from within the common school system: already the cities were moving to consolidate, to grade the schools, and within the schools the classes.[81] Such hurrying toward the future aroused considerable opposition, among Reform sympathizers especially. Their instincts for localism and voluntaryism were offended by visions of "Prussian despotism."[82] Readers of the *Mirror* were warned to beware "the destructive snare of the Prussian saddlebag centralizer" and his "educational police system" whose local school inspectors were "detectives."[83] The Gore District Council memorialized the Legislature in November 1847 to have the School Act repealed as being without a redeeming feature: the system was unwieldy, the normal school unnecessary, the paying of superintendents extravagant. A realistic assessment of Upper-Canadian society indicated that the schools must remain very much the way they are, for teachers were either immigrants on their way to better things, or "those whose Physical Disabilities from age, render this mode of obtaining a livelihood the one suited to their Decaying Energies."[84]

But visions of the future were at the centre of the appeal which the common school system had for its supporters. Ryerson and the other "common sense practical" men concerned with the "well being of the middle classes of society" did not focus on the present for it was changing too quickly. The last twenty years had transformed Upper-Canadian society and the experience of this, combined with a Victorian's belief in progress, fostered impatience for tomorrow. No one could stand still. "How is the uneducated and unskilful man to succeed in these times of sharp and skilful competition and sleepless activity? And these times are but the commencement of a spirit of competition and enterprise in the country. The rising generation should, therefore, be educated not for Canada as it has been, or even now is, but for Canada as it is likely to be half a generation hence."[85] The United States tantalized with an image of what was to come: the people, the railways, the factories, and cities both exhilarated and appalled. If "the youth of the rural districts . . . are much behind the age," with education the rising generation might "be prepared, at least, to make some near approach to that place in the social scale, which their more intelligent, because better educated, neighbours, now threaten to monopolize."[86] Public apathy was the obstacle, "the deadliest enemy to improvement." But in responding to the educational needs of a growing community, a provincial system of common schools had time on its side. The attractions of localism and voluntaryism proved fragile barriers against the inroads of efficiency. Those who, with Ryerson, saw the common school as a force for social cohesion, a unifying tendency with which to counter the pluralism implicit in the increasing complexity of Upper-Canadian society, swelled the ranks of educational promoters.

An educational system is not like a school, a bank, or an industry, any one of which might be described in terms of one man's "achievement." Thus an overemphasis on Egerton Ryerson's long career as chief superintendent has distorted the extent to which the educational debate encompassed fundamental issues of social organization. Social, economic, and demographic circumstances had contrived by the 1840's to involve the aspirations of many Upper Canadians with the issue of public education. Thus the establishment of a common school system in 1846 bears witness to the pervasive influence of attitudes susceptible to the promises of an educational solution to social problems. From then on, the development and internal elaboration of the public school system would provide the middle class with their main strategy for meeting the problems of their changing society.

NOTES

1. See: J. S. Moir, *Church and State in Canada West* (Toronto, 1959).
2. Ellwood P. Cubberly, *Public Education in the United States* (Boston, rev. ed., 1934), and Charles E. Phillips, *The Development of Education in Canada* (Toronto, 1957), provide classic statements of the progressive view. For an overview of recent European work in this field, see: Gillian Sutherland, "The Study of the History of Education," *History*, LIV (1969), 49-59.
3. See Leroy Stone, *Urban Development in Canada* (Ottawa, 1967); Jacob Spelt, *The Urban Development in South-central Ontario* (Assen, 1955).

4. J. M. S. Careless, "Mid-Victorian Liberalism in Central Canadian Newspapers, 1850-67," *CHR*, XXXI, 3 (1950), 221-36.
5. F. H. Armstrong, "Toronto in Transition, 1828-1838" (Ph.D. thesis, University of Toronto, 1965); J. M. S. Careless, "Frontierism, Metropolitanism, and Canadian History," *CHR*, XXXV, 1 (1954), 1-21.
6. R. H. Bonnycastle, *Canada and the Canadians* (London, 1849), I, 195.
7. Mr. Speaker Bidwell in debate on the school bill, 30 March 1835, *Christian Guardian*, 8 April 1835.
8. Bonnycastle, *Canada and the Canadians,* I, 196.
9. J. S. Hogan, *Canada: An Essay* (Montreal, 1855), 27. Commenting on rural Upper-Canadian fashion, Hogan observed that "the coats of the men are indistinguishable from those worn by professional men and merchants in town."
10. See: M. B. Katz, *The Hamilton Project: Interim Reports, I & II* (Toronto, 1969, 1970); also, Peter Goheen, *Victorian Toronto, 1850-1900* (Chicago, 1970).
11. Support for common or elementary schooling, of course, carries no implications for support of educational facilities at other levels: Lawrence Stone, "Literacy and Education in England, 1640-1900," *Past and Present*, XLII (1969), 69-139.
12. J. George Hodgins, *Documentary History of Education in Upper Canada* [*DHE*] (Toronto, 1897), II, 15. Strachan was also president of the Council and much of the membership was overlapping.
13. *Christian Guardian*, 15 January 1834.
14. *Ibid.*, 7 December 1831.
15. *Ibid.*, 15 January 1834.
16. *DHE*, II, 198-9.
17. G. M. Craig, *Upper Canada: The Formative Years, 1784-1841* (Toronto, 1963), 198-9; Judson Purdy, "John Strachan and Education in Canada, 1800-1851" (Ph.D. thesis, University of Toronto, 1962), 108, 130-1. In a letter to Draper, 22 April 1846, Ryerson suggested that although Reform educational policy was deliberately modelled on American practices, the inevitable time lag rendered it always slightly passé: J. George Hodgins, ed., *Ryerson Memorial Volume* (Toronto, 1889), 77-8.
18. Upper Canada, *Journals* of the House of Assembly [*Journals*] (1836), App. 35, 64.
19. M. B. Katz, *The Irony of Early School Reform* (Cambridge, Mass., 1968).
20. *Journals* (1836), App. 30, 71.
21. *Ibid.*, App. 71, 4.
22. *Ibid.*, App. 35, 57-60.
23. *Ibid.*, 11.

24. *DHE*, II, 339.
25. PAO, Hodgins Papers, Ryerson to Draper, 14 May 1846, provides insight into the problems Ryerson perceived in securing membership on the Board of Education, which reflected the various religious denominations and at the same time preserved the necessary aura of social respectability.
26. *Report of the Committee on Education: Appendix to the Fifth Report of the General Board* (3 *Vic.* 1840). Also in *DHE*, III, 243-83.
27. *DHE*, III, Strachan's reply to the Commission's circular of inquiry, 12 December 1839, 267.
28. PAO, Education Office, Canada West, Letter Book A, Murray to P. Thornton, 28 March 1843, 239-40.
29. Francis Hincks, *Reminiscences of His Public Life* (Montreal, 1884), 175-7; quoted in *DHE*, IV, 242.
30. Apparently Baldwin's commitment to the taxation principle was strong as early as 1841: Egerton Ryerson, *Introductory Sketch of the System of Public Elementary Instruction in Upper Canada* (Toronto, 1851), 4-5.
31. *DHE*, IV, Report of the educational proceedings of the Legislature, 1843, 240.
32. PAO, Education Office, Letter Book A, Murray to Alex. McMillan, 12 April 1843, 251-2.
33. Historians at least are virtually unanimous in their assessment of Ryerson as a "conservative": Goldwin French, *Parsons and Politics* (Toronto, 1962), 103; Clara Thomas, *Ryerson of Upper Canada* (Toronto, 1969), 52; C. B. Sissons, *Egerton Ryerson: His Life and Letters* (Toronto, 1937), I, 3.
34. Sissons, *Ryerson*, I, Ryerson to Sydenham, 5 October 1840, 562.
35. "Observations made by the Rev. Egerton Ryerson at the commencement of the session, 1841, Victoria College," *Christian Guardian*, 3 November 1841. Both Goldwin French, *Parsons and Politics*, and G. W. Brown, *Canada in the Making* (Toronto, 1953), document the Canadian theme in the history of Methodism in Upper Canada in the first half of the nineteenth century.
36. J. G. Hodgins, "History and Systems of Education in Upper Canada, 1855," a paper read before the American Association for the Advancement of Education (New York, 1855).
37. *DHE*, VI, Ryerson to Horace Mann, 23 December 1846, 213.
38. PAO, Hodgins Papers, Ryerson to W. H. Draper, 30 March 1846.
39. *DHE*, V, Ryerson to Higginson, 8 March 1845, 108.
40. *DHE*, V, Ryerson to Higginson, 30 April 1845, 240.
41. *Christian Guardian*, 15 January 1834.
42. *DHE*, V, Ryerson to Higginson, 30 April 1845, 239.
43. Egerton Ryerson, *Special Report on the Measures which have been*

adopted for the Establishment of a Normal School and for Carrying into Effect Generally the Common School Act (Montreal, 1847), 14-5.

44. *DHE*, VII, Special Report on the operation of the Common School Act of 1846, 110-11.

45. The elimination of alien teachers prescribed by the 1843 act was to take effect on 1 January 1846. In the debate on the 1846 bill, Baldwin and Price tried to secure an extension of the right of aliens to teach until such time as the normal school was functioning. They lost.

46. *Copies of Correspondence Between Members of the Government and the Chief Superintendent of Schools on the Subject of the School Law for Upper Canada and Education Generally* (Toronto, 1850), Chief Superintendent to Hon. James Leslie, 14 October 1848.

47. *Annual Report of the Normal, Model, Grammar and Common School for 1851*, 19-21; see also, Timothy Smith, "Protestant Schooling and American Nationality, 1800-1850," *Journal of American History*, LIII (1967), 679-95.

48. *Copies of Correspondence*, Ryerson to Hon. D. Daly, 3 March 1846; also *DHE*, VI, 72.

49. *Circular* no. 3, Wardens of the District Municipal Councils, 1 October 1846.

50. Sissons, *Ryerson*, II, Ryerson to Rev. A. MacNab, 26 October 1844, 77.

51. Harmony provided Ryerson with an enduring cause. For example, "The tendencies of the age and all the institutions and enterprises of our country, are to co-operation and union among all classes of citizens, rather than to isolation and estrangement from each other": *Dr. Ryerson's Letters in Reply to the Attacks of the Hon. George Brown* (Toronto, 1859), 22.

52. Ryerson publicly regretted separate schools "on this account and almost on this account alone"; the isolation of Catholic children "from intellectual competitions and friendships with the other children of the land": *Annual Report*, 1857, 24.

53. *DHE*, VI, Report on a System of Public Elementary Instruction for Upper Canada 1846, 158.

54. *Annual Report*, 1855, 13.

55. *DHE*, VI, Report on a System of Public Elementary Instruction, 142.

56. *Ibid.*, 146. At a public meeting, 10 January 1852, the chairman of the Toronto Board of Trustees testified that his inspection of the common schools had revealed that the majority of the students were "those called poor classes . . . the respectable mechanics, small traders, the honest labourers of the city": Toronto Public School Board, *Report of the Past History and Present Condition of*

the Common or Public Schools of the City of Toronto (Toronto, 1859), 35.

57. *Ibid.*, Ryerson's speech, 10 January 1852, 36. In a letter to his daughter Sophie in 1862, Ryerson asks for help in persuading Charley to go to an English public school, in the footsteps of Judge Hagarty's boy. Sophie is to point out to her brother "how pleasant and useful it would be to him all his life": United Church Archives, Toronto, Ryerson, Letters to Sophie, 2-5 January 1862.

58. *DHE*, VI, Report on a System of Public Elementary Instruction, 143-5.

59. Egerton Ryerson, "The Importance of Education to a Manufacturing and a Free People," speech given on tour, fall 1847, *Journal of Education of Upper Canada* (October, 1848), 300.

60. Sissons, *Ryerson*, II, Ryerson to Rev. A. MacNab, 31 March 1845, 87-8.

61. *Annual Report*, 1851, 21.

62. PAO, Hodgins Papers, Draft of a Bill for the Better Establishment and Maintenance of Common Schools in Upper Canada (now slightly changed), 9 Vic., c. 20, Education Office West, March 1846, sec. XXVI, 5 and 6, 25.

63. *Copies of Correspondence*, Ryerson to Hon. D. Daly, 3 March 1846, 23.

64. *Mirror of Parliament of the Province of Canada, March 20-June 9, 1846* (Montreal, 1846), House of Assembly, 16 April 1846, 73.

65. PAO, Hodgins Papers, Draper to Ryerson, 22 April 1846. There is some disagreement as to how badly Draper was beaten as the vote has not been recorded. Ryerson used the phrase "by a small majority," which Hodgins interpreted as "a majority of four or five": PAO, Hodgins Papers, Remarks and Suggestions on the Common School Act, 7 Vic. c. XXIX, Accompanying a Draft of a Bill (now), 9 Vic. CXX, Education Office (West), 3 March 1846.

66. Sissons, *Ryerson*, II, Ryerson to Draper, 20 April 1846, 101.

67. *DHE*, VI, Ryerson to James Wallace, 9 November 1846, 291.

68. *Mirror of Parliament*, 69. Oddly, Draper insisted that it was his bill despite Ryerson having submitted a draft, 3 March 1846. That the measure was given first reading as an *amending* bill suggests that Ryerson might not have had such a *carte blanche* with educational legislation as commentators have assumed.

69. George Metcalfe, "Draper Conservatism and Responsible Government in the Canadas, 1836-1847," *CHR*, XLII, 4 (1961), 300-24.

70. PAO, Hodgins Papers, Ryerson to Draper, 30 April 1846.

71. *Mirror of Parliament*, 73.

72. PAO, Hodgins Papers, Ryerson to Draper, 14 May 1846.

73. *Mirror of Parliament*, 73.

74. *DHE*, VII, Hamnett Pinhey, warden of the Dalhousie District, to Ryerson, 7 February 1847, 128-9.

75. *Dundas Warder*, 12 May 1846. Robert Spence, editor, attacked Ryerson throughout 1847-8. Also, *Examiner*, Toronto, 10 May 1848.
76. *Globe*, Toronto, 31 January, 5, 17 February 1852.
77. For a discussion of the reversal of Reform policy on free schools in Toronto, see: Peter N. Ross, "Free Schools in Toronto, 1848-52" (unpublished ms., Ontario Institute for Studies in Education, 1968).
78. PAO, Hodgins Papers, Ryerson to Draper, 30 March 1846.
79. *DHE*, VI, Ryerson to Daly, 3 March 1846, 72.
80. PAO, Hodgins Papers, Ryerson to Draper, 30 April 1846.
81. *Copies of Correspondence*, Chief Superintendent to Hon. D. Daly, 20 March 1847, 25-9. Also, *Annual Report*, 1850, sec. 15.
82. For a report of the *Banner* and *British Colonist* charges, see *DHE*, VI, 214-15; also *Globe*, 6 January 1847; and *Examiner*, 29 April, 22 July, 12 November, 9 December 1846.
83. *Mirror*, Toronto, 12 May 1848.
84. *DHE*, VII, Memorial of the Gore District Council, 10 November 1847, 114-16.
85. Ryerson, "The Importance of Education," 300.
86. *DHE*, VII, Report of the Colborne District Council on the Gore Memorial, 116-18.

VI
Women

The new history is very new and its scope has been correspondingly narrowed. Sylvia Van Kirk deals with several of the still undeveloped areas of social history. The history of women has attracted a good deal of attention very recently but much of the first wave of feminist writings has been essentially political rather than social. The pre-settlement West has remained the domain of those interested in the fur trade and those romantically attracted to explorers. And, for the most part, historians have not seen the native peoples, at least not beyond Louis Riel. Van Kirk breaks new ground in all these areas. At the same time, some familiar bells are sounded. The role of Indian women in tribal politics and the fur trade echoes the discussions of lower-class culture we read in the essays by Fingard and Bleasdale. The subtleties of class relations, so confused by ethnicity, are as present on the Prairies as in colonial British North America. Sylvia Van Kirk demonstrates how the study of a small and relatively powerless group can connect into general and important questions.

FURTHER READING:
Sylvia Van Kirk has produced several articles on these themes, including: "The Impact of White Women on Fur Trade Society," in Susan Mann Trofimenkoff and Alison Prentice, eds., *The Neglected Majority* (Toronto, 1977), 27-48; and a book, *"Many Tender Ties": Women in Fur-Trade Society, 1760-1870* (Winnipeg, 1980). The standard work on the economy remains

H. A. Innis, *The Fur Trade in Canada* (New Haven, 1930). A stimulating later work is Arthur Ray's *Indians in the Fur Trade* (Toronto, 1974). Some of the better essays on women are to be found in Trofimenkoff and Prentice, eds., *The Neglected Majority*. A survey of the history of native peoples is E. Palmer Patterson, *The Canadian Indian: A History Since 1500* (Don Mills, 1972).

Sylvia Van Kirk is in the History Department at the University of Toronto.

"Women in Between": Indian Women in Fur Trade Society in Western Canada

by Sylvia Van Kirk

In attempting to analyse the life of the Indian woman in fur trade society in Western Canada, especially from her own point of view, one is immediately confronted by a challenging historiographical problem. Can the Indian woman's perspective be constructed from historical sources that were almost exclusively written by European men? Coming from a non-literate society, no Indian women have left us, for example, their views on the fur trade or their reasons for becoming traders' wives.[1] Yet if one amasses the sources available for fur trade social history, such as contemporary narratives, journals, correspondence, and wills, a surprisingly rich store of information on Indian women emerges. One must, of course, be wary of the traders' cultural and sexual bias, but then even modern anthropologists have difficulty maintaining complete objectivity. Furthermore the fur traders had the advantage of knowing Indian women intimately – these women became their wives, the mothers of their children. Narratives such as that of Andrew Graham in the late eighteenth century and David Thompson in the nineteenth, both of whom had native wives, comment perceptively on the implications of Indian-white social contact.[2] The key to constructing the Indian woman's perspective must lie in the kinds of questions applied to the data;[3] regrettably the picture will not be complete, but it is hoped that a careful reading of the traders' observations can result in a useful

From Canadian Historical Association, *Historical Papers* (1977), 30-46. Reprinted by permission.

and illuminating account of the Indian woman's life in fur trade society.

The fur trade was based on the complex interaction between two different racial groups. On the one hand are the various Indian tribes, most importantly the Ojibway, the Cree, and the Chipewyan. These Indians may be designated the "host" group in that they remain within their traditional environment. On the other hand are the European traders, the "visiting" group, who enter the Northwest by both the Hudson Bay and St. Lawrence-Great Lakes routes. They are significantly different from the Indians in that they constitute only a small, all-male fragment of their own society. For a variety of factors to be discussed, this created a unique situation for the Indian women. They became the "women in between" two groups of males. Because of their sex, Indian women were able to become an integral part of fur trade society in a sense that Indian men never could. As country wives[4] of the traders, Indian women lived substantially different lives when they moved within the forts. Even within the tribes, women who acted as allies of the whites can also be observed; certain circumstances permitted individual women to gain positions of influence and act as "social brokers" between the two groups.

It is a major contention of this study that Indian women themselves were active agents in the development of Indian-white relations.[5] A major concern then must be to determine what motivated their actions. Some themes to be discussed are the extent to which the Indian woman was able to utilize her position as "woman in between" to increase her influence and status, and the extent to which the Indian woman valued the economic advantage brought by the traders. It must be emphasized, however, that Indian-white relations were by no means static during the fur trade period.[6] After assessing the positive and negative aspects of the Indian woman's life in fur trade society, the paper will conclude by discussing the reasons for the demise of her position.

I

Miscegenation was the basic social fact of the western Canadian fur trade. That this was so indicates active co-operation on both sides. From the male perspective, both white and Indian, the formation of marital alliances between Indian women and the traders had its advantages. The European traders had both social and economic reasons for taking Indian mates. Not only did they fill the sexual void created by the absence of white women,[7] but they performed such valuable economic tasks as making moccasins and netting snowshoes that they became an integral if unofficial part of the fur trade work force.[8] The traders also realized that these alliances were useful in cementing trade ties; officers in both the Hudson's Bay and North West companies often married daughters of trading captains or chiefs.[9] From the Indian point of view, the marital alliance created a reciprocal social bond which served to consolidate his economic relationship with the trader. The exchange of women was common in Indian society where it was viewed as "a reciprocal alliance and series of good offices . . . between the friends of both parties; each is ready to assist and protect the other."[10] It was not loose morality or even hospitality which prompted the Indians to be so generous with their offers of women. This was their way of drawing the traders into their kinship circle, and in return for giving the traders sexual and domestic rights to their women, the Indians expected equitable privileges such as free access to the posts and provisions.[11] It is evident that the traders often did not understand the Indian concept of these alliances and a flagrant violation of Indian sensibilities could lead to retaliation such as the Henley House massacre in 1755.[12]

But what of the women themselves? Were they just pawns in this exchange, passive, exploited victims? Fur trade sources do not support this view; there are numerous examples of Indian women actively seeking to become connected with the traders. According to an early Nor'Wester, Cree women considered it an honour to be selected as wives by the voyageurs, and any husband who refused to lend his wife would be subject to the general condemnation of the women.[13] Alexander Ross observed that Chinook women on the Pacific coast showed a preference for living with a white man. If deserted by one husband, they would return to their tribe in a state of widowhood to await the opportunity of marrying another fur trader.[14] Nor'Wester Daniel Harmon voiced the widely held opinion that most of the Indian women were "better pleased to remain with the White People than with their own Relations," while his contemporary George Nelson affirmed "some too would even desert to live with the white."[15] Although Alexander Henry the Younger may have exaggerated his difficulties in fending off young Indian women, his personal experiences underline the fact that the women often took the initiative. On one occasion when travelling with his brigade in the summer of 1800, Henry was confronted in his tent by a handsome woman, dressed in her best finery, who told him boldly that she had come to live with him as she did not care for her husband or any other Indian. But Henry, anxious to avoid this entanglement partly because it was not sanctioned by the husband whom he knew to be insatiably jealous, forced the woman to return to her Indian partner.[16] A year or so later in the lower Red River district, the daughter of an Ojibway chief had more luck. Henry returned from New Year's festivities to find that "Liard's daughter" had taken possession of his room and "the devil could not have got her out."[17] This time, having become more acculturated to fur trade life, Henry acquiesced and "Liard's daughter" became his country wife. The trader, however, resisted his father-in-law's argument that he should also take his second daughter because all great men should have a plurality of wives.[18]

The fur traders also comment extensively on the assistance and loyalty of Indian women who remained within the tribes. An outstanding example is the young Chipewyan Thanadelthur, known to the traders as the "Slave Woman."[19] In the early eighteenth century after being captured by the Cree, Thanadelthur managed to escape to York Factory. Her knowledge of Chipewyan made her valuable to the traders, and in 1715-16, she led a Hudson's Bay Company (HBC) expedition to establish peace between the Cree and the Chipewyan, a necessary prelude to the founding of Fort Churchill. Governor James Knight's journals give us a vivid picture of this woman, of whom he declared: "She was one of a Very high Spirit and of the Firmest Resolution that ever I see any Body in my Days."[20]

Post journals contain numerous references to Indian women warning the traders of impending treachery. In 1797, Charles Chaboillez, having been warned by an old woman that the Indians intended to pillage his post, was able to nip this intrigue in the bud.[21] George Nelson and one of his men only escaped an attack by some Indians in 1805 by being "clandestinely assisted by the women."[22] It appears that women were particularly instrumental in saving the lives of the whites among the turbulent tribes of the lower Columbia.[23] One of the traders' most notable allies was the well-connected Chinook princess known as Lady Calpo, the wife of a Clatsop chief. In 1814, she helped restore peaceful relations after the Nor'Westers had suffered a raid on their canoes by giving them important information about Indian custom in settling disputes. Handsome rewards cemented her attachment to the traders with the result that Lady Calpo reputedly saved Fort George from several attacks by warning of the hostile plans of the Indians.[24]

The reasons for the Indian women's action are hinted at in the traders' observations. It was the generally held opinion of the traders that the status of women in Indian society was deplorably low. As Nor'Wester Gabriel Franchère summed it up:

> Some Indian tribes think that women have no souls, but die altogether like the brutes; others assign them a different paradise from that of men, which indeed they might have reason to prefer . . . unless their relative condition were to be ameliorated in the next world.[25]

Whether as "social brokers" or as wives, Indian women attempted to manipulate their position as "women in between" to increase their influence and status. Certainly women such as Thanadelthur and Lady Calpo were able to work themselves into positions of real power. It is rather paradoxical that in Thanadelthur's case it was her escape from captivity that brought her into contact with the traders in the first place; if she had not been a woman, she would never have been carried off by the Cree as a prize of war. Once inside the HBC fort, she was able to use her position as the only Chipewyan to advantage by acting as guide and consultant to the Governor. The protection and regard she was given by the whites enabled Thanadelthur to dictate to Indian men, both Cree and Chipewyan, in a manner they would not previously have tolerated. Anxious to promote the traders' interests, she assaulted an old Chipewyan on one occasion when he attempted to trade less than prime furs; she "ketcht him by the nose Push'd him backwards & call'd him fool and told him if they brought any but Such as they ware directed they would not be traded."[26] Thanadelthur did take a Chipewyan husband but was quite prepared to leave him if he would not accompany her on the arduous second journey she was planning to undertake for the Governor.[27] It is possible that the role played by Thanadelthur and subsequent "slave women" in establishing trade relations with the whites may have enhanced the status of Chipewyan women. Nearly a century later, Alexander Mackenzie noted that, in spite of their burdensome existence, Chipewyan women possessed "a very considerable influence in the traffic with Europeans."[28]

Lady Calpo retained a position of influence for a long time. When Governor Simpson visited Fort George in 1824, he found she had to be treated with respect because she was "the best News Monger in the Parish"; from her he learned "More of the Scandal, Secrets and politics both of the out & inside of the Fort than from Any other source."[29] Significantly, Lady Calpo endeavoured to further improve her rank by arranging a marriage alliance between the Governor and her carefully raised daughter. Although Simpson declared he wished "to keep clear of the Daughter," he succumbed in order "to continue on good terms with the Mother."[30] Many years later, a friend visiting the Columbia wrote to Simpson that Lady Calpo, that " 'fast friend' of the Whites," was still thriving.[31]

As wives of the traders, Indian women could also manoeuvre themselves into positions of influence. In fact, a somewhat perturbed discussion emerges in fur trade literature over the excessive influence some Indian women exerted over their fur trader husbands. The young North West Company (NWC) clerk George Nelson appears to have spent long hours contemplating the insoluble perplexities of womankind. Nelson claimed that initially Cree women when married to whites were incredibly attentive and submissive, but this did not last long. Once they had gained a little footing, they knew well "how to take advantage & what use they ought to make of it."[32] On one of his first trips into the interior, Nelson was considerably annoyed by the shenanigans of the Indian wife of Brunet, one of his voyageurs. A jealous, headstrong woman, she completely dominated her husband by a mixture of "caresses, promises & menaces." Not only did this woman render her husband a most unreliable servant, but Nelson also caught her helping herself to the Company's rum. Brunet's wife, Nelson fumed, was as great "a vixen & hussy" as the tinsmith's wife at the marketplace in Montreal: "I now began to think that women were women not only in civilized countries but elsewhere also."[33]

Another fur trader observed a paradoxical situation among the Chipewyan women. In their own society, they seemed condemned to a most servile existence, but upon becoming wives of the French-Canadian voyageurs, they assumed "an importance to themselves and instead of serving as formerly they exact submission from the descendants of the Gauls."[34] One of the most remarkable examples of a Chipewyan wife rising to prominence was the case of Madam Lamallice, the wife of the brigade guide at the HBC post on Lake Athabasca. During the difficult winter of 1820-21, Madam Lamallice was accorded a favoured position because she was the post's only interpreter and possessed considerable influence with the Indians.[35] George Simpson, then experiencing his first winter in the Indian Country, felt obliged to give in to her demands for extra rations and preferred treatment in order to prevent her defection. He had observed that the Nor'Westers' strong position was partly due to the fact that "their Women are faithful to their cause and good Interpreters whereas we have but one in the Fort that can talk Chipewyan."[36] Madam Lamallice exploited her position to such an extent that she even defied fort regulations by carrying on a private trade in provisions.[37] A few years later on a trip to the Columbia, Governor Simpson was annoyed to discover that Chinook women when married to the whites often gained such an ascendancy "that they give law to their Lords."[38] In fact, he expressed general concern about the influence of these "petticoat politicians" whose demands were "more injurious to the Companys interests that I am well able to describe."[39] The Governor deplored Chief Factor James Bird's management of Red River in the early 1820's because of his habit of discussing every matter "however trifling or important" with "his Copper Cold. Mate," who then spread the news freely around the colony.[40] Too many of his officers, Simpson declared, tended to sacrifice business for private interests. Particular expense and delay were occasioned in providing transport for families. Simpson never forgave Chief Factor John Clarke for abandoning some of the goods destined for Athabasca in 1820 to make a light canoe for his native wife and her servant.[41]

It is likely that Simpson's single-minded concern for business efficiency caused him to exaggerate the extent of the Indian women's influence. Nevertheless, they do seem to have attempted to take advantage of their unique position as women "in between" two groups of men. This fact is supported by the traders' observation that the choice of a husband, Indian or white, gave the Indian woman leverage to improve her lot. Now she could threaten to desert to the whites or vice-versa if she felt she were not being well-treated: "She has always enough of policy to insinuate how well off she was while living with the white people and in like manner when with the latter she drops some hints to the same purpose."[42] Although Chipewyan women who had lived with the voyageurs had to resume their former domestic tasks when they returned to their own people, they reputedly evinced a greater spirit of independence.[43] Considerable prestige accrued to Chinook women who had lived with the traders; upon rejoining the tribes, they remained "very friendly" to the whites and "never fail to influence their connections to the same effect."[44]

From the Indian woman's point of view, material advantage was closely tied to the question of improved influence or status. The women within the tribes had a vested interest in promoting cordial relations with the whites. While George Nelson mused that it was a universal maternal instinct which prompted the women to try to prevent clashes between Indian and white,[45] they were more likely motivated by practical, economic considerations. If the traders were driven from the country, the Indian woman would lose the source of European goods, which had revolutionized her life just as much if not more than that of the Indian man. It was much easier to boil water in a metal kettle than to have to laboriously heat it by means of dropping hot stones into a bark container. Cotton and woolen goods saved long hours of tanning hides. "Show them an awl or a strong needle," declared David Thompson, "and they will gladly give the finest Beaver or Wolf skin they have to purchase it."[46]

Furthermore, it can be argued that the tendency of the Indians to regard the fur trade post as a kind of welfare centre was of more relevance to the women than to the men. In times of scarcity, which were not infrequent in Indian society, the women were usually the first to suffer.[47] Whereas before they would often have perished, many now sought relief at the companies' posts. To cite but one of many examples: at Albany during the winter of 1706, Governor Beale gave shelter to three starving Cree women whose husband had sent them away as he could only provide for his two children.[48] The post was also a source of medical aid and succour. The story is told of a young Carrier woman in New Caledonia, who having been severely beaten by her husband managed to struggle to the nearest NWC post. Being nearly starved, she was slowly nursed back to health and allowed to remain at the post when it became apparent that her relatives had abandoned her.[49] The desire for European goods, coupled with the assistance to be found at the fur trade posts, helps to explain why Indian women often became devoted allies of the traders.

In becoming the actual wife of a fur trader, the Indian woman was offered even greater relief from the burdens of her traditional existence. In fact, marriage to a trader offered an alternative lifestyle. The fur traders themselves had no doubt that an Indian woman was much better off with a white man. The literature presents a dreary recital of their abhorrence of the degraded, slave-like position of the Indian woman. The life of a Cree woman, declared Alexander Mackenzie, was "an uninterrupted success of toil and pain."[50] Nor'Wester Duncan McGillivray decided that the rather singular lack of affection evinced by Plains Indian women for their mates arose from the barbarous treatment the women received.[51] Although David Thompson found the Chipewyan a good people in many ways, he considered their attitudes toward women a disgrace; he had known Chipewyan women to kill female infants as "an act of kindness" to spare them the hardships they would have to face.[52]

The extent to which the fur traders' observations represent an accurate reflection of the actual status of Indian women in their own societies presents a complex dilemma which requires deeper investigation. The cultural and class biases of the traders are obvious. Their horror at the toilsome burdens imposed upon Indian women stems from their narrow, chivalrous view of women as the "frail, weaker sex." This is scarcely an appropriate description of Indian women, particularly the Chipewyan who were acknowledged to be twice as strong as their male counterparts.[53] Furthermore, while the sharp sexual division of labour inflicted a burdensome role upon the women, their duties were essential and the women possessed considerable autonomy within their own sphere.[54] Some traders did think it curious that the women seemed to possess a degree of influence in spite of their degraded situation; indeed, some of the bolder ones occasionally succeeded in making themselves quite independent and "wore the breeches."[55]

A possible way of explaining the discrepancy between the women's perceived and actual status is suggested in a recent anthropological study of the Mundurucú of Amazonian Brazil. In this society, the authors discovered that while the official (male) ideology relegates women to an inferior, subservient position, in the reality of daily life, the women are able to assume considerable autonomy and influence.[56] Most significantly, however, Mundurucú women in order to alleviate their onerous domestic duties, have actively championed the erosion of traditional village life and the concomitant blurring of economic sex roles which have come with the introduction of the rubber trade. According to the authors, the Mundurucú woman "has seen another way of life, and she has opted for it."[57]

This statement could well be applied to the Indian woman who was attracted to the easier life of the fur trade post. In the first place, she now became involved in a much more sedentary routine. With a stationary home, the Indian woman was no longer required to act as a beast of burden, hauling or carrying the accoutrements of camp from place to place. The traders often expressed astonishment and pity at the heavy loads which Indian women were obliged to transport.[58] In fur trade society, the unenviable role of carrier was assumed by the voyageur. The male servants at the fort were now responsible for providing firewood and water, although the women might help. In contrast to Indian practice, the women of the fort were not sent to fetch home the produce of the hunt.[59] The wife of an officer, benefiting from her husband's rank, enjoyed a privileged status. She herself was carried in and out of the canoe[60] and could expect to have all her baggage portaged by a voyageur. At Fond du Lac in 1804 when the wife of NWC *bourgeois* John Sayer decided to go on a sugar-making expedition, four men went with her to carry her baggage and provisions and later returned to fetch home her things.[61]

While the Indian woman performed a variety of valuable economic tasks around the post, her domestic duties were relatively lighter than they had traditionally been. Now her energies were concentrated on making moccasins and snowshoes. As one Nor'Wester declared, with the whites, Indian women could lead "a comparatively easy and free life" in contrast to the "servile slavish mode" of their own.[62] The prospect of superior comforts reputedly motivated some Spokan women to marry voyageurs.[63] The ready supply of both finery and trinkets, which *bourgeois* and voyageurs were seen to lavish on their women, may also have had an appeal.[64] Rival traders noted that luxury items such as lace, ribbons, rings, and vermilion, which "greatly gain the Love of the Women," were important in attracting the Indians to trade.[65] The private orders placed by HBC officers and servants in the 1790's and later include a wide range of cloth goods, shawls, gartering, earrings, and brooches for the women.[66] When taken by a trader *à la façon du pays*, it became common for an Indian woman to go through a ritual performed by the other women of the fort; she was scoured of grease and paint and exchanged her native garments for those of a more civilized fashion. At the NWC posts, wives were clothed in "Canadian fashion," which consisted of a shirt, short gown, petticoat, and leggings.[67]

The traders further thought that Indian women benefited by being freed from certain taboos and customs which they had to bear in Indian society. Among the Ojibway and other tribes, for example, the choicest part of an animal was always reserved for the men; death it was believed would come to any woman who dared to eat such sacred portions. The Nor'Westers paid little heed to such observances. As Duncan Cameron sarcastically wrote: "I have often seen several women living with the white men eat of those forbidden morsels without the least inconvenience."[68] The traders were also convinced that Indian women welcomed a monogamous as opposed to a polygamous state. Polygamy, several HBC officers observed, often gave rise to jealous and sometimes murderous quarrels.[69] It is possible, however, that the traders' own cultural abhorrence of polygamy[70] made them exaggerate the women's antipathy toward it. As a practical scheme for the sharing of heavy domestic tasks, polygamy may in fact have been welcomed by the women.

II

Thus far the advantages which the fur trade brought to Indian women have been emphasized in order to help explain Indian women's reactions to it. It would be erroneous, however, to paint the life of an Indian wife as idyllic. In spite of the traders' belief in the superior benefits they offered, there is evidence that fur trade life had an adverse effect on Indian women. Certainly, a deterioration in her position over time can be detected.

First there is the paradox that the supposedly superior material culture of the fur trade had a deleterious effect on Indian women. It was as if, mused Reverend John West, the first Anglican missionary, "the habits of civilized life" exerted an injurious influence over their general constitutions.[71] Apart from being more exposed to European diseases, the Indian wives of traders suffered more in childbirth than they had in the primitive state.[72] Dr. John Richardson, who accompanied the Franklin Expedition of the 1820's, noted that not only did Indian women now have children more frequently and for longer periods, but that they were more susceptible to the disorders and diseases connected with pregnancy and childbirth.[73] It was not uncommon for fur traders' wives to give birth to from eight to twelve children, whereas four children were the average in Cree society.[74]

The reasons for this dramatic rise in the birth rate deserve further investigation, but several reasons can be advanced. As recent medical research has suggested, the less fatiguing lifestyle and more regular diet offered the Indian wife could have resulted in greater fecundity.[75] The daily ration for the women of the forts was four pounds of meat or fish (one half that for the men);[76] when Governor Simpson jokingly remarked that the whitefish diet at Fort Chipewyan seemed conducive to procreation he may have hit upon a medical truth.[77] Furthermore, sexual activity in Indian society was circumscribed by a variety of taboos, and evidence suggests that Indian men regarded their European counterparts as very licentious.[78] Not only did Indian women now have sex more often, but the attitudes of European husbands also may have interfered with traditional modes of restricting family size. The practice of infanticide was, of course, condemned by the whites, but the Europeans may also have discouraged the traditional long nursing periods of from two to four years for each child.[79] In their view this custom resulted in the premature aging of the mothers,[80] but the fact that Indian children were born at intervals of approximately three years tends to support the recent theory that lactation depresses fertility.[81]

The cultural conflict resulting over the upbringing of the children must have caused the Indian women considerable anguish. An extreme example of the tragedy which could result related to the Chinook practice of head-flattening. In Chinook society, a flat forehead, achieved by strapping a board against the baby's head when in its cradle, was a mark of class; only slaves were not so distinguished. Thus it was only natural that a Chinook woman, though married to a fur trader, would desire to bind her baby's head, but white fathers found this custom abhorrent. The insistence of some fathers that their infants' heads not be flattened resulted in the mothers murdering their babies rather than have them suffer the ignominy of looking like slaves. Gradually European preference prevailed. When Governor Simpson visited the Columbia in the early 1820's, he reported that Chinook wives were abiding by their husbands' wishes and no cases of infanticide had been reported for some years.[82]

In Indian society, children were the virtual "property" of the women who were responsible for their upbringing;[83] in fur trade society, Indian women could find themselves divested of these rights. While the traders acknowledged that Indian women were devoted and affectionate mothers, this did not prevent them from exercising patriarchal authority, particularly in sending young children to Britain or Canada so that they might receive a "civilized" education.[84] It must have been nearly impossible to explain the rationale for such a decision to the Indian mothers; their grief at being separated from their children was compounded by the fact that the children, who were especially vulnerable to respiratory diseases, often died.[85]

It is difficult to know if the general treatment accorded Indian women by European traders met with the women's acceptance. How much significance should be attached to the views of outside observers in the early 1800's who did not think the Indian woman's status had been much improved? Some of the officers of the Franklin Expedition felt the fur traders had been corrupted by Indian attitudes toward women; Indian wives were not treated with "the tenderness and attention due to every female" because the Indians would despise the traders for such unmanly action.[86] The first missionaries were even stronger in denouncing fur trade marital relations. John West considered the traders' treatment of their women disgraceful: "They do not admit them as their companions, nor do they allow them to eat at their tables, but degrade them *merely* as slaves to their arbitrary inclinations."[87] Such statements invite skepticism because of the writers' limited contact with fur trade society, and in the case of the missionaries because of their avowedly hostile view of fur trade customs. Furthermore, the above statements project a European ideal about the way women should be treated, which, apart from being widely violated in their own society, would have had little relevance for Indian women. It is doubtful, for example, that the Indian women themselves would have viewed the fact that they did not come to table, a custom partly dictated by the quasi-military organization of the posts, as proof of their debased position.[88] The segregation of the sexes at meals was common in Indian society, but now, at least, the women did not have to suffice with the left-overs of the men.[89]

Nevertheless, there is evidence to suggest that Indian women were misused by the traders. In Indian society, women were accustomed to greater freedom of action with regard to marital relationships than the traders were prepared to accord them. It was quite within a woman's rights, for example, to institute a divorce if her marriage proved unsatisfactory.[90] In fur trade society, Indian women were more subject to arbitrary arrangements devised by the men. Upon retiring from the Indian Country, it became customary for a trader to place his country wife and family with another, a practice known as "turning off." Although there was often little they could do about it, a few cases were cited of women who tried to resist. At a post in the Peace River district in 1798, the Indian wife of an *engagé*, who was growing tired of wintering *en derouine*, absolutely rejected her husband's attempt to pass her to the man who agreed to take his place.[91] At Fort Chipewyan in 1800, the estranged wife of the voyageur Morin foiled the attempt of his *bourgeois* to find her a temporary "protector": she stoutly refused three different prospects.[92] Indian women also did not take kindly to the long separations which fur trade life imposed on them and their European mates. Although the Indian wife of Chief Factor Joseph Colen was to receive every attention during his absence in England in the late 1790's, Colen's successor could not dissuade her from taking an Indian lover and leaving York Factory.[93]

Indian wives seem to have been particularly victimized during the violent days of the trade war when rivals went so far as to debauch and intimidate each other's women. In 1819 at Pelican Lake, for example, HBC servant Deshau took furs from a NWC servant and raped his wife in retaliation for having had his own wife debauched by a Nor'Wester earlier in the season.[94] A notorious instance involved the Indian wife of HBC servant Andrew Kirkness at Isle à la Crosse in 1810-11. In the late summer, this woman in a fit of pique had deserted her husband and sought refuge at the Nor'Westers' post. She soon regretted her action, however, for she was kept a virtual prisoner by the Canadians, and all efforts of the HBC men to get her back failed. The upshot was that Kirkness himself deserted to the rival post, leaving the English in dire straits since he was their only fisherman. Kirkness was intimidated into remaining with the Nor'Westers until the spring with the threat that should he try to leave "every Canadian in the House would ravish his woman before his eyes." Eventually Kirkness was released, but only after his wife had been coerced into saying that she did not want to accompany him. As the HBC party were evacuating their post, the woman tried to escape but was forcibly dragged back by the Nor'Westers and ultimately became the "property" of an *engagé*.[95]

Such abusive tactics were also applied to the Indians. By the turn of the century, relations between the Indians and the Nor'Westers in particular showed a marked deterioration. In what seems to have been a classic case of "familiarity breeding contempt," the Nor'Westers now retained their mastery through coercion and brute force and frequently transgressed the bounds of Indian morality. An especially flagrant case was the Nor'Westers' exploitation of Chipewyan women at its posts in the Athabasca district. By the end of the eighteenth century, they had apparently built up a nefarious traffic in these women: the *bourgeois* did not scruple at seizing Chipewyan women by force, ostensibly in lieu of trade debts, and then selling them to the men for large sums.[96] The situation became so bad that the Chipewyan began leaving their women behind when they came to trade, and when Hudson's Bay traders appeared on Lake Athabasca in 1792, the Indians hoped to secure their support and drive out their rivals. The English, however, were too weak to offer any effective check to the Nor'Westers who continued to assault both fathers and husbands if they tried to resist the seizure of their women. Since they were not powerful enough to mount an attack, the Chipewyan connived at the escape of their women during the summer months when most of the traders were away. Resentful of their treatment, many of the women welcomed the chance to slip back to their own people so that the summer master at Fort Chipewyan was almost solely preoccupied with keeping watch over the *engagés'* women.[97] By 1800 at least one voyageur had been killed by irate Chipewyan, and the *bourgeois* contemplated offering a reward for the hunting down of "any d--nd rascal" who caused a Frenchman's woman to desert.[98]

The Indians appear to have become openly contemptuous of the white man and his so-called morality. A northern tribe called the Beaver Indians took a particularly strong stand. At first they had welcomed the Canadians but, having rapidly lost respect for them, now forbade any intercourse between their women and the traders.[99] Elsewhere individual hunters boycotted the traders owing to the maltreatment of their women.[100] Sporadic reprisals became more frequent. Whereas Indian women had previously played a positive role as a liaison between Indian and white, they were now becoming an increasing source of friction between the two groups. Governor Simpson summed up the deteriorating situation:

> It is a lamentable fact that almost every difficulty we have had with Indians throughout the country may be traced to our interference with their Women or their intrigues with the Women of the Forts in short 9 murders out of 10 Committed on Whites by Indians have arisen through Women.[101]

Although there is little direct evidence available, it is possible that the Indian women themselves were becoming increasingly dissatisfied with their treatment from the whites. In spite of the initiative which the women have been seen to exercise in forming and terminating relationships with the traders, there were undoubtedly times when they were the unwilling objects of a transaction between Indians and white men. Certainly not all Indian women looked upon the whites as desirable husbands, a view that was probably reinforced with experience. George Nelson did observe in 1811 that there were some Indian women who showed "an extraordinary predilection" for their own people and could not be prevailed upon to live with the traders.[102]

The increasing hostility of the Indians, coupled with the fact that in well-established areas marriage alliances were no longer a significant factor in trade relations, led to a decline in the practice of taking an Indian wife. In fact, in 1806 the North West Company passed a ruling prohibiting any of its employees from taking a country wife from among the tribes.[103] One of the significant factors which changed the traders' attitudes toward Indian women, however, was that they were now no longer "women in between." By the turn of the century a sizable group of mixed-blood women had emerged, and for social and economic reasons fur traders preferred mixed-blood women as wives. In this way the Indian women lost their important place in fur trade society.

The introduction of the Indian woman's perspective on Indian-white relations serves to underscore the tremendous complexity of intercultural contact. It is argued that Indian women saw definite advantages to be gained from the fur trade, and in their unique position as "women in between" they endeavoured to manipulate the situation to improve their existence. That the limits of their influence were certainly circumscribed, and that the ultimate benefits brought by the traders were questionable, does not negate the fact that the Indian women played a much more active and important role in the fur trade than has previously been acknowledged.[104]

NOTES

1. The lack of written Indian history is, of course, a general problem for the ethnohistorian. Indeed, all social scientists must rely heavily on the historical observations of the agents of white contact such as fur traders, explorers, and missionaries. Little seems to have been done to determine if the oral tradition of the Indians is a viable source of information on Indian-white relations in the fur trade period.

2. Glyndwr Williams, ed., *Andrew Graham's Observations on Hudson's Bay, 1769-91*, Hudson's Bay Record Society, XXVII (London, 1969); Richard Glover, ed., *David Thompson's Narrative, 1784-1812*, Champlain Society, XL (Toronto, 1962).

3. A fascinating study which indicates how the application of a different perspective to the same data can produce new insights is *Women of the Forest* by Yolanda and Robert Murphy (New York, 1974). Based on field work conducted twenty years earlier in Amazonian Brazil, the authors found that by looking at the life of the Mundurucú tribe from the woman's point of view, their understanding of the actual as opposed to the official functioning of that society was much enlarged.

4. Marriages between European traders and Indian women were contracted according to indigenous rites derived from Indian custom. For a detailed explanation, see Sylvia Van Kirk, " 'The Custom of the Country': An Examination of Fur Trade Marriage Practices," in L. H. Thomas, ed., *Essays in Western History* (Edmonton, 1976), 49-70.

5. See Murphy, *Women of the Forest*, Ch. 6, for a useful comparison. Mundurucú women actively welcomed the social change brought about by the introduction of the rubber trade into their traditional economy.

6. An instructive study of the Indians' economic role in the fur trade is provided by Arthur Ray in *Indians in the Fur Trade* (Toronto, 1974). He shows that the Indian played a much more active, although changing role in the dynamics of the fur trade than had previously been acknowledged.

7. HBC men were prohibited from bringing women to Hudson Bay. It was not until the early nineteenth century that the first white women came to the Northwest.

8. In 1802 HBC men defended their practice of keeping Indian women in the posts by informing the London Committee that they were "Virtually your Honors Servants": Hudson's Bay Company Archives, [HBCA] B.239/b/79, f. 40d-41. For a discussion of the important economic role played by native women in the fur trade, see Sylvia Van Kirk, "The Role of Women in the Fur Trade Society of the Canadian West, 1700-1850" (Ph.D. thesis, University of London, 1975).

9. HBCA, B.31/a/63, f. 18d; Albany Journal, 24 January 1771: "Connolly vs Woolrich," Superior Court, 9 July 1867, *Lower Canada Jurist*, 11, 234.

10. Charles Bishop, "The Henley House Massacres," *The Beaver* (Autumn, 1976), 40.

11. *Ibid.*, 39. For a more technical look at the socio-economic relationship between the Indians and the traders, see the discussion of "balanced reciprocity" in Marshall Sahlins, *Stone Age Economics* (Chicago, 1972), Ch. 5.

12. In this instance the Indian captain Woudby attacked Henley House because the master was keeping two of his female relatives but denying him access to the post and its provisions.

13. Alexander Henry, *Travels and Adventures in Canada and the Indian Territories 1760-1776*, ed. by Jas. Bain. (Boston, 1901), 248.

14. Alexander Ross, *The Fur Hunters of the Far West* (London, 1855), I, 296-7.

15. W. Kaye Lamb, ed., *Sixteen Years in the Indian Country: The Journal of Daniel Williams Harmon, 1800-1816* (Toronto, 1957), 29; TPL, George Nelson papers, Journal 1810-11, 24 April 1811, 42.

16. Elliott Coues, ed., *New Light on the Early History of the Greater North West: The Manuscript Journals of Alexander Henry and David Thompson, 1799-1814* (Minneapolis, 1965), 71-3.

17. *Ibid.*, 163.

18. *Ibid.*, 211.

19. For a detailed account of the story of this woman, see Sylvia Van Kirk, "Thanadelthur," *The Beaver* (Spring, 1974), 40-5.

20. *Ibid.*, 45.

21. PAC, Masson Collection, Journal of Charles Chaboillez, 13 December 1797, 24.

22. TPL, Nelson Papers, Journal and Reminiscences, 1825-26, 66.

23. Ross, *Fur Hunters*, I, 296.

24. Coues, *New Light*, 793; Frederick Merk, ed., *Fur Trade and Empire: George Simpson's Journal, 1824-25* (Cambridge, Mass., 1931), 104.

25. Gabriel Franchère, *Narrative of a Voyage to the Northwest Coast of America, 1811-14*, ed. by R. G. Thwaites (Cleveland, 1904), 327.

26. Van Kirk, "Thanadelthur," 44.

27. *Ibid.*, 45.

28. W. Kaye Lamb, ed., *The Journals and Letters of Sir Alexander Mackenzie* (Cambridge, Eng., 1970), 152.
29. Merk, *Fur Trade and Empire*, 104.
30. *Ibid.*, 104-5.
31. HBCA, D.5/8, f. 147, R. Crooks to G. Simpson, 15 March 1843.
32. TPL, Nelson Papers, Journal 1810-11, 41-2.
33. *Ibid.*, 1803-04, 10-28 *passim*.
34. PAC, Masson Collection, "An Account of the Chipwean Indians," 23.
35. E. E. Rich, ed., *Simpson's Athabaska Journal and Report, 1820-21*, Hudson's Bay Record Society, I (London, 1938), 74.
36. *Ibid.*, 231.
37. HBCA, B.39/a/16, f. 6-21d. *Fort Chipewyan Journal,* 1820-1, *passim*.
38. Merk, *Fur Trade and Empire*, 99.
39. *Ibid.*, 11-12, 58.
40. HBCA, D.3/3, f. 52, George Simpson's Journal, 1821-22.
41. Rich, *Athabasca Journal*, 23-4; see also Merk, *Fur Trade and Empire*, 131.
42. PAC, Masson Collection, "Account of Chipwean Indians," 23-4.
43. *Ibid.*, 23.
44. Ross, *Fur Hunters*, I, 297.
45. TPL, Nelson Papers, Journal and Reminiscences, 1825-6, 66. Nelson claimed that around 1780 some Indian women had warned the Canadian pedlars of impending attack because in their "tender and affectionate breast (for women are lovely all the world over) still lurked compassion for the mothers of those destined to be sacrificed."
46. Glover, *Thompson's Narrative*, 45. Cf. with the Mundurucú women's desire for European goods: Murphy, *Women of the Forest*, 182.
47. Samuel Hearne, *A Journey to the Northern Ocean*, ed. Richard Glover (Toronto, 1958), 190.
48. HBCA, B.3/a/1, f. 28, Albany Journal, 23 February 1706.
49. Ross Cox, *The Columbia River*, eds. Jane and Edgar Stewart (Norman, Okla., 1957), 377.
50. Lamb, *Journals of Mackenzie*, 135.
51. A. S. Morton, *The Journal of Duncan McGillivray . . . at Fort George on the Saskatchewan 1794-95* (Toronto, 1929), 60.
52. Glover, *Thompson's Narrative*, 106.
53. Hearne, *Journey to Northern Ocean*, 35: "Women," declared the Chipewyan chief Matonabee, "were made for labour; one of them can carry, or haul, as much as two men can do."
54. There has been a trend in recent literature to exalt the Indian woman's status by pointing out that in spite of her labour she had more independence than the pioneer farm wife. See: Nancy O.

Lurie, "Indian Women: A Legacy of Freedom," *The American Way*, 5 (1972), 28-35.

55. Morton, *McGillivray's Journal*, 34; L. R. F. Masson, *Les Bourgeois de la Campagnie du Nord-Ouest* (Quebec, 1889), I, 256.

56. Murphy, *Women of the Forest*, 87, 112.

57. *Ibid.*, 202.

58. Lamb, *Journals of Mackenzie*, 254; Glover, *Thompson's Narrative*, 125.

59. PAC, Masson Collection, Journal of John Thomson, 15 October 1798, 10.

60. J. B. Tyrrell, *Journals of Samuel Hearne and Philip Turnor, 1774-92*, Champlain Society, XXI (Toronto, 1934), 252.

61. Michel Curot, "A Wisconsin Fur Trader's Journal, 1803-4," Wisconsin Historical Society *Collections*, 20 (1911), 449, 453.

62. TPL, Nelson Papers, Journal, 1810-11, 41; Reminiscences, Part 5, 225.

63. Cox, *Columbia River*, 148.

64. Coues, *New Light*, 914; Ross, *Fur Hunters*, II, 236.

65. Tyrrell, *Journals of Hearne and Turnor*, 273.

66. HBCA, A.16/111-2, *passim*, Book of Servants Commissions.

67. Lamb, *Sixteen Years*, 28-9.

68. Masson, *Les Bourgeois*, II, 263.

69. Hearne, *Journey to Northern Ocean*, 80; Williams, *Graham's Observations*, 158.

70. Alexander Ross, *Adventures of the First Settlers on the Oregon or Columbia River* (London, 1849), 280-1; Glover, *Thompson's Narrative*, 251.

71. John West, *The Substance of a Journal during a residence at the Red River Colony 1820-23* (London, 1827), 54.

72. The traders were astonished at the little concern shown for pregnancy and childbirth in Indian society. See, for example: Lamb, *Journals of Mackenzie*, 250, and Williams, *Graham's Observations*, 177.

73. John Franklin, *Narrative of a Journey to the Shores of the Polar Sea 1819-22* (London, 1824), 86.

74. *Ibid.*, 60. The Indian wives of Alexander Ross and Peter Fidler, for example, had thirteen and fourteen children respectively.

75. Jennifer Brown, "A Demographic Transition in the Fur Trade Country: Family Sizes and Fertility of Company Officers and Country Wives, Ca. 1750-1850, 61-71," *Western Canadian Journal of Anthropology*, VI, 1 (1976), 68.

76. Cox, *Columbia River*, 354.

77. J. S. Galbraith, *The Little Emperor* (Toronto, 1976), 68.

78. TPL, Nelson Papers, Reminiscences, Part 5, 225.

79. Brown, "A Demographic Transition," 67.

80. Margaret MacLeod, ed., *The Letters of Letitia Hargrave*,

Champlain Society, XXVII (Toronto, 1947), 94-5; Alexander Ross, *The Red River Settlement* (Minneapolis, 1975), 95, 192.

81. Brown, "A Demographic Transition," 65.
82. Merk, *Fur Trade and Empire*, 101.
83. Williams, *Graham's Observations*, 176, 178.
84. Ross, *Adventures on the Columbia*, 280; W. J. Healy, *Women of Red River* (Winnipeg, 1923), 163-6.
85. Lamb, *Sixteen Years*, 138, 186.
86. Franklin, *Narrative of a Journey*, 101, 106.
87. West, *Red River Journal*, 16.
88. Cox, *Columbia River*, 360.
89. Hearne, *Journey to Northern Ocean*, 57.
90. Williams, *Graham's Observations*, 176.
91. PAC, Masson Collection, Thomson's Journal, 19 November 1798, 20.
92. Masson, *Les Bourgeois*, II, 384-5. We are not told whether she also escaped being sold when the brigades arrived in the spring as the *bourgeois* intended.
93. HBCA, B.239/a/103, f. 14d, York Journal, 2 December 1798.
94. HBCA, D.158/a/1, f. 7d, Pelican Lake Journal, 18 January 1819.
95. This account is derived from the Isle à la Crosse Journal, HBCA, B.89/a/2, f. 5-36 d., *passim*.
96. Tyrrell, *Journals of Hearne and Turnor*, 446n, 449.
97. *Ibid.*, 449-50.
98. Masson, *Les Bourgeois*, II, 387-8.
99. Lamb, *Journals of Mackenzie*, 255; Rich, *Athabasca Journal*, 388.
100. PAC, Masson Collection, Journal of Ferdinand Wentzel, 13 January 1805, 41.
101. Merk, *Fur Trade and Empire*, 127.
102. TPL, Nelson Papers, Journal, 1810-11, 41-2.
103. W. S. Wallace, ed., *Documents Relating to the North West Company*, Champlain Society, XXII (Toronto, 1934), 211. This ruling was not enforced in outlying districts such as the Columbia. Even after the union in 1821, Governor Simcoe continued to favour the formation of marital alliances in remote regions as the best way to secure friendly relations with the Indians. See: Rich, *Athabasca Journal*, 392.
104. For a discussion of the role played by mixed-blood women in fur trade society, see: Van Kirk, "Role of Women in Fur Trade Society."

Readings in Canadian Social History